Trans Philosophy

Trans
Philosophy

Perry Zurn, Andrea J. Pitts,
Talia Mae Bettcher, and PJ DiPietro
Editors

University of Minnesota Press
Minneapolis
London

Talia Mae Bettcher, "What Is Trans Philosophy?" was originally published in *Hypatia* 34, no. 4 (2019): 644–67.

Published by the University of Minnesota Press
111 Third Avenue South, Suite 290
Minneapolis, MN 55401-2520
http://www.upress.umn.edu

ISBN 978-1-5179-1703-6 (hc)
ISBN 978-1-5179-1704-3 (pb)

A Cataloging-in-Publication record for this book is available from the Library of Congress.

Printed in the United States of America on acid-free paper

The University of Minnesota is an equal-opportunity educator and employer.

33 32 31 30 29 28 27 26 25 24   10 9 8 7 6 5 4 3 2

Contents

PART III. Temporality, Technicity, and
Bioethics of Becoming

PART IV. Politics, Institutions, and World-Making

Introduction
Situating and Desituating Trans Philosophy

Perry Zurn, Andrea J. Pitts,
Talia Mae Bettcher, and PJ DiPietro

Recently, philosophers have had much to say about trans people. Whether as a new favorite thought experiment or as a policy problem, a growing number of philosophers have turned to trans people as objects of curiosity and concern. This has notably occurred within the broader cultural context of increased trans visibility, as well as renewed social scrutiny and legislative backlash. Trans philosophers and allies, in turn, have become more vocal not only about the difficulties of being trans in philosophy but also about the necessity of a new field: trans philosophy. While significant trans philosophical work has been done over the last several decades, trans philosophy as a subfield is new. Trans philosophical work at its best is characterized by a commitment to justice for trans people, including people whose relationships to the term and category "trans" remain at once affirming and disorienting. This commitment persists in the face of a steady stream of material and discursive injustices that mark our positionality in the world.

Trans Philosophy is the first collection to establish trans philosophy as a unique field of inquiry—characterizing an emerging and polymorphous landscape. It defines *trans philosophy* with an open hand as philosophical work that is accountable to and illuminative of cross-cultural and transnational trans experiences, histories, cultural productions, and politics. The book showcases work from a range of fresh and established voices in this nascent field. It addresses a variety of topics (e.g., discrimination, embodiment, identity, language, law, policy, and politics), utilizes diverse philosophical methods (e.g., theoretical, experimental, and applied), and attends to significant intersections between gender and class, disability, ethnicity, language, nationality, race, and sexuality. Across language and politics, feminism and phenomenology, decolonial theory and disability studies, trans philosophy concerns itself with trans world-making in all its excruciating beauty and mundanity. Positioned primarily in the United States but stretching across North and South America, *Trans Philosophy* understands itself as an opening missive. Not in the business of sanctioning or of restrictively defining either *trans* or *philosophy,* the collection honors the capaciousness of these terms by working from within multiple geopolitical landscapes, fields, and directions in the knowledge that what trans philosophy is and will become already exceeds it in scope.

At a time when thinly thought trans-exclusionary views are gaining traction in politics as well as in philosophy, it is important that philosophers redraw the contours of the conversation, highlighting the wisdom already generated in trans and gender-variant communities and the insights still to be gained through philosophical work accountable to those communities. *Trans Philosophy* does just that. Critically, this philosophical project centralizes the contributions of trans philosophers, as well as gender-disruptive philosophers who contend with the experience and positionality of *trans* and other gender formations to which *trans* points but does not fully contain.

In this introduction, we set the stage for readers to constructively engage with the contents of the book itself. We begin by positioning ourselves in relationship to the project before situating the terms *trans* and *philosophy* in historical and critical context. We then give a brief overview of the history of trans philosophy in the United States and transnationally, including defining moments of transphobic backlash. Following that, we reflect on what trans philosophy is and could be, grappling with some of the complexities of "founding a field" that is often rooted outside of or adjacent to philosophy proper and academia itself. We also characterize the intimacies and distinctions between trans philosophy, trans theory, and other sites of inquiry where "trans" loses its Westernizing, Euro-America–centered legibility. After a brief description of the book's contents, we close with a reflection on the capaciousness of a trans reading/writing/thinking praxis within which trans philosophy sits.

Situating Trans Philosophy

As editors, we represent a variety of embodiments and geopolitical lineages, as well as differing relationships to the term *trans,* the field of philosophy, and academia itself. We each understand ourselves to be a trans philosopher (some more easily and some less). All four of us live and make home in the United States, from West to East Coast. Two of us originally hail from the United States (via families who immigrated and settled here), one of us from Argentina, and one from Canada. Two of us are Latinx scholars, two of us are white. We are complexly gendered and embodied, with various relationships to ability and disability, sanity, and what Cameron Awkward-Rich calls "trans maladjustment."[1] Three of us were assistant professors at the time of conceiving and completing most of the work on this volume, while one of us was (and remains) a full professor. Two of us work in philosophy departments with additional affiliations, one of us works in a women's and gender studies department, and another works in comparative literature. We come to this project having different personal and professional histories with trans embodiment, philosophy, and trans studies, and we did not always see eye to eye on the project. But we share a conviction that trans theorizing happens in more places within and outside the university than anyone thinks. And we share a commitment to facilitating greater accountability and creativity in that theorizing, as it becomes increasingly rooted in trans and gender-disruptive lives and communities.

We understand *trans* and *philosophy* to have unstable, capacious, and contested referents. Following parallel genealogies in trans studies, we take the term *trans* as an umbrella term for gender disruptions (e.g., agender, genderqueer, gendertrash, genderfuck, genderfluid, nonbinary, transgender, transsexual); as "prefixial flesh" through which the movement of disruptive genders links up with other axes of analysis, whether social identities or institutions; and, perhaps most importantly, as an abyssal embodiment among intertwined technologies of dehumanization and dispossession.[2] As capacious as *trans* is, we are also fully aware that it cannot name everything about gender disruption and that in fact its attempt to do so, especially within white Euro-American trans scholarship, has betrayed a disavowal of intersex struggles and a troubling coloniality at the heart of trans studies. We stay with the term *trans,* then, for all it brings but also to reckon with its failures and to press beyond it. We take a similar stance toward *philosophy.* Following the well-established tradition of philosophies of difference, we take *philosophy* to refer to a range of incongruous communities of praxis, consciously including Africana philosophy; Asian and Asian American philosophies; feminist philosophy; Indigenous philosophy; Afro-Latinx, Latinx, Latin American, and Caribbean philosophy; LGBTQ and queer philosophy; philosophy of disability; and postcolonial and decolonial philosophy.[3] Equally informed by critical theory, we take philosophy to be a praxis of inquiry that must, consistently, become strange even to itself, ruthlessly challenging practitioners' various attachments to one or another preferred method or canon of philosophical inquiry.[4]

We take trans philosophy to be a critical project, a grounded project, and a collective project. As a critical project, trans philosophy analyzes the conditions of possibility for trans experience, questions the social institutions and structures that impinge on trans life, and works reflexively to interrogate its own implicit biases and complicities in systems of oppression. That critical project may well derail concepts and methods already entrenched in philosophy in order to explore trans experience, but it will equally draw concepts and methods from trans experience and weave them back into philosophy.

As a grounded project, trans philosophy is rooted in, as Viviane Namaste puts it, "the banality of buying some bread, of making photocopies, of getting your shoe fixed."[5] Negotiated in this everydayness, trans philosophy is necessarily refracted through the geopolitical landscapes—and lands—in which trans, gender-disruptive, and allied peoples theorize in the midst of conviviality. Nothing about this rootedness requires the university, and in fact everything about this rootedness requires breaking from the university's centrality to theory.

Finally, as a collective project, trans philosophy is a set of conversations. Being a part of those conversations involves being a part of trans worlds, sometimes building resonances within and across them but just as often honoring the discordance within and between them. To paraphrase Audre Lorde's magnificent ode to coalitional work, this tensed collectivity embedded in trans philosophy reflects belonging as much as it requires humility, accountability, and engagement for and with differences.[6]

Given our critical comportment toward *trans* and *philosophy*, it is no surprise that we approach the emergence of the academic subfield of trans philosophy with equal parts excitement and trepidation. We are eager for more trans philosophical work, accountable to and illuminative of cross-cultural and transnational trans experiences, histories, cultural productions, and politics, to flourish in the field. And we understand the promise of this book to lie in expanding and energizing the many shapes that trans philosophical work can take. But we also are not so naive as to think that the emergence of such a subfield is essentially liberatory, sure to unleash suppressed voices and histories into the bright light of a noonday sun. We are cognizant of the already-existing complicities of simply calling trans philosophy "trans philosophy." We are also aware of the university's repeated co-optation of radical theorizing from marginalized communities into neutralized enclaves of "difference studies."[7] It is our commitment, as practitioners of trans philosophy, to keep alive its capacity to make incisive inroads into the academy but also to keep its creative impetus and centerweight well outside of it. To do so, we will continue to forefront the unsettling and unsettled nature of both *trans* and *philosophy*.

While trans philosophy has distinct and identifiable contours, even today in its relatively nascent state, what those contours become is an open question. Our commitment to trans philosophy's undetermined futures, moreover, is matched only by our correlative commitment to its multiplicitous histories. It is to some of those that we now turn.

Histories of Trans Philosophy

Philosophy in the United States, over the past several decades at least, has consistently taken up trans people as overt objects of critique (as in the case of trans-exclusionary radical feminism) or as mere thought experiments. As trans philosophy has found its voice, it is perhaps no real surprise that a parallel strand of philosophy, traveling under the title "gender-critical feminism," has sprung up in the United Kingdom (and Australia) and found significant resonance across the pond.[8] Meanwhile, legislative backlash has increased in regularity and vehemence around the globe, especially targeting, in the United States, for example, trans children and athletes; in Spain, gender self-determination; and in Argentina, gender-inclusive language. What is it, in this moment, then, to tell the story of trans philosophy? To imagine a form of philosophy rooted in and explorative of trans life and community, while granting the limitations of the term *trans* itself? How can such a story be told in a way that makes room for its unique account-abilities and its distinct geographies? For the rejection of the term *trans* by gender-variant people in and beyond U.S. contexts and the vast theoretical resources being generated outside of philosophy departments? Insofar as this volume focuses on contributions to trans philosophy in North and South America, including Indigenous communities in these occupied lands, the history we offer here acquires a distinct valence. We do not presume to tell a single story. Rather, we offer threads of various histories that stretch far beyond what we do here. We track how "trans philosophy" travels, but also how "trans" and "philosophy" do not always travel well.

Having committed ourselves to a multiplicitous, mycorrhizal story of trans philosophy, there nevertheless remain innumerable ways of telling it.[9] As a motley group from contrasting geopolitical locales and viewpoints, we could, for example, focus on the intricacies and incursions of Canadian trans theorists, or between the parallel but remarkably alienated worlds of the United States and Argentina, or the suppression of Indigenous theorizing in Canada, the United States, and Latin and Latinx Americas. We could anchor the story in the discipline proper, tracing in the United States, for example, the development of trans philosophy conversations in key academic organizations such as the American Philosophical Association, the Society for Phenomenology and Existential Philosophy, the Association for Feminist Ethics and Social Theory, the Society for the Advancement of American Philosophy, and philoSOPHIA. Or we could tell the story of trans philosophy through the development of trans activism, where community building and the poetics of being with one another in struggle fuels trans theorizing.[10] In what follows, we offer a constellation of beginnings to the story of trans philosophy. We offer that constellation as always preliminary, emphasizing its incongruous roots and complex futures.

It is no simple task, of course, to locate the origin of trans life, let alone trans philosophy. One could begin telling a story of trans philosophy in the 1990s, just as the word *transgender* came into rich circulation within resistantly theorizing trans communities. But of course, this is only a recent chapter of a long history of gender deviance and gender resistance.[11] In this light, one history of trans philosophy might extend back to Judith Butler's *Gender Trouble* and contemporaneous work in gay, lesbian, and queer theory, or indeed to the gender transgressiveness of feminist philosophy itself and even of (especially women) philosophers for several millennia. But the story is more complicated still. Contemporary trans philosophy and trans theorizing in multiple countries have differing genealogies, and a number of cultures have long traditions of embodiment and theorizing that defy and exceed gender binaries and norms. Thinking trans, as a fleshly and philosophical practice, is far from a unitary project; it spans multiple geographies, cultures, and histories, some newly emergent and some violently submerged. These differing and diasporic histories not only actively inform what trans philosophy is and can be but also demand a crucial practice of geopolitical accountability. This accountability requires pushing at the limits and contours of trans philosophy as it responds to the varied ways in which trans and philosophical communities are often located outside of or precariously positioned within the white, Eurocentric norms of universities and noncritical, issue-driven social movements.

To trace one of trans philosophy's many beginnings in the United States, we might start with the *Transgender Studies Reader,* published in 2006, which collected some early trans philosophical work.[12] Shortly thereafter, in 2009, Talia Mae Bettcher and Ann

Garry edited a special issue of *Hypatia* on trans studies and feminist philosophy, while Laurie J. Shrage edited *"You've Changed": Sex Reassignment and Personal Identity*.[13] Including luminaries such as Paisley Currah, C. Jacob Hale, Cressida J. Heyes, Viviane Namaste, Gayle Salamon, and C. Riley Snorton, these two projects aimed to explore the interaction and interplay between trans studies and feminist philosophy, especially on questions of intersectionality, public policy, personal identity, and theoretical method. Following the publication of the *Transgender Studies Reader 2* in 2013, in which still more trans philosophical work was collected, trans philosophy coalesced both as a term and as a project in 2016 with the Trans* Experience in Philosophy Conference at the University of Oregon, the same year that *TSQ: Transgender Studies Quarterly* published their "Trans/Feminisms" issue, coedited by Susan Stryker and Talia Mae Bettcher.[14] This turn was followed by the establishment of the Trans Philosophy Project in 2018, funded by the American Philosophical Association and *Hypatia,* and the associated Thinking Trans // Trans Thinking Conference, whose keynotes and plenaries to date have included Cameron Awkward-Rich, Talia Mae Bettcher, Mel Y. Chen, Eli Clare, Jules Gill-Peterson, Che Gossett, C. Riley Snorton, and Marlene Wayar.[15]

Some of the earliest North American trans philosophers were Canadian. Miqqi Alicia Gilbert and Talia Mae Bettcher both studied at York University in Toronto, where Gilbert went on to teach while Bettcher moved to California State University, Los Angeles. Importantly, both Gilbert's and Bettcher's trans philosophical reflections are deeply rooted in trans subcultures (especially at Fantasia Fair and in Los Angeles, respectively). While sociologists by training, Canadians Aaron Devor, Viviane Namaste, and Alexandre Baril have and continue to do important theoretical work to guide trans history, trans epistemology, and trans bioethics. Cressida J. Heyes, of the University of Alberta, also stands out as an early trans ally in feminist philosophy circles at the turn of the twenty-first century. Of note, the comparatively robust conversations about Indigenous sovereignty that have marked Canadian cultural theory have not yet richly informed trans Canadian philosophy.

From its earliest moments, trans philosophy in the United States has been informed by other philosophies of difference and minority discourses. Always in conversation with feminist philosophy, trans philosophy by Sandy Stone, C. Jacob Hale, Talia Mae Bettcher, and others was influenced, as early as the 1980s and 1990s, by Latina feminism, especially the work of Gloria Anzaldúa and María Lugones.[16] Their concepts and themes of borders, worlds, and multiplicitous selves help illuminate gender ambiguity and subaltern community. Those roots continue to flourish today among Chicanx and Latinx authors who are doing philosophically rich work on Latina feminism and trans issues, including micha cárdenas, T. Jackie Cuevas, PJ DiPietro, Francisco J. Galarte, L Heidenreich, and Andrea J. Pitts, among others.[17] Disability theory, with its critique of pathologization and its reclamation of monsters and misfits, is likewise important. Scholars working on the border between disability studies and trans studies, such as Cameron Awkward-Rich, Alexandre Baril, Cavar, Mel Y. Chen, and Eli Clare, emphasize the imbrication of sanism, ableism, racialization, and environmental injustice.[18] The unique relationship between blackness and transness, moreover, is a focus of work by C. Riley Snorton and others, such as Marquis Bey, Che Gossett, and Kai M. Green, who argue that (trans)gender has been racialized in specific ways and that blackness and the transatlantic slave trade, as ontological prefigurations of embodiment and being, are crucial parts of that story.[19] Trans Marxism, in turn, analyzes gender nonconformity in a capitalist context of widespread socioeconomic inequality and precarity, and in relation to reproductive labor and labor histories.[20] And discourses of abolitionism, furthermore, extend trans philosophical analysis to neoliberalism, the prison industrial complex, and carceral medicine.[21] These are just some of the navigational stars through which trans philosophy in the United States has formed. They carry with them an incisive critique of both trans studies and philosophy and, as such, continue to challenge trans philosophy to cultivate intersectional, materialist, and political commitments.

In a parallel but distinct vein, the philosophical roots of trans and *travesti* critique in Argentina, which leads the Americas in trans-inclusive policies, emerged in dialogue with the grassroots struggles of trans, travesti, and transsexual activists such as Nadia Echazú, Lohana Berkins, and Diana Sacayán, including their efforts to transform the legislative, representational, and institutional conditions for gender-variant peoples across the country.[22] It continues with the work of the Independent Chair in Trans* Studies at the University of Buenos Aires. Common to this work is a critical comportment toward the term *trans*, as well as trans theoretical discourse, as predominantly U.S.–based and Global-North–centric.[23] This comportment is paired with a concomitant insistence that local lineages and embodiments of gender disruption and gender discontent be thought with equal complexity. Reflective of this turn, Lohana Berkins, for example, asserts that something "gets lost" with the overemphasis or singular emphasis on "trans identity" and that is transversality *(transversalidad)* or the transversal coalitions that, in fact, mobilize trans and travesti folks in political resistance alongside a host of other marginalized groups.[24] In these ways, trans philosophy and travesti theory grapple with the reality of material precarity for and beyond trans people from the start, including the ways in which academic forms of tokenization and marginalization extract from trans and other oppressed communities without providing just compensation to or participating in coalitional resistance with said peoples. As such, many practitioners of trans philosophy insist that if trans philosophy is to flourish, these emphases must remain in place.

Across Canada, the United States, Central America, and South America, theoretical conversations among trans people whose ancestors settled there often happen in remarkable isolation from theoretical conversations among two-spirit and otherwise gender-variant and gender-disruptive Indigenous peoples. In turn, Indigenous and decolonial theory are consistently subjugated in academic environments (despite, and perhaps even through, recent efforts at neoliberal inclusion). While the cost of this exclusion is recognized by early trans theorists such as Sandy Stone and Leslie Feinberg, in settler contexts, (trans)gender theorizing is increasingly flourishing within Indigenous communities and allied groups.[25] Leanne Betasamosake Simpson, for example, makes a clarion call to Indigenous communities to resist the cisnormative frameworks they have inherited through colonization.[26] In turn, Indigenous scholars such as Kai Pyle have taken up the work of uncovering queer, gender-disruptive, and trans stories and terms within Indigenous histories.[27] If today's gender system is a colonial/modern gender system, as María Lugones argues, then decolonial struggle is arguably tied (despite Lugones's problematic relation to transness) to new relations to land, sovereignty, nature, kinship, and embodiment beyond colonial and (neo)liberal relationalities. Accountability to Indigenous communities in this struggle is thereby necessary to trans philosophical futures.[28]

Given its critical comportment to both *trans* and *philosophy,* and given these geopolitically varied histories, trans philosophical praxis has a tensed, although generative relationship to the academic fields of trans studies and philosophy. How have we and might we best navigate that terrain?

Trans Philosophy: Field or Foe?

There are, of course, some concerns with dubbing trans philosophy a "subfield." Trans philosophy, similar to other subfields rooted in experiences of marginalization, might be better described as an *approach,* a distinctive set of aims and methodologies that can be applied to almost all philosophical subfields—philosophy of language, metaphysics, ethics, and so on. To be sure, like other grounded "philosophies of difference," trans philosophy does tend to have a topical focus—in this case, gender broadly construed and issues of concern to trans and gender-variant people more specifically. However, the reduction to mere area risks the very reduction of trans people themselves to puzzles and thought experiments— the reduction that first appears to introduce gender variance into academic philosophy.

The tension between *area* and *approach* points to the ways in which grounded "philosophies of difference" do not fit well within a hegemonically crafted taxonomy of disciplinary philosophy. Indeed, as these philosophies challenge dominant conceptions of philosophy, as well as the dominant methodologies of the practice, their integration within the dominant taxonomy ought to be viewed as a sort of invisibility that is sometimes quite useful and other times a hindrance.

As trans philosophy emerges within the discipline now as something that might be denominated a "subfield," at any rate, both trans political and metaphilosophical questions—often intertwined— present themselves for reflection. These sorts of questions are particularly acute among grounded philosophies of difference.

They concern the work that philosophical discourse can accomplish in the service of resistance, oppression, obfuscation, and illumination.

Consider, for instance, the decision to engage with a literature that is decidedly antitrans—a literature subjecting the validity of trans identities to an undermining scrutiny. The engagement requires putting aside a trans philosophical starting point that trans identities are presumptively valid, thereby ceding political ground while eschewing a philosophical exploration that might have proved more illuminating for trans people themselves than the one undertaken. Nonetheless, this philosophical move might be useful or even required for strategic reasons such as helping to undermine or at least to contest transphobia in the profession (and the many other oppressions with which it intersects) to make life a little better for trans philosophers who, with their multiplicitous selves, attempt to survive and even flourish therein. Trans philosophy is beset with such decisions as par for the course.

The emergence of trans philosophy as a subfield raises questions about what sort of work is accomplished thereby. Certainly, to the extent that such a subfield both contests transphobia and helps legitimate work in trans philosophy within the profession, lives can be made better for at least some trans people. We might, however, proceed cautiously, worrying about possible obstacles to trans philosophical investigation instituted consequently. Consider, for instance, the practice of philosophy to bring intelligibility to one's life in response to what one of us calls the "WTF questions" that arise under conditions of oppression.[29] How might the quest for philosophical illumination as resistance be thwarted by the solidification of trans philosophy as a subfield?

Certainly, we should expect the development of a literature or, rather, set of literatures, as we would find in all subfields. Specific topics would be brought into prominence from the clustering together of various writings, formal talks, and discussions. This, in turn, would set a kind of agenda in the subfield, particularly when certain topics were hot. Such an arrangement would be beneficial to trans philosophers by providing publishing niches and, therewith, publishing opportunities. However, this arrangement could likewise exert a controlling force in de-emphasizing or even rendering invisible other topics. Worse, the literature cluster may depend upon uncontested philosophical assumptions hidden, in part, by the submergence of other topics or their relegation to the periphery.

Such dangers beset all philosophical subfields, no doubt. Philosophy has this feature of, on the one hand, requiring or at least generating a literature and, on the other, falling prey to that literature's obfuscation. Yet, trans philosophy, as other grounded philosophies of difference, cannot afford such obfuscation when the quest for illumination is itself a form of resistance. Ironically, because we have already had to understand the hostile political work of various philosophical maneuvers, trans philosophers are well-accustomed to taking the metaphilosophical stance required to negotiate the dangerous terrain. Certainly, we editors are wary of the dangers in contributing to philosophical foreclosure. We are also hopeful that this collection, aimed at showcasing emergent trans philosophy and thereby, perhaps, inflecting that emergence, will continue to expand the possibilities for trans philosophy rather than curtail them.

One intriguing feature inherent in the emergence of trans philosophy is that it includes thinkers who operate both within and without the profession of philosophy. This is not inconsequential in light of the following two givens. The first is the existence of what Judith Butler calls "philosophy's Other"—otherwise known as "theory"—which they regard as produced through professional philosophy's exclusionary tendencies and the fact that rich philosophical investigation continues to develop elsewhere, nonetheless.[30] The second is the fact that the theoretical basis for trans studies—trans theory—was developed in the bosom of philosophy's Other at a time when professional philosophy had absolutely no interest in trans people. In one respect, one might simply maintain that—petty prejudices aside—there is no difference between "philosophy" and its "Other"—it is all just "philosophy" in some suitable sense. In another, however, one might entertain the hope that, ultimately, unquestioned assumptions at the root of professional trans theory or trans theories might be challenged while so too might the unquestioned presumptions of professional philosophy itself. Philosophy, in fact, has many theoretical Others, within interdisciplinary fields like Africana studies, Asian and Asian American studies, Black studies, disability studies, environmental studies, feminist theory, Indigenous studies, intersex studies, Latin American and Caribbean studies, Latinx and Chicanx studies, queer studies, and studies of social class. For some trans scholars, these subfields are equally (if not more) valuable than "trans theory" as a field of reference. Such interdisciplinary fields are theoretical kin and thereby core sites for both philosophical learning and critique for trans philosophers.

Indeed, one of the greatest dangers inherent in the emergence of this subfield is the distortion afforded by the selection of (trans)gender over race, sexuality, disability, class, species, and other bases of oppression. To be clear, this distortion remains uncontested regardless of the capaciousness or the inclusiveness of *trans* since—as there's invariably some sort of intermeshing among gender, race, sexuality, disability, class, (in)humanity, and the like—the undeniable prioritization of one through the very selection of a qualifier of philosophy must necessarily create distortion. To be sure, similar distortions can likewise be attributed to any grounded philosophy of difference, including those that proceed from the intermeshing of two such areas.

However, it is difficult to fathom how distortion can somehow be lessened through its own multiplication. One expects that any such philosophy must remain transparently inadequate, as well as permeable. More than that, one suspects that a necessary ingredient is philosophical engagement among these grounded philosophies of difference—an interplay that is as relationship-building as it is illuminating. Here again, trans philosophy strains at the domesticating force of "field," as we contend it must invariably do.

Guiding Questions and Entanglements

Given these expansive historical and scholarly trajectories, this volume seeks to engage a number of questions that are beginning to coalesce as central themes within trans philosophy, themes that likewise honor the field's own experimental and exploratory practices. For example, the essays gathered here reflect on questions of self-expression and self-interpretation, tarrying with the forms

of intimacy, kinship, affective alliances, and embodied relationalities that allow gender variance in communal and historically
rooted ways to meaningfully cohere. Within such self-directed
focus, questions of geopolitical negotiations with institutional,
state, and extralegal power emerge as well, often becoming coor-
dinated sites of confrontation or as opportunities for subversion
and co-optation. In this, academic spaces, clinical contexts, and
legal settings each are marked by violence. Yet they are not only
this. Rather, the chapters offered here invite readers to the multiplicitous worlds of trans experience within and beyond the sanc-
tioned reach of existing medical, legal, and scholarly domains. The
authors in this collection thereby forage and play with conceptions
of embodiment, nature, desire, and temporality, showing readers where and how to survive, often against the odds. They also
guide us in the practice of learning how to remember with care
and nuance those who are no longer in the world of the living. As
such, the works offered here show readers more than the human,
more than its prescribed contours and curious habits. Threading
through differential planetary moments and interspecies dependencies, the collection thereby shares with readers the locatedness
of the experience of gender variance and its invitations away from
the strictures of the human under modernity/coloniality.

The chapters are arranged in four sections. Part I, "Metaphilosophy, Categories, and Kinds," tackles the ever-present challenge of taking trans experience as a philosophical ground rather
than as a marginalized afterthought. Whether addressing the nature of trans philosophy itself, gendered terms and gender kinds,
or critiquing the machinations whereby trans people are made
laughable, these essays consider both the ways in which categories harm and also the power of theorizing from trans life itself. In
"What Is Trans Philosophy?," Talia Mae Bettcher contrasts trans
philosophy with generic philosophy about trans people, aiming
to draw out some of the former's methodological distinctiveness.
In "Reimagining Transgender," Robin Dembroff distinguishes between transgender identity and transgender experience; while
the former is a contemporary label built on a definable category,
they argue, the latter refers to any instance of willful and costly
gender deviance. In "Replicating Gender: Reflections on Gender

Concepts, Gender Kinds, and History," Stephanie Kapusta critiques social ontologies of gender kinds (especially that of Theodore Bach) for centralizing the supposedly standard elements in a category and neglecting the resistant processes that always also mark social gender systems. Then, in "Laughing at Trans Women: A Theory of Transmisogyny," Amy Marvin develops an account of the mechanics of transphobic laughter, analyzing how trans women become a category of thing subject to disgust, social isolation, and subjugation. Across these markedly distinct projects, authors in this section open up the world of naming and name-calling—a world that, although often marked by epistemic violence, is also a location of trans creativity and resistance.

Part II, "Embodiment, Materiality, and Phenomenologies of Flesh," grapples with a central feature of trans philosophical work to date: the experience of trans embodiment. Refusing to repeat a basic (and universalizing) reduction of trans life to nonnormative gendered and sexual embodiment, these essays use critical phenomenology and decolonial, Black, and Indigenous theory to track trans materiality across multiple geographies and architectures, histories, and positionalities. In "Thinking Trans Embodiment: On Contingent 'Home' and Trans Fatigue," Ryan Gustafsson explores the physics of trans people finding and making "home" not only in different macrocontexts of societies and cultures but also in the microcontexts of rooms, streets, public transit systems, office spaces, and community hangouts. In "'I Look Too Good Not to Be Seen': Multiple Meaning Realism and Sociosomatics," PJ DiPietro rethinks trans embodiments at the crossroads of racialization and various iterations of the nonhuman, querying language and performance as traces of unseen and unfamiliar forms of carnal kinship. Finally, Che Gossett, in "The Art(s) of Ecstasy: Black Trans Art in the Afterlife of Slavery," then takes up the relationship between blackness and transness, arguing that they are sites of inhabitation rather than identity, coming together in shared flesh and haptic movement. Together, the essays in this section illuminate the multiple economies and ecologies within and against which trans bodies come to mean, matter, and even turn on themselves.

Part III, "Temporality, Technicity, and Bioethics of Becoming," offers a series of critical commentaries on the assumed link between time and sociomaterial transformation, including themes of human development, betterment, and (neo)liberal promises of redress and accessibility for trans peoples. The section opens with Hil Malatino's chapter, "Genealogies of Trans Technicity," in which Malatino addresses the Eurocentric roots of Cold War–era narratives of technological progress and military dominance and the function of these narratives within white trans theorizing in the late twentieth and early twenty-first centuries. Malatino describes a form of "white trans futurism" that emerges from the cybernetic imagery developed among several trans theorists in the 1990s and early 2000s and that reflects narratives of somatechnical mastery reminiscent of sex studies of the 1950s. The following chapter, Megan Burke's "Misgendering as Temporal Capture," adds a phenomenological layer of analysis to psychological accounts of the harms caused by practices of misgendering. Burke proposes an account of "temporal capture" as a cisnormative feature of colonial racializing processes that shape and configure trans relations to an assumed originating event of gender assignment, thus harkening to forms of temporal (dis)placement. The next two chapters explicitly address medicalized narratives of progress and advancement. Andrea J. Pitts, for example, in "Sylvia Rivera and the Fight against Carceral Medicine," offers a reading of interviews with trans Latina activist Sylvia Rivera and Rivera's prescient insights regarding the mutual relationship between punishment and health industries in the late twentieth and early twenty-first centuries. Pitts points to Rivera's remarks on neoliberal patterns of social welfare reform, housing and food insecurity, and medicalized confinement as sites where both carceral and health-care systems converge. The final chapter in the section, Tamsin Kimoto's "tRacing Face: A Racial Genealogy of Beauty," examines facial feminization surgery among trans people as a site that enacts a racialized history of the face. Such cosmetic surgical practices, Kimoto proposes, extend many of the same forms of aesthetic investments in racial physiognomy that circulated in classical-era physical anthropology. Accordingly, Kimoto's chapter, along with the others in the section, examines the historical contours of previous narratives of medical, psychological, anthropological, or technological advancement and places these narratives in critical dialogue with trans theorizing today.

Part IV, "Politics, Institutions, and World-Making," addresses the increasingly urgent intersections between trans welfare and institutional politics. Crossing loci as diverse as the university and the street, law and the environment, authors in this cluster centralize the insights of trans world-making in and against socially ordering policies, discourses, vocabularies, and grammars. In "Scatter: A Trans/Crip Analytic," Perry Zurn uses archival and ethnographic research into trans activism in higher education to dramatize the fundamental intimacies between trans and crip life, even or perhaps especially when they are disavowed. In "The Racializing Work of Biological Sex," Marie Draz, in dialogue with Paisley Currah and María Lugones, argues that antitrans law and politics are predicated on the construction of "biological sex" and that a decolonial feminist methodology is crucial for its undoing. Finally, in "Latin American *Travesti*/Trans Theory," Marlene Wayar elucidates two key concepts from her recent book *Travesti: A Good Enough Theory*: sexual/gender dissidence and travesti. Importantly, for her, these concepts are generated within travesti community and, as such, represent a praxis of theorization that begins with listening and ends by producing "joint actions." Whatever the political is and whatever it does, these essays argue for the profound changes trans life necessitates in how politics gets thought and gets lived.

There is more love and thought here than can be contained within the covers of a book or the properties of a digital file. The rich worlds from and for which this work has been drawn will continue to lead and challenge the field of trans philosophy going forward.

Trans Thinking

Trans philosophy is but one species of trans thinking, and trans thinking is a capacious, incongruous praxis of reading and writing our worlds. As such, trans philosophy can learn much about its art from discussions of trans method more broadly. For some time now, trans studies has taken *trans-* to be a rich invitation to iterative crossings of multiple borders and boundaries at once. In their field-defining 2008 special issue of *Women's Studies Quarterly*,

Susan Stryker, Paisley Currah, and Lisa Jean Moore characterize *transing* as a movement by which so-called fixed entities are transgressed and unsettled.[31] *Trans-,* as such, undoes many of the structures, relations, and concepts we have inherited in and about our world, but it also links up with—thereby making new monstrous formations in and through—unexpected embodiments, identitarian axes, social institutions, and units of sense. At its best, what *trans-* can do and where it can go remains fundamentally, constitutively, open. While trans thinking is rooted in trans life and specific geopolitical histories, then, it has the potential to remain in some significant way unmoored and unmooring. As Tey Meadow argues, taking *trans-* (and *trans**) seriously involves granting that we cannot know in advance how it is we come to know ourselves and the world; instead, a "relational, contingent, iterative, . . . infinitely complex" process occurs in which the contours of reader and read are constantly redrawn.[32]

Because trans thinking undertakes the unmaking and making of worlds, especially through sociosymbolic creation, there lies a certain poetics at its heart. TC Tolbert describes trans poetics as writing that "challenges the idea of a single trans narrative, interrogates binaries of all sorts, and plays with, delighting in, explorations (explosions) of form," much like trans embodiments.[33] Indeed, the resonances between gender and genre, flesh and text, and trans lives as poem-bodies have been grounds of trans studies since its inception.[34] In that uneasy place between, where the making of sense and of each other happens,[35] trans thinking maintains an ear for the undecidable mutation of concept and creature;[36] a hand for irreconcilable entanglements;[37] an eye for gender and racial, linguistic and geographical, disciplinary and spiritual ambiguity;[38] a nose for questioning, the sort of questioning that creates space for a differently enfleshed notion of gender;[39] and a tongue for what we cannot yet (or ever) speak.[40] This interplay of illuminations and opacities, congealments and scatterings defines—without offering a definition of—trans thinking and, by extension, trans philosophy.

We invite readers to engage this text with these resonances and reverberations in mind. Read across it. Unsettle it. Be unmoored by it. Connect it to other networks of sense (and non-sense) with which you and yours are coconstructing paths of embodiment and coalition. Tarry with what is incoherent and discordant within this collection—what ways of reading and writing the world are incommensurate with one another. Settle into that ambiguity and its still uneasy resolution in accountable listening. Whatever trans philosophy is or might be, we hope it maintains a concrete sense of its own limitations (and occlusions) alongside this sense of collectively shaped, fostered, and cultivated indeterminacy.

Notes

1. Cameron Awkward-Rich, *The Terrible We: Thinking with Trans Maladjustment* (Durham, N.C.: Duke University Press, 2022).
2. Susan Stryker, Paisley Currah, and Lisa Jean Moore, "Trans-, Trans, or Transgender?," *Women's Studies Quarterly* 36, no. 3–4 (2008): 11–22; Eva Hayward, "More Lessons from a Starfish: Prefixial Flesh and Trans-speciated Selves," *Women's Studies Quarterly* 36, no. 3–4 (2008): 64–85; C. Riley Snorton, *Black on Both Sides: A Racial History of Trans Identity* (Minneapolis: University of Minnesota Press, 2017); Roderick A. Ferguson, *Aberrations in Black: Toward a Queer of Color Critique* (Minneapolis: University of Minnesota Press, 2003); Hortense Spillers, *Black, White, and in Color* (Chicago: University of Chicago Press, 2003).
3. Kristie Dotson, "How Is This Paper Philosophy?," *Comparative Philosophy* 3, no. 1 (2012): 3–29.
4. Judith Butler, "What Is Critique? An Essay on Foucault's Virtue," in *The Judith Butler Reader,* ed. Sara Salih (Oxford: Blackwell, 2004), 302–22; Judith Butler, "Can the Other of Philosophy Speak?," in *Undoing Gender* (New York: Routledge, 2004), 232–50.
5. Viviane Namaste, *Sex Change, Social Change: Reflections on Identity, Institutions, and Imperialism* (London: Women's Press, 2008), 25.
6. Audre Lorde, "Age, Race, Class, and Sex: Women Redefining Difference," in *Sister Outsider: Essays and Speeches* (Freedom, Calif.: Crossing Press, 1984), 114–23.
7. See, for example, the analysis in Roderick A. Ferguson, *The Reorder of Things: The University and Its Pedagogies of Minority Difference* (Minneapolis: University of Minnesota Press, 2012).
8. For an iteration of gender-critical feminism in Spanish-speaking Europe, see Alicia H. Puleo, *Ser Feministas: Pensamiento y Acción* (Madrid: Cátedra, 2017), and the public statements of another feminist philosopher, Amelia Valcárcel, "El debate sobre la ley trans se está tratando de un modo sentimental que no es el adecuado," Universidad Internacional Menéndez Pelayo, July 9, 2021, https://www.uimp.es/actualidad-uimp/amelia-valcarcel-debate-sobre-ley-trans.html.

9. Mycorrhizae are rhizomatic fungal roots that grow in symbiotic relationship with roots from other neighboring plants.

10. Perry Zurn and Andrea J. Pitts, "Trans Philosophy: The Early Years," a Conversation with Talia Mae Bettcher, Loren Cannon, Miqqi Gilbert, and C. Jacob Hale, *APA Newsletter on LGBT Issues in Philosophy* 20, no. 1 (2020): 1–11; Marlene Wayar, *Travesti: Una teoria lo suficientemente buena* (Buenos Aires: Muchas Nueces, 2019). Compare with Fred Moten's construction of poetics in *The Poetics of the Undercommons* (Brooklyn: Sputnik & Fizzle, 2016).

11. See, for example, Leslie Feinberg, *Transgender Warriors: Making History from Joan of Arc to RuPaul* (Boston: Beacon Press, 1996).

12. Susan Stryker and Stephen Whittle, eds., *The Transgender Studies Reader* (New York: Routledge, 2006).

13. Talia Mae Bettcher and Ann Garry, "Transgender Studies and Feminism: Theory, Politics, and Gender Realities," special issue, *Hypatia* 24, no. 3 (2009); Laurie J. Shrage, ed., *"You've Changed": Sex Reassignment and Personal Identity* (Oxford: Oxford University Press, 2009).

14. Susan Stryker and Aren Aizura, eds., *The Transgender Studies Reader 2* (New York: Routledge, 2013); Perry Zurn, "Trans Experience in Philosophy," *Blog of the APA,* August 11, 2016, https://blog.apaonline.org /2016/08/11/trans-experience-in-philosophy/; Susan Stryker and Talia Mae Bettcher, "Trans/Feminisms," special issue, *TSQ: Transgender Studies Quarterly* 3, no. 1–2 (2016).

15. Trans Philosophy Project, https://www.transphilosophyproject.com/.

16. Gloria Anzaldúa, *Borderlands / La Frontera* (San Francisco: Aunt Lute Books, 1987); María Lugones, *Pilgrimages / Peregrinajes: Theorizing Coalition against Multiple Oppressions* (Lanham, Md.: Rowman & Littlefield, 2003). For commentary on that influence, see Andrea J. Pitts, *Nos/ Otras: Gloria E. Anzaldúa, Multiplicitous Agency, and Resistance* (New York: State University of New York Press, 2021), chap. 5; Talia Mae Bettcher, "How I Became a Trans Philosopher," *Journal of World Philosophies* 7 (2022): 145–56; Perry Zurn, "The Path of Friction: Revisiting Hale's 'Rules' for Accountability to and within Trans Communities," *TSQ: Transgender Studies Quarterly* 10, no. 1 (2023): 71–85. This is not to suggest either that gender-dissident theory does not already exist in Latinx feminisms or that such theory occurs exclusively in work produced in academic contexts. See, for example, the artwork of Maya González (http://www.mayagonzalez.com/artist/bio/) and Diane Gamboa (Laura Elisa Perez, *Chicana Art* [Durham, N.C.: Duke University Press, 2007], 68–80).

17. micha cárdenas, *Poetic Operations: Trans of Color Art in Digital Media* (Durham, N.C.: Duke University Press, 2021); T. Jackie Cuevas, *Post-Borderlandia: Chicana Literature and Gender Variant Critique* (New Brunswick, N.J.: Rutgers University Press, 2018); PJ DiPietro, *Sideways*

Selves: The Politics of Transing Matter across the Americas (Austin: University of Texas Press, forthcoming); Francisco J. Galarte, *Brown Trans Figurations: Rethinking Race, Gender, and Sexuality in Chicanx/Latinx Studies* (Durham, N.C.: Duke University Press, 2021); L Heidenreich, *Nepantla Squared: Transgender Mestiz@* (Lincoln: University of Nebraska Press, 2020); Pitts, *Nos/Otras.*

18. Awkward-Rich, *Terrible We*; Alexandre Baril, *Undoing Suicidism: A Trans, Queer, Crip Approach to Rethinking (Assisted) Suicide* (Philadelphia: Temple University Press, 2023); Cavar, "Toward TransMad Epistemologies: A Working Text," *Spark: A 4C4Equality Journal* 4 (2022): https://sparkactivism.com/toward-transmad-epistemologies/; Mel Y. Chen, *Animacies: Biopolitics, Racial Mattering, and Queer Affect* (Durham, N.C.: Duke University Press, 2012); Mel Y. Chen, "Tranimacies: An Interview with Mel Y. Chen," *TSQ: Transgender Studies Quarterly* 2, no. 2 (2015): 317–23; Eli Clare, *Exile and Pride: Disability, Queerness, and Liberation* (Durham, N.C.: Duke University Press, 2015); Eli Clare, *Brilliant Imperfection: Grappling with Cure* (Durham, N.C.: Duke University Press, 2017).

19. Marquis Bey, *Cistem Failure* (Durham, N.C.: Duke University Press, 2021); Che Gossett, "Blackness and the Trouble of Trans Visibility," in *Trap Door: Trans Cultural Production and the Politics of Visibility,* ed. Reina Gossett, Eric A. Stanley, and Johanna Burton (Cambridge, Mass.: MIT Press, 2017), 183–90; Treva Ellison, Kai M. Green, Matt Richardson, and C. Riley Snorton, eds., "The Issue of Blackness," special issue, *TSQ: Transgender Studies Quarterly* 4, no. 2 (2017); Snorton, *Black on Both Sides.*

20. Jules Joanne Gleeson and Elle O'Rourke, eds., *Transgender Marxism* (London: Pluto Press, 2021).

21. E.g., Dean Spade, *Normal Life: Administrative Violence, Critical Trans Politics, and the Limits of Law* (2011; Durham, N.C.: Duke University Press, 2015); Eric A. Stanley, Nick Mitchell, Che Gossett, and Liat Ben-Moshe, "Critical Theory, Queer Resistance, and the Ends of Capture," in *Death and Other Penalties: Continental Philosophers on Prisons and Capital Punishment,* ed. Lisa Guenther, Scott Zeman, and Geoffrey Adelsberg (New York: Fordham University Press, 2015), 266–96.

22. Martín De Mauro Rucovsky, "The Travesti Critique of the Gender Identity Law in Argentina," trans. Ian Russell, *TSQ: Transgender Studies Quarterly* 6, no. 2 (2019): 223–38; DiPietro, *Sideways Selves.*

23. Lohana Berkins, "Un itinerario político del travestismo," in *Sexualidades Migrantes: Género y Transgénero,* ed. D. Maffía (Buenos Aires: Femimaría Editora, 2003), 127–37; Lohana Berkins, *Cumbia, copeteo y lágrimas: Informe nacional sobre la situación de las travestis, transexuales y transgéneros* (Buenos Aires: Asociación de Lucha por la Identidad Travesti-Transexual, 2007). See also Blas Radi, "On Trans* Epistemol-

ogy: Critiques, Contributions, and Challenges," *TSQ: Transgender Studies Quarterly* 6, no. 1 (2019): 43–63; Wayar, *Travesti*.

24. Lohana Berkins cited in PJ DiPietro, "Decolonizing Travesti Space in Buenos Aires: Race, Sexuality, and Sideways Relationality," *Gender, Place & Culture: A Journal of Feminist Geography* 23, no. 5 (2016): 683; cf. Lohana Berkins, *Selected Writings,* trans. Jamie Berrout (self-pub., 2019).

25. See DiPietro, *Sideways Selves*; Jennie Luna and Gabriel S. Estrada, "Trans*lating the Genderqueer-x through Caxcan, Nahua, and Xicanx Indigenous Knowledge," in *Decolonizing Latinx Masculinities,* ed. Arturo J. Aldama and Frederick Luis Aldama (Tucson: University of Arizona Press, 2020), 251–74; Pitts, *Nos/Otras*; Susy J. Zepeda, *Queering Mesoamerican Diasporas: Remembering Xicanx Indígena Ancestries* (Champaign: University of Illinois Press, 2022).

26. Leanne Betasamosake Simpson, *As We Have Always Done: Indigenous Freedom through Radical Resistance* (2017; Minneapolis: University of Minnesota Press, 2020).

27. Kai Pyle, "Naming and Claiming: Recovering Ojibwe and Plains Cree Two-Spirit Language," *TSQ: Transgender Studies Quarterly* 5, no. 4 (2018): 574–88.

28. María Lugones, "Heterosexualism and the Colonial/Modern Gender System," *Hypatia* 22, no. 1 (2007): 186–209; Aníbal Quijano, "Coloniality and Modernity/Rationality," *Cultural Studies* 21, no. 2–3 (2007): 168–78.

29. See Talia Mae Bettcher, "What Is Trans Philosophy?," this volume.

30. Butler, "Can the Other of Philosophy Speak?"

31. Stryker, Currah, and Moore, "Trans-, Trans, or Transgender?" See also Aren Z. Aizura, Marquis Bey, Toby Beauchamp, Treva Ellison, Jules Gill-Peterson, and Eliza Steinbock, "Thinking with Trans Now," *Social Text* 38, no. 4 (145) (2020): 125–47.

32. Tey Meadow, "Toward Trans* Epistemology: Imagining the Lives of Transgender People," *Women's Studies Quarterly* 44, no. 3/4 (2016): 320, 322.

33. TC Tolbert, "Open, and Always, Opening—An Introduction in 3 Parts," in *Troubling the Line: Trans and Genderqueer Poetry and Poetics,* ed. TC Tolbert and Trace Peterson (New York: Nightboat Books, 2013), 10.

34. See Sandy Stone, "The 'Empire' Strikes Back: A Posttranssexual Manifesto" (1987), in Stryker and Whittle, *Transgender Studies Reader,* 221–35.

35. Perry Zurn, *How We Make Each Other: Trans Life at the Edge of the University* (Durham, N.C.: Duke University Press, forthcoming).

36. DiPietro, *Sideways Selves*.

37. Christina León, *Matters of Inscription: Reading Figures of Latinidad* (New York: NYU Press, 2024).

38. Anzaldúa, *Borderlands / La Frontera*; Lugones, *Pilgrimages / Peregrinajes*, 121–50.
39. Marquis Bey, *Black Trans Feminism* (Durham, N.C.: Duke University Press, 2022), 145–74.
40. J. Logan Smilges, *Queer Silence: On Disability and Rhetorical Absence* (Minneapolis: University of Minnesota Press, 2022).

PART I
Metaphilosophy, Categories, and Kinds

What Is Trans Philosophy?

Talia Mae Bettcher

> I can only speak for myself. But what I write and how I write
> is done in order to save my own life.
> —*Barbara Christian, "The Race for Theory"*

In an important sense, trans philosophy didn't exist at all perhaps
as recently as ten years ago.[1] Back then, I would have described my
own research as situated at the intersections of disciplinary feminist philosophy and the inter- and multidisciplinary field of trans
studies. The expression "trans philosophy" wasn't quite available,
or at least it didn't say very much. Perhaps that seems remarkable now.

For so long there had been so few trans folks working on trans
issues in the profession: there was the pioneering work of C. Jacob
Hale, Miqqi Alicia Gilbert, and Jamie Lindemann Nelson in the
1990s. Loren Cannon, C. Riley Snorton, and I were writing in the
first decade of the 2000s. But trans philosophers were few and far
between. Admittedly, an anthology on trans issues and personal
identity as well as a special *Hypatia* issue on feminist philosophy
and trans issues made their appearances as early as 2009.[2] But both
milestones demonstrated just how difficult it was to find trans philosophers publishing at all, let alone publishing in the profession.

Now, however, there's a marked generational change—a wave
of trans and nonbinary scholars who have begun to publish or are
getting ready to publish in the area—philosophers such as Megan
Burke, Robin Dembroff, Grayson Hunt, Stephanie Kapusta, Tamsin

Kimoto, Amy Marvin, Rachel McKinnon, Andrea J. Pitts, and Perry Zurn, to name some.

The turning point was marked by the first-ever trans philosophy conference, Trans* Experience in Philosophy, that took place at the University of Oregon in 2016, sponsored by *Hypatia*. The Trans Philosophy Project has since been sponsored by *Hypatia*.[3] Not only did the project provide funding for a second trans philosophy conference in 2018—Trans Thinking // Thinking Trans—it includes a resource initiative for compiling a bibliography of trans philosophy, as well as pedagogical materials for teaching it and for developing a set of best practices for philosophy organizations that want to support trans philosophers and trans philosophy.

This is not to say, however, that there haven't been some recent growing pains—if by "growing pains" we mean "explosive controversies." Several years ago, there was considerable discussion of philosopher Kathleen Stock's so-called gender-critical feminism that she published online.[4] Her work was taken up on the *Leiter Reports* and *Daily Nous,* mainstream philosophy blogs.[5] Many philosophers entirely unfamiliar with trans issues or trans scholarship enthusiastically embraced what they took to be the exposure of a politically correct trans agenda that had little intellectual merit. Meanwhile, several trans scholars and largely feminist allies complained that the engagement seemed to ignore the existence of trans studies in general and trans philosophy in particular.

The most notable controversy, however, concerned *Hypatia* itself and, in particular, the publication of an essay about transgender people and so-called transracialism in Spring 2017. There was a community backlash, particularly on social media, about the essay's lack of engagement with the existing literature in critical race theory and trans studies, its unacknowledged political positioning with regard to race and transness, and deeper questions about how it came to be published in the first place. The controversy blew up enough to be covered in the *New York Times* and, by the end of it, *Hypatia* had been shaken to its core.[6] Regardless of one's thoughts on the controversy, one thing was clear (well, at least to me)—namely, that trans philosophy has (or is) coming of age.

The question "What *is* trans philosophy?" is therefore timely. This essay considers it from a place of long-standing engagement, of seeing some things change and others stay the same. This essay has a historical sensibility as well as a practical, political one as I see the increased visibility of trans philosophy in the profession in tandem with a wave of these young, new trans and gender-nonconforming scholars. I'm more than a little worried about the climate.[7]

For me, the question is also deeply personal. My groping toward answers comes from my own experiences attempting to do "trans philosophy" in the first place. Much of what I have to say is a reflection on what I've been trying to do for years and what I aim to do now. My goal is not to give *the* answers but simply to shed some light on the question. Or, to put it differently, there are different ways of answering this question, and what I offer here is one.

Despite its idiosyncrasy, however, this essay is also not much more than a shiny new version of an old wheel. Much of what I have to say resembles the earlier ideas of philosophers who have been marginalized in the profession in various ways—perhaps most centrally, by way of racism and ethnocentrism, but also in ways that haven't begun to be reckoned with, such as ableism, and ways that have, such as sexism. To be sure, trans philosophy differs from other forms of "philosophies of difference" in some respects. For example, trans people have a rather marked relation to theories that have been written about us by nontrans people and the effect of this authorial-topic arrangement has consequences in our lives. However, I'm not interested in sorting through which things are more specific to trans philosophy and which are not. Such an endeavor rests on some rather problematic views that we will discuss in due course. My hope, instead, is that this article will constitute a "newish" arrangement of a rather old number.

Preliminaries

The metaphilosophical question "What is trans philosophy?" might be viewed merely as an instance of the general question "What is philosophy?" If so, the only distinctive thing about it would be the subject matter. But that wouldn't tell us anything particularly fascinating about trans philosophy; it certainly won't enable trans philosophy to reveal something important about philosophy in general. Most important, it would simply miss the point.

I take my cue from trans studies—the multi- and interdisciplinary field of study that began in the early 1990s. I start with Sandy Stone's pioneering essay "The *Empire* Strikes Back: A Posttranssexual Manifesto" in which she wonders, "Whose story is this anyway?" and "If the transsexual were to speak, what would s/he say?"[8] She writes: "The people who have no voice in this theorizing are the transsexuals themselves. . . . Transsexuals have been resolutely complicit by failing to develop an effective counterdiscourse."[9] And I rely heavily on Susan Stryker's crucial distinction between the mere study of trans phenomena and the field of trans studies proper: "Transgender studies considers the embodied experience of the speaking subject, who claims constative knowledge of the referent topic, to be a proper—indeed essential— component of the analysis of transgender phenomena."[10] I take it Stryker is drawing a contrast between traditional theories of trans phenomena, on the one hand, and trans theories that articulate broader answers to Stone's questions above or that contribute to this "counterdiscourse," on the other.

I put it this way: we trans people live under constant theoretical pressure. Theories float on high, dogging our moves, questioning our motives, limiting or opening our options. Some of these theories are hostile; they're like hovering weapons taking shots at us while we try to get through the business of life. Others are friendlier; they come to saturate our lives. We avail ourselves of them to explain ourselves to others or to make sense of our own lives. We breathe those theories, try to embody them. Sometimes, we just try to figure it out on our own. We have an intimate relation to theory. It gets stuck to our bodies. One of the reasons trans people exist under theoretical pressure is precisely that we don't conform to everyday expectations—we're considered anomalous. But, from the other side of the theory, we "anomalies" want to know what's going on. For us, our very relation to theory needs to be subject to inquiry. It's an important question: What is it to philosophize from underneath the theory, on the other side of theory?[11]

Crucially, although trans studies often does concern trans people and trans issues, it's also much broader. General and often deep questions arise when we reconsider what has been taken for granted, when we bring a broadly "trans perspective" into focus. How should we understand gender itself? What about sexual orientation and sexuality more generally? What does gender have to do with personhood? What effect does the acknowledgment of trans oppression/resistance have on how we understand multiple forms of oppression? What is it to say that gender oppression is not reducible to sexist oppression? What question does this raise for the important concept of intersectionality? The list goes on.

If trans philosophy is understood in light of this, it obviously cannot be determined by subject alone. It must be undertaken, rather, with an overarching aim of exposing and combating trans oppression, of illuminating and enacting a kind of trans resistance. Otherwise, what's the point? This in turn greatly affects one's philosophical approach: one's methodology.

To pursue these methodological effects, I consider three related questions in this essay. First, what is philosophical about trans philosophy? Second, on what is trans philosophy grounded? Third, what is the relation of trans philosophy to "the literature"?

What Can Trans Philosophy Offer?
Philosophical Perplexity and the WTF

In arguing against both Ludwig Wittgenstein's and Richard Rorty's accounts of philosophy, Graham Priest writes:

> Philosophy is precisely that intellectual inquiry in which anything is open to critical challenge and scrutiny. This, at least, explains many of its salient features. Philosophy is subversive. Time and again, philosophers have shot at religions, political systems, public mores. They do this because they are prepared to challenge things which everybody else takes for granted, or whose rejection most people do not countenance.[12]

How exciting! Of course, the quote raises pertinent questions, like "What happened to philosophy? Why is its failure to live up to this promise so spectacular?" and "How might trans philosophy do better?" But Priest does capture a sense of what philosophy is (or is supposed to be) that appeals to both philosophers and nonphilosophers alike.

According to Priest, philosophy has both a negative and a positive side. The negative side (the side that critiques other theories, the side that asks penetrating, relentless questions) is primary. The positive side (the side that provides theory, answers questions), though important, is secondary and subservient to the former. One of the main values of a positive theory is precisely that it gives added heft to one's critique of contending theories. That is, constructive philosophy is ultimately subsumable under the critical aspect of philosophy. Crucially, what makes philosophy distinctive is that anything is up for criticism. There are no disciplinary or methodological restrictions.

> It is exactly here, it seems to me, that philosophy is to be distinguished from other intellectual inquiries. In religion, one is explicitly not allowed to question certain things. In history, one is not allowed to question the view that other historians have minds. And in science, one may be expected to be critical of novel ideas and results, but one is not encouraged to question well-entrenched and established parts of the scientific corpus.[13]

To be clear, Priest does not require that all philosophy be primarily critical. He recognizes that philosophers differ in approach: some are chiefly critical, whereas others are builders, yet others are both. His claim, rather, is that the positive theory-building is ultimately parasitic on unfettered philosophical criticism. The latter best captures the spirit of philosophy, its distinctive feature.

I find myself dissatisfied, however. I don't see my philosophical projects as ultimately serving the project of critique; I see them as ultimately serving the project of illumination. And I suspect that my departure from Priest concerns a fundamental disagreement about the nature of philosophy itself, a disagreement concerning the relation between philosophy and the everyday world of common sense that is worth taking some time to elaborate.

Philosophy has a reputation for spinning its wheels, for beating its head against unsolvable problems, for losing itself in quicksand. The notion of "philosophical perplexity" has been a longstanding philosophical topic that reaches back at least to the early modern philosophers: What's wrong (or right) with philosophy such that it seems not to make scientific progress? There have been many answers about the source of such perplexity. One is just that the subject matter is so extraordinarily challenging that it's easy to take a disastrous misstep, a wrong turn, that could lead one in the wrong direction for hundreds of years. Another is that many of the questions philosophy seeks to answer are simply beyond the limits of human understanding; we're just not cognitively constituted to answer some of these questions, so confusion and a lack of progress is to be expected. Yet another says philosophy itself creates the problems and confusions when everything was just fine to begin with.

Regardless, there's considerable agreement that philosophy plays an important role in leading us to such perplexity, forcing us to consider tough questions, forcing us to explore ever deeper. Even if philosophy isn't itself the source of perplexity, certainly it's our guide, the practice that strips back a seemingly coherent commonsense reality to reveal a seething cauldron of confusion, and it does so by asking so many critical questions.

There's something intuitively appealing about this view; it gets at a deep conception of what philosophy is. As Bertrand Russell explains: "As soon as we begin to philosophize . . . we find that even the most everyday things lead to problems to which only very incomplete answers can be given."[14] What I want to suggest, however, is that this conception of philosophy rests on a highly controversial assumption: namely, that for the "prephilosophical man" the "world tends to become obvious" and "common objects rouse no questions" and that this man is "imprisoned in the prejudices derived from common sense."[15] In short, this is to assume that all appeared well and good before philosophy arrived on the scene: Our common sense, our everyday understanding of the world was, if superficial, happily undisturbed. In other words, this is to assume a close fit between individuals and their "everyday."

This assumption is baseless.[16] The baselessness is plain to those of us for whom this everyday has seemed utterly confusing—often hostile. It is hard to make sense of oneself as a trans person. Coming out to oneself and transitioning can be brutal. For us, the so-called everyday and any common sense that accrues to it does not suit us, is disorienting at best, and is violent at worst. It is shot through with questions.

What does it mean to say that I'm a woman, I've wondered. And why does so much appear to hinge on it? How do I make sense, for example, of being assaulted in the middle of Santa Monica

Boulevard by someone who wanted to prove I was really a man?[17] Why do people want to kill us? WTF?

Seriously—WTF?

We trans people live an "everyday" shot through with perplexity, shot through with WTF questions. We live in the WTF. We did not need philosophy to uncover this perplexity. It was already there. If philosophy is going to give us anything at all, it had better be answers or at least some partial, provisional illumination. Otherwise, it cannot help us. In this light, therefore, I do not see the chief function of trans philosophy as negative or critical. I see it as primarily constructive, positive, illuminating, and orienting. I do think here that philosophy is uniquely positioned to address the WTF rather than, say, sociology or psychology or anthropology—precisely because the WTF is so all-embracing, so personal, indeed, so existential in nature. Or, in other words, I think the attempt to provide illumination in response to these WTF questions is necessarily philosophical.

Crucially, this is not to say that this constructive approach aims to answer all questions—as if that were possible. In attempting to illuminate that which perplexes, new questions invariably arise—questions that cannot be readily answered. And of course, this unearthing of new questions is part and parcel of the philosophical enterprise. It is to say, however, that these new questions serve as breadcrumbs on one's way to answering those original questions with which one began—questions that were present before one began philosophizing.

The key thing is that for what I'll call "ground-bound" philosophy, perplexity isn't philosophical because it is exposed through philosophical critique but, rather, because it cries out for philosophical illumination. One difficulty with Graham Priest's view, then, which defines philosophy as "that intellectual inquiry in which anything is open to critical challenge and scrutiny," is that it recognizes only what might be called "pristine philosophy"—a philosophy that leads us to a state of perplexity through philosophical practice itself, whereas the "prephilosophical" was, to begin with, happily undisturbed.[18] This is less the fault of Priest, however, and more a reflection of the pervasive underlying conception of philosophy. By challenging this conception, we become open to the possibility that the relations among perplexity, philosophy, and the everyday are not uniform.

By recognizing both pristine and ground-bound philosophy, we have a preliminary way of making sense of the difference between trans philosophy and philosophizing about trans people. In the latter we should expect to see trans phenomena as the topic of or possibly used as part of some critical philosophical intervention. What such an approach will invariably lack is any hint of an effort to confer intelligibility upon trans experiences in the WTF. And this, of course, is because a particular conception of philosophy is presupposed.

Down the Rabbit Hole

Critical intervention is built right into the project of shedding light on the WTF. Specifically, the critical assessment and possible rejection of prevailing theoretical models, political frameworks, and taken-for-granted assumptions that impede our capacity to shed light on the WTF is plainly required. Indeed, when viewed in this way, the very failure of some positive account to provide adequate illumination constitutes a serious philosophical challenge to it.

Yet this is not to deny that there are starting points built right into trans philosophy. I see it as a necessary starting point that we take trans self-identities as at least presumptively valid. It should be taken for granted, for example, that if a trans man says he is a man, he is, indeed, a man. This opens me up to the charge of being "dogmatic" and ultimately "not philosophical" insofar as I'm not allowing for everything to be up for grabs. It is important to see why this is not so.

Trans philosophy is much like queer theory, feminist theory and philosophy, and critical race theory and philosophy. There are certain presuppositions, that is to say, starting points. For example, it would be odd if the question whether homosexuality was immoral were a hot topic in queer theory. It would be bizarre to see the question whether women ought to be subjected to the rule of men as the central area of discussion in feminist philosophy.

And similarly, the question whether trans people are who we say we are should not be central in trans philosophy. To be clear, nothing that I have said makes these presumptions out of bounds in philosophy in general (I shall return to this later). At present, I'm simply claiming that if one ends up arguing that such presumptions are false, one is not doing queer, feminist, or trans philosophy at all; one is doing something else. At least on the face of it, this "something else" looks, in part, like an attempt to undermine the validity of these very domains of inquiry. If somehow, some way, it were established beyond doubt that men ought to rule over women, feminist philosophical inquiry would be off the table.

Of course, one might respond that in all of these examples, the acceptance of starting points runs against the spirit of philosophical investigation. Feminist, antiracist, queer, and trans philosophy are all dogmatic. But this is to falsely suppose that philosophy ought to have no starting points at all. It ought to be plain to philosophical practitioners that we invariably rely on starting points in order to conduct our investigations. It's impossible to do philosophy without them.

Consider, for example, the quest for illumination in the WTF. As a trans woman, I do want to know how it is that I am a woman in this world that denies this. The presumption that my identity is valid hardly answers this. This is to say, even given the presumption, we don't know yet what the universe must be like in order for this to be so. Surely, we would like to know that. That is, I think, a valid question. Indeed, it's one of deep philosophical importance that can—and ought to—be included within trans philosophical investigations.

What Grounds Our Contribution?

Unless we have some sort of robust a priori knowledge of the world (which we don't), it seems philosophers must proceed from a place of worldly engagement. We eat, read, sleep. We walk around. We talk to people. Perhaps we buy milk. We live in some everyday, and we possess a worldly perception that I take to include not only our lived experiences but also our knowledge of local common sense, as well as familiarity with the social practices that shape experiences and in which "common sense" inheres.

Certainly, any philosophical project centralizing some aspect of the everyday—either as obvious or perplexing—as a topic has ipso facto involved worldly perception. To take aim at "religions, political systems, [and] public mores" requires a worldly grasp of them. But even philosophical projects that don't focus on the everyday still must deploy worldly perception in philosophical judgments, regardless of how abstract and attenuated, about what seems wrong/right, im/plausible, and un/important.

There's a sense in which perhaps all disciplines rely to some extent on this worldly perception. But to the extent that philosophy isn't data-driven and not even usually expressly empiricist, this worldly perception surely plays a crucial methodological role—either acknowledged or not. This forces the embarrassing admission that a single person's worldly perception appears to be playing a rather conflated methodological role in much of what passes for philosophical research.

One solution is to reject any philosophy that isn't more solidly grounded in empirical data, of course. Another solution is to simply own it—at least to some degree. What can be said on behalf of the latter?

It has its benefits. In relying on one's worldly perception rather than on some dataset, the worldly contact that guides one's reflections is oriented to practice. The world is revealed through an ongoing engagement within it. Indeed, worldly perception might be said to yield "data" organized in the shape of a life—a life with both a history and a future. There is, in this sense, something inherently first-personal about the worldly perception tethering philosophical reflection to something other than its own literature. It is good, in my view, to have some disciplines like that. Such an approach seems particularly well suited to addressing WTF questions that are often so deeply personal in character. And there's the hint of an undeveloped critical upshot here: namely, that philosophizing that maintains an increasingly attenuated relation to worldly perception through repeated iterations of literature engagement alone (informally a "cottage industry") has a greater likelihood of producing obfuscation than illumination.

Unfortunately, when one lives in deep tension with the everyday, when the prevailing common sense scarcely countenances one's existence, when the deepest questions arise from the ground on which one fails to stand, well before one has even begun to philosophize, one will surely need an alternative worldly perception, and therefore an alternative form of the social. Although the perplexing character of the everyday may make a good starting point in the quest for illumination, it's tough to rely on one's chief source of confusion as one's ground for philosophical judgment about what seems wrong/right, im/plausible, and un/important. Trans philosophy needs to proceed from pretheoretical sociality among trans people—whatever form that takes—standing in a relation of resistance to the prevailing mainstream world of the WTF. What else does one have to draw on that could provide the worldly perception necessary for life-affirming, rather than suicidal, philosophical illuminations?

Recognizing both the centrality of worldly perception in philosophical method and the heterogeneous character of the social, however, forces a frank acknowledgment of the limitations of philosophical inquiry. Philosophers' worldly perceptions are obviously shaped and limited by their social milieu; they're culturally, geographically, and temporally indexed. I write from my own personal experiences in various Los Angeles trans subcultures from around the mid-1990s to the present. Saying this is important. It's to clarify scope and limitations. But this is no less true for philosophers who fail to announce their locatedness—philosophers who can pretend their worldly perception is universal. To be sure, philosophizing locally seems almost oxymoronic in light of the long history of philosophy's grand aspirations. It's certainly a serious comedown. But it's also more philosophical if we take philosophy to be at all concerned with the truth.

To see what I mean, consider the deployment of philosophical intuitions in conceptual analysis. Consider the question "What is a woman?" then, which is to be taken as a question about the concept of a woman. Suppose one has intuitions that trans women are, at best, "hard cases" with respect to the concept.[19] That is, depending upon the particular facts about any particular trans woman, she is going to end up as only marginally counting or as being "in-between" or as not counting at all.

The problem is that I have entirely different intuitions. My intuitions are that trans women are women and, moreover, that we are not merely marginal women. Furthermore, my intuitions are that this is so regardless of whether a trans woman has a penis or a vagina. Indeed, I think that questions about genitalia and even chromosomes are not relevant to the question of womanhood.

To be sure, my intuitions might be rejected out of hand. But as a matter of fact, they're grounded in my embeddedness in trans subcultures—including my familiarity with trans discursive and nondiscursive practices there. This points to the ways in which trans philosophy is supported not only by its methodological commitments but also by alternative forms of the everyday that guide philosophical judgment.

If this is right, it seems clear that, in general, philosophy as a discipline needs to acknowledge the locatedness of worldly perception. What María Lugones calls "world-traveling" becomes integral to philosophy when worldly perception plays such a key methodological role.[20] It promotes a double worldly perception; the capacity to be "bicultural" with regard to the "everydays" in which we are embedded is fostered. This notion of double perception is scarcely new, of course.[21] But what's crucial to note is that it can enable a more penetrating analysis of the social quotidians (as now they are multiple). When one occupies a liminal space between alternative forms of the social quotidian, worldly perception as a double perception enables a deeper, more ruthless interrogation of an everyday by enabling one to look at an everyday from the perspective of another.[22]

Any ground-bound philosophical approach, including trans philosophy, can be said to proceed from a double worldly perception— both a perception of resistant forms of trans sociality and a perception of the dominant ones. It is a necessary condition of its existence. In this way, ground-bound approaches are particularly well-positioned to accomplish the challenging of "common sense" that we found in Priest and Russell.

Nonetheless, such double perception is local and therefore limited. It can conceal power imbalances even within a resistant form of sociality. Good philosophizing requires being able to recognize such hegemony and erasure, and this is not possible when one remains static. Although imperfect, such world-traveling is imperative to any ground-bound philosophy—it works to render ever more complex one's starting point, one's life experience, one's fluency in multiple everydays. In this way, how one lives one's life, with whom one develops bonds of sociality and intimacy, becomes an integral component of philosophical methodology. This, in turn, suggests the beginning of an answer to the question of just how nontrans philosophers can contribute to trans philosophy in a significant way.

With Whom Should We Speak? The Work of Philosophy

Let's return to a pristine take on the question of whether trans women are women. Suppose, for example, that we're interested in raising philosophical perplexity about the concept "woman" and we think that an appeal to trans women will help. What's going on?

There will probably be a failure to recognize the existence of ground-bound philosophy at all. Specifically, any attempt to confer intelligibility on living while trans in the WTF may not seem particularly important in the glowing light of the intriguing conceptual question "What is a woman?" The question "Why do people want to kill us?" will likely not appear on the radar. There will likely be the erasure of trans subcultural worlds, or at least a strong presumption that they are irrelevant (rather than methodologically crucial to trans philosophy). The question about which intuitions count and why is certainly off the table.

What work does such an approach do? It can have consequences in terms of how trans scholars are actually treated in the profession. It can communicate that trans identities are up for negotiation "in the real world." It can erase trans philosophy as a viable approach—it can say that there is no room in philosophy for trans philosophers to make sense of a transphobic world.

Recognizing this can help us better understand the various kinds of work that trans philosophy itself performs. For those of us who live under theoretical pressure, philosophical critique doesn't always flow from some philosophical penchant for asking questions. It's life and death once "the literature" starts to have material consequences in our lives. It's about outright survival. It's about clearing space.

There are several ways of doing this. One obvious way is pedagogical. It may be necessary to bring philosophers to that place where they're equipped to engage in a more advanced form of inquiry. At a lower undergraduate level, I may very cautiously raise the question whether homosexuality is immoral in order to show that there is no good argument that it is. However, I wouldn't dream of raising such a question in an advanced course in LGBT philosophy—for one thing, the posing of the question is heterosexist. I make—and expressly problematize—my concession in the lower division course for pedagogical reasons.

A second way involves replying to the philosopher who barges into a room full of trans scholars, demanding that someone prove the validity of trans identities. Here, the critical intervention may involve responding to such philosophers in their own terms. This means, very likely, that one will not have the chance to do the careful framing in the pedagogical approach above. Such a response therefore runs the risk of complicity in the centralization of pristine philosophy, in the erasure of trans philosophy.

Another way of responding involves engaging in this problematizing work—actually doing the metaphilosophy. Whereas the first two approaches require accepting starting points and intuitions that are not one's own, this approach includes exposing this very fact. The danger, here, of course, is that the work will simply be misunderstood. In effect, one argues that before one can take up the question whether P, one must first consider whether Q, only to receive the angry response that one has just given a rather shoddy argument for P. Here, one sees the interesting work that such a response accomplishes—namely it prevents the very discussion of Q. It insists that the only question of importance is P. As Amy Marvin remarks:

> Asking people who want to do critical scholarship on this subject to "read the literature" seems to often get dismissed as a near-ad hominem, or as a tactic for uncritical dismissal without any engagement (and thus intellectually shallow). . . . I worry that the difficulty of having a conversation about whether or not trans women are women (it stands out to me, by the way, that this yet again focuses on trans women rather than trans men) amounts to a suggestion that the conversation

should not include our scholarly and personal voices, and continue to cast us as people who scholarship should be about rather than with.[23]

Note that in all three cases, a defensive posture is taken. Although one is doing philosophy, one is certainly not doing philosophy-as-illumination; one is doing critique. But neither is the critique pristine. I don't claim to provide a common feature of trans philosophy; this is one of the reasons why. Trans philosophy can do many things; illumination in the WTF is just one.

Defensive responses are important and require philosophical acumen; however, they don't involve the philosophical depth that illumination of the WTF provides. By contrast, illumination seems useful in guiding these defensive responses. It's nice to have a clearer picture of what's going on before one replies. And, of course, illumination is survival-rich in its own right. Unfortunately, illumination must be undertaken with some caution. There's a danger in even going there (or at least going there publicly), since what we say can also be weaponized against us. Indeed, one of the functions of this threat is precisely this foreclosure of self-understanding, of illumination. Keeping us off balance with unproductive battles, and then threatening to use our own self-critique against us, renders philosophical reflection nearly impossible as we are backed into a corner. But this also speaks to the importance of attempting to do just this.

The point, at any rate, is that once philosophy is understood to accomplish different kinds of work, our view of philosophy is rendered more complex. We must concern ourselves not only with what philosophy says but also with what it does. We must philosophize with our eyes wide open: Whose interests are being served? To what end? What work does it perform?

In my view, reflection on the different kinds of work a piece of philosophy performs is constitutive of doing philosophy at all. This is evident to anyone who does ground-bound philosophy. But it should also be accepted by pristine practitioners. The "work of philosophy" may often be nothing more than a Priest-style back-and-forth debate, but this doesn't mean this is the only work for which philosophy is used. Certainly, in light of what I've said, a purely pristine approach to trans issues cannot be treated as on par with a pristine approach to the metaphysics of time. There's work being accomplished in the former that is not in the latter. By failing to understand this, one fails as a philosopher. Not only does one fail to comprehend how others are using philosophy, one fails to comprehend one's own philosophical actions. In effect, one does not know what one is doing. If one pays full attention only to the back-and-forth of pristine engagement, one fails to comprehend what is really going on.

Once we open our minds to what's really going on, questions around philosophical practice and the ethics thereof come immediately into view. What do we say of the philosopher who understands that trans philosophers are trying to figure things out for ourselves, who recognizes the importance of ground-bound philosophy, who understands the effect of theories in our lives, and yet who continues to raise pristine questions about whether or not trans people are who we say we are? There's a willful ignorance, a patent disregard, that surely should be subject to ethical scrutiny: Why are you behaving like that? These discussions about the ethics of philosophical practice are critical, in my view, although now isn't the time to jump into the deep end. Rather, I return to Priest's thought that any assumption is up for grabs in philosophy. This is true. The point I'm pressing, however, is that it still doesn't follow that key ethical considerations don't arise. These questions matter to the practice of trans philosophy as well. Specifically, we might ask what work we ought to be doing.

Philosophy's Other?

As I wrap up, I want to consider Judith Butler's essay "Can the 'Other' of Philosophy Speak?"[24] Butler points to work that is philosophical, that draws from philosophical traditions, and that nonetheless exists outside of the purview of professional philosophy within much broader cross-disciplinary theoretical conversations. This "Other" arises largely due to the efforts of professional philosophy in enforcing its own disciplinary boundaries too obsessively. This, then, raises the frightful possibility that philosophy has lost itself to the very thing it has excluded.

The Other is important since, from the beginning, most of the theoretical work in trans studies has developed outside the bounds of disciplinary philosophy. A key question therefore is this: Insofar as disciplinary trans philosophy has begun to come into its own, what exactly is being claimed when it calls itself "philosophy"? How is it understood in relation to philosophy's Other from which trans studies itself has blossomed? Do we ignore all of the pertinent trans philosophical work that does not originate from scholars in philosophy departments? What, then, of Gayle Salamon's crucial contributions?[25] What, then, of the groundbreaking work of C. Riley Snorton?[26] Or should disciplinary trans philosophy simply "lose itself" to the Other? After all, to insist upon boundary-drawing between the "real" philosophy and the "other" surely replicates the problem. Perhaps. But if so, we still can't ignore the recent appearance of trans philosophy within the discipline, minimally because to do so would be to ignore the distinctive issues that confront trans and nonbinary philosophers who are trying to eke out an existence there.

Butler makes it seem that nobody works at the "margins" of the profession in philosophy.[27] They suggest, for example, that all the feminist philosophers have left the profession. But that's not true. There are plenty of ground-bound philosophers working at the margins. To work at the margins of the profession is often to work in the liminal space between philosophy and its Other—a space Butler seems not to acknowledge.

In light of this, there are different ways of sketching the topography. The distinction between pristine and ground-bound philosophy is perhaps more important than the one between philosophy and its Other, as we find both approaches within and outside the profession of philosophy. It's important to remember, after all, that Butler's work, and queer theory more generally, has been criticized by trans scholars precisely for using trans phenomena for conducting more abstract investigations into gender.[28] We might understand the charge as, in part, the complaint that such investigations fail to recognize the existence of trans experiences in the WTF, trans attempts to find illumination in the WTF.

Most important, however, is the fragmentation of these ground-bound investigations, the inherent limitations and distortions mentioned above, and consequently, the possibilities of misunderstanding and misrepresenting one another in our philosophical work. Butler's work can scarcely be described as pristine. Their early, foundational queer theory came from a particular location in queer space—one that concerned misrepresentation of butch–femme relations as mere replications of heterosexuality.[29] What this suggests is the importance of communication and engagement among different ground-bound philosophies. Such engagement is another kind of important work that philosophy can perform. But here caution is required. If what I have said is right, it cannot be conducted through pristine attempts to referee the conflicts, nor can be it accomplished through ground-bound philosophers passing themselves off as pristine in order to secure referee status.

On the contrary, once we centralize this challenge of communication, the question "What literature should we engage with and why?" takes on a different tone. If something like world travel is an important practice in opening up one's experiences—experiences that guide one's philosophical judgment—then it might also be that literature travel is likewise crucial.

This applies equally to trans philosophy itself, of course. We ought to think long and hard about the literature with which we engage, particularly if we're interested at all in the crucial project of communicating across ground-bound philosophies. Is it most important to engage with pristine philosophers? Is it most important to draw from and contribute to philosophy's Other? Must trans philosophy be grounded in a European "postmodern" literature, for example? Might it not, instead, head toward a more decolonial feminism?[30] With whom are we philosophizing and why?

Such questions matter, in part, because our original question "What is trans philosophy?" is not merely the traditional, ahistorical one that could be raised exclusively within the discipline of philosophy. The question, rather, is living and contemporary, grounded in part in this doubling of philosophy. This sociohistorically situated rendering of the question asks not merely for the conclusion of well-crafted arguments, but for the bold creation and enactment of new possibilities. If it's metaphilosophical, it's nonetheless also a question of praxis: it's future-oriented. No doubt, the question in the end isn't merely what trans philosophy is but also what it could be.

Notes

This is an abbreviated version of a longer essay published under the same title, "What Is Trans Philosophy?," *Hypatia* 34, no. 4 (2019): 644–67.

1. In this article, I use *trans* to include those who do not identify with fixed binary identities, who are gender-fluid, and who disown any gender identity, along with binary-identified trans people.
2. Laurie Shrage, ed., *"You've Changed": Sex Reassignment and Personal Identity* (Oxford: Oxford University Press, 2009); Talia Mae Bettcher and Ann Garry, eds., "Transgender Studies and Feminism: Theory, Politics, and Gender Realities," special issue, *Hypatia* 24, no. 3 (2009).
3. See Trans Philosophy Project, https://www.transphilosophyproject .com/.
4. Talia Mae Bettcher, "'When Tables Speak': On the Existence of Trans Philosophy," Daily Nous, May 30, 2018, http://dailynous.com/2018/05/30 /tables-speak-existence-trans-philosophy-guest-talia-mae-bettcher/; Kathleen Stock, "Response to Professor Talia Mae Bettcher," Medium, May 31, 2018, https://medium.com/@kathleenstock/response-to -professor-talia-mae-bettcher-21263ffd87c8.
5. Stock argued against counting trans women as women in certain spaces—such as restrooms, changing rooms, domestic violence centers, and so forth. Her complaints centered around the United Kingdom's Gender Recognition Act. For the controversy, see especially "Monthly Archives: May 2018," *Daily Nous,* May 2018, http://dailynous .com/2018/05/; "May 2018," *Leiter Reports: A Philosophy Blog,* https:// leiterreports.typepad.com/blog/2018/05/index.html. For related issues, see Lori Watson, "The Woman Question," *TSQ: Transgender Studies Quarterly* 3, no. 1–2 (2016): 248–55; Talia Mae Bettcher, "Through the Looking Glass: Transgender Theory Meets Feminist Philosophy," in *Routledge Handbook of Feminist Philosophy,* ed. Ann Garry, Serene Khader, and Allison Stone (London: Routledge, 2017), 393–404.
6. See Jennifer Schussler, "A Defense of 'Transracial' Identity Roils Philosophy World," *New York Times,* May 19, 2017.
7. For a discussion of the difficulties that trans scholars face in the profession of philosophy, see Perry Zurn, "Trans Experience in Philosophy," *Blog of the American Philosophical Association,* August 11, 2016, https:// blog.apaonline.org/2016/08/11/trans-experience-in-philosophy/.
8. Sandy Stone, "The *Empire* Strikes Back: A Posttranssexual Manifesto," in *The Transgender Studies Reader,* ed. Susan Stryker and Stephen Whittle (New York: Routledge, 2006), 229, 230.

9. Stone, 229–30.

10. Susan Stryker, "(De)subjugated Knowledges: An Introduction to Transgender Studies," in Stryker and Whittle, *Transgender Studies Reader,* 12.

11. The objectification of trans people in this approach is also usefully explored in terms of curiosity—for example, through what Perry Zurn calls "autopsic" and "therapeutic" modes, in his reading of Jacques Derrida. This raises the question about the potential for liberatory or at least resistant forms of curiosity. See Perry Zurn, "The Curiosity at Work in Deconstruction," *Journal of French and Francophone Philosophy* 27, no. 1 (2018): 84–106; Perry Zurn "Puzzle Pieces: Shapes of Trans Curiosity," *APA Newsletter on LGBT Issues in Philosophy* 18, no. 1 (2018): 10–16; Grayson Hunt, "Loving Curiosity: On the Intersection of Bisexual and Transgender Oppression," *Philosopher* (blog), June 2, 2017, https://politicalphilosopher.net/2017/06/02/featured-philosopher -grayson-hunt/.

12. Graham Priest, "What Is Philosophy?," *Philosophy* 81, no. 316 (2006): 202.

13. Priest, "What Is Philosophy?," 201–2.

14. Bertrand Russell, *The Problems of Philosophy* (Oxford: Oxford University Press, 1912), 157.

15. Russell, *Problems of Philosophy,* 157.

16. For a related discussion of disruptions of the everyday, see Mariana Ortega, *In-between: Latina Feminist Phenomenology, Multiplicity, and the Self* (Albany: State University of New York Press, 2016).

17. Talia Mae Bettcher, "Other 'Worldly' Philosophy," *Philosopher* (blog), August 16, 2015, https://politicalphilosopher.net/2015/08/16/featured -philosop-her-talia-bettcher/.

18. Priest, "What Is Philosophy?," 202.

19. See, for example, Natalie Stoljar, "Essence, Identity, and the Concept of Woman," *Philosophical Topics* 23, no. 2 (1995): 262–93; Mari Mikkola, "Gender Concepts and Intuitions," *Canadian Journal of Philosophy* 39, no. 4 (2009): 559–83. Stephanie Kapusta provides an excellent discussion of some of these issues from a trans philosophical perspective in "Misgendering and Its Moral Contestability," *Hypatia* 31, no. 3 (2016): 502–19.

20. María Lugones, *Pilgrimages/Peregrinajes: Theorizing Coalition against Multiple Oppressions* (Lanham, Md.: Rowman & Littlefield, 2003).

21. For example, W. E. B. Du Bois's notion of "double consciousness," Gloria Anzaldúa's notion of "mestiza consciousness," María Lugones's notion of "'world'-traveling," and Mariana Ortega's notion of "the multiplicitous self." See W. E. B. Du Bois, *The Souls of Black Folk* (New York: W. W. Norton, 1999), 11; Gloria Anzaldúa, *Borderlands/La Frontera: The New Mestiza* (San Francisco: Aunt Lute, 1987), 99–113; María Lugones, *Pilgrimages/Peregrinajes,* 85–90; Ortega, *In-between.*

22. Of course, much of this accords with some of the basic ideas of feminist standpoint epistemology. See Rachel McKinnon, "Trans*formative Experiences," *Res Philosophical* 92, no. 2 (2015): 419–40.
23. Amy Marvin, May 20, 2018, comments on "Talking about Talking," *Feminist Philosophers* (blog), May 17, 2018, https://feministphilosophers.wordpress.com/2018/05/17/talking-about-talking/#comment-163853.
24. Judith Butler, "Can the 'Other' of Philosophy Speak?," in *Undoing Gender* (New York: Routledge, 2004), 232–50.
25. Gayle Salamon, *Assuming a Body: Transgender and Rhetorics of Materiality* (New York: Columbia University Press, 2010); Gayle Salamon, *The Life and Death of Latisha King: A Critical Phenomenology of Transphobia* (New York: New York University Press, 2018).
26. C. Riley Snorton, *Black on Both Sides: A Racial History of Trans Identity* (Minneapolis: University of Minnesota Press, 2018).
27. Bettcher, "Through the Looking Glass."
28. Viviane Namaste, *Invisible Lives: The Erasure of Transsexual and Transgendered People* (Chicago: University of Chicago Press, 2000); Viviane Namaste, "Undoing Theory: The 'Transgender Question' and the Epistemic Violence of Anglo-American Feminist Theory," *Hypatia* 24, no. 3 (2009): 11–32.
29. Judith Butler, "Imitation and Gender Insubordination," in *The Lesbian and Gay Studies Reader,* ed. Henry Abelove, Michèle Aina Barale, and David M. Halperin (New York: Routledge, 1993), 312.
30. María Lugones, "Toward a Decolonial Feminism," *Hypatia* 25, no. 4 (2010): 742–59.

Reimagining Transgender

Robin Dembroff

Let's begin with a political reality. Transgender lives are being fashioned into a cultural debate that serves to distract from a dying planet, a widening wealth gap, disappearing worker protections, shrinking social safety nets, and intentional undermining of democracy. Authoritarian leaders paint transgender people as extremists, using genocidal rhetoric to justify denying us health care, housing, employment, and parental rights.[1] Supporters who flock to their sides see us as delusional, all the while demanding that the size of a child's genitals settles the shape of their desirable future.

This context—this here and now—frames what I have to say in this essay, as well as the way that I have chosen to say it. In the most direct words that I can find, my hope is to get beneath *transgender* as an identity and to argue that *transgender* centers an experience. "Transgender experience," as I'll call it, is the experience of risking severe penalty through self-directed gender nonconformity. Understood this way, transgender experience is not the same thing as, or coextensive with, having a transgender identity. Far more people have transgender experience than would describe themselves as "transgender" or reject the gender category that they were initially assigned.

I believe that grasping the difference between transgender experience and transgender identity is vital for getting a clear picture on what is at stake in the so-called culture war over so-called transgender issues. Restrictions on gender-affirming health care, the demonization of drag, the eradication of LGBTQ education, and other sadistic legislative measures absolutely affect people with transgender identities. But these measures do not only target people with transgender identities; they target everyone with transgender experience. Authoritarians are not only waging war against the acceptance of transgender identity. Even more fundamentally, they are battling to uphold a social order where self-directed gender nonconformity is and will be punished. These punishments are not felt by everyone equally, but they do restrict everyone's freedom to pursue gender-nonconforming desires.

I Know What I Am

In his ethnography, *Imagining Transgender,* David Valentine describes his experience of interviewing "fem queens" in the Meatpacking District of New York City during the late 1990s.[2] Going into these interviews, Valentine expected that most of the queens would consider themselves transgender and avail themselves of community services promoted as serving transgender people. He soon discovered that, while some of the queens did use these services, many others did not. They did not see "transgender" as a label that applied to them. As a result, they did not think that these services were intended for them. Consider Valentine's interview with Anita, a twenty-four-year-old Puerto Rican queen:

> **David Valentine:** Do you know what this term "transgender" means?
> **Anita:** No.
> **DV:** You never heard it before?
> **Anita:** No.
> **DV:** Um, but, OK do you know what transexual means?
> **Anita:** Transexual means a sex change right?
> **DV:** Uh, yeah. You don't consider yourself to be transexual?
> **Anita:** No.
> **DV:** No, OK. But, and do you consider yourself to be a woman?
> **Anita:** I consider . . . yes, yes, but *I know what I—I know what I am,* but I . . . I . . . you know, I treat myself like a woman, you know I do everything like a woman. . . .
> **DV:** You . . . do you consider yourself to be gay then?

Anita: Yes! . . .

DV: Even though you live as a woman.

Anita: Yes.

DV: Right, OK.

Anita: I know I'm gay and I know I'm a man.[3]

In this exchange, we see Valentine, a scholar of gender and sexuality, struggle to understand and be understood by Anita. In certain ways, Anita perfectly fits Valentine's paradigm of "transgender." Although assigned male at birth, Anita began feminizing hormones in adolescence, lives every day as a woman, and considers herself a woman. But in another, essential way, Anita does not fit Valentine's paradigm. According to Anita, she does not reject the gender category that she was initially assigned. Anita considers herself a woman, but she also considers herself a man. She is a "gay . . . man," she tells Valentine, who "know[s] what [she] is."

Anita's insistence is the starting point for this essay. Whatever labels or categories Anita uses to describe herself, she knows what she is. I resonate with this insistence. Until I was in my mid-twenties, I begrudgingly reported to those who asked—and many did—that I was a girl or a woman. I accepted this classification, prescribed to me by my family, church, and broader society, as immutable and inevitable. I did not have the conceptual tools or community that I would have needed to step outside of these prevailing ideas of gender. And so, I carved out spaces to exist within them. As a kid, this meant calling myself a "tomboy." Later, I tacked the word *butch* onto *woman* or *lesbian*. Since then, my ideas of gender have changed. Today, if asked, I will report that I am a man to some and a woman to others, but neither to myself. I call myself "transgender" as shorthand for a personal history, both painful and joyous, that is saturated with self-directed gender nonconformity.

Whatever the categories, though, I know what I am. I am a person whose happiness requires pursuing desires that conflict with my society's fundamental rules of gender. Directed by this knowledge, I have pursued—and continue to pursue—those desires. That choice has been life-saving and life-affirming, but it also has come with some severe costs. I suspect that my racial and class privileges have kept these costs still lower than those that Anita has paid.

Those who pursue forms of life that defy society's entrenched rules of gender know that this choice always is accompanied by a demand for justification. This demand is an interrogation that, as Gayle Salamon writes, is at once "both politics and ethics."⁴ People who lead lives of relative gender conformity often feel an urgent need to know why we have rejected their "normal," "natural," or "commonsense" way of being in favor of something "weird," "disgusting," or "unnatural."⁵ The response "I know what I am, and this is me" will not satisfy their demand. For the demand is that they must know what we are, and they must come to know using only the "logics of . . . seeing" that are already familiar to them.⁶

The demand sets an impossible task. Although this is rapidly changing (thus the "culture war"), most people think about gender in ways that distort or erase the lives of those who follow their internal compass deep into the territory of gender nonconformity.⁷ Faced with their justificatory demands, we do what we can. We stitch words and concepts together in an attempt to make ourselves understood, or else we invent new words altogether. For this reason, you'll find a wide array of self-affixed titles among us. We are "trans men" and "trans women," we are "transmasculine" and "transfeminine," we are "butches" and "femmes" and "bois" and "queens," and so many other things besides. But beneath this explosive bouquet of labels, we share something in common. We all desire to live in ways that deeply conflict with the gender rules that surround us, and we risk severe punishments by following those desires. We choose to break established rules of gender, but in a similar way to choosing to eat food or drink water. A choice is there, but it is a choice that is essential to our pursuit of happiness.

In this essay, I want to suggest that, given the work that we ask the term *transgender* to do, its attendant concept is not only or even primarily one of identity. At an even deeper level, I think that *transgender* centers this experience of engaging in heavily penalized forms of self-directed gender nonconformity.⁸ Understood this way, transgender people are those who brave what Lauren Berlant describes as the "costs of not acceding to normatively sexualized life narratives."⁹ This group does not include everyone. No one is perfectly gender conforming, but not everyone has taken on great risks through self-directed gender nonconformity. At the same time, this group is much larger than the group of people who embrace "transgender" as a label or who reject the gender category that they were assigned at birth. Many who have transgender experience do not have transgender identity.

In its exploration of these ideas, this essay uses a methodology outside the norm of analytic philosophy. We often assume that an answer to a question of the form "What is X?" will delineate necessary and sufficient conditions for something being X or an instance of X. For example, answers to questions like "What is a person?" or "What is free will?" typically go something like "Something is a person if and only if . . ." or "Someone has free will just in case . . ." I have many concerns with this methodology.[10] For present purposes, my most pressing worry is that this approach is ill-suited for an inquiry into "transgender," which I do not think has definitive or fixed boundaries. This exploration calls for a different approach. In particular, I believe that it calls for us to consider the work that we ask "transgender" to do and to then rebuild our concept using core meanings suggested by that conceptual labor.[11] The essay before you is an exercise in this method. My focus is on the center of "transgender," not its borders.

What I have to say is limited in scope. I will offer considerations in favor of the idea that we ask *transgender* to highlight expressions of self-directed gender nonconformity that risk severe penalty. I'll argue that this meaning does not reduce to identity, nor does it include the full spectrum of gender nonconformity. I won't provide a complete picture of gender nonconformity or offer a schema for determining when gender nonconformity is self-directed or heavily penalized. I will not speculate on why, for people like me, flourishing requires the pursuit of gender-nonconforming desires, or comment on the important connections between transgender identity and related identities from the past, such as "transsexual," "transvestite," or "invert."[12] As for the historical and cultural scope of transgender experience, my only view is that wherever we find self-directed gender nonconformity that breaks stringently enforced rules of gender, there we find transgender experience.[13] Whatever words and concepts we mix, match, and produce to answer others' demands for justification, we know what we are.[14]

Transgender Experience and Transgender Identity

The idea that *transgender* centers on transgender experience contrasts with a common definition of *transgender* as an identity that each person either has or does not have. According to this picture, to say that someone is "transgender" has less to do with their experience and more to do with the labels that they use to describe themself. A transgender person, taken this way, is someone who rejects the gender categorization that they were given at birth. A cisgender person, by contrast, is someone who accepts (or, at least, does not reject) this categorization. That picture produces what is now a widely assumed binary: you're transgender if you reject your initial gender categorization, and you're cisgender otherwise.

This binary is rooted in an all-or-none perspective. It implies that every person either straightforwardly rejects their initial gender classification or they do not—an implication that has been rightly resisted by feminists and lesbians with ambivalent relationships to the category "woman."[15] For these reasons, I am skeptical of the transgender/cisgender binary, but I won't dwell on that point now. Setting aside the binary, it is true that some people do not identify with their original gender categorization and most (but not all) other people unreflectively do. This fact alone, as well as the growing number of people moving out of the second group—sometimes, into the first—is significant.

But *transgender* and *cisgender* are not only asked to describe groups distinguished by self-identifications. These words are regularly relied upon to provide information about which people risk penalty for their unwillingness to live by the rules of gender and which people stand to gain from these penalties. As philosopher Luce deLire writes, "To be cis means to benefit from hostility toward trans people."[16] This description is particularly apt in the context of institutional settings, where *cisgender* and *transgender* are used to communicate information about distinct institutional experiences and needs. Yet even in these contexts, *transgender* is typically defined as identity, creating a mismatch between this term's explicit description and actual use. Although *transgender* is defined as identity, it is asked to highlight people who risk penalty for self-directed gender nonconformity.

There is some reason to think that the two meanings coincide.

Rejecting your original gender categorization is extremely taboo; it is itself a heavily penalized form of gender nonconformity. We are forbidden from articulating self-conceptions that conflict with what others insist is an unshakable and unquestionable truth—that we always have been and must be either a girl/woman or a boy/man.[17] Anyone who refuses this narrative thereby challenges its essentialist ideology. Confronted with transgender identity, then, those in the grip of this ideology must choose among three possibilities. They can insist that transgender identities are deceptive. They can claim that transgender identities are delusional.[18] Or they can question their internalized essentialism. Unfortunately, many people are too existentially committed to the idea of their own gender identities being rooted in supposed nature to take the third path. Often, they resort instead to attacking, belittling, and excluding people with transgender identities. Transgender identity, for this reason, is reliably accompanied by transgender experience.

The reverse is where the synonymy breaks down. Transgender experience is not reliably accompanied by transgender identity. This is what Valentine discovered through his conversations with people like Anita, who experience severe costs for their self-directed gender nonconformity but do not reject their original gender categorization. Faced with someone like Anita, transgender identity can no longer serve as a proxy for transgender experience. To say that Anita is not transgender (or worse, to say that Anita is cisgender) would in many contexts communicate the weighty falsehood that Anita benefits from a life of relative gender conformity. But to say that Anita is transgender, when we define it in terms of identity, patronizingly misrepresents Anita's own description of herself.

When we understand *transgender* only in terms of identity, or when we assume that transgender experience entails transgender identity, we forget that many social differences (e.g., historical, geographical, racial, class) mediate the conceptual and linguistic tools that we use to describe ourselves. What we desire and how we articulate those desires are shaped and directed, even if not determined, by the material and cultural conditions that we inhabit. As Dean Spade and Valentine point out, ignoring this variability has serious costs in the context of organizations and social services designed to aid transgender communities.[19] When these organizations reduce *transgender* to identity, Valentine writes, they "cannot account for the experiences of the most socially vulnerable gendervariant people."[20] They end up further marginalizing the very people that they intend to serve.

The same is true within feminist and gender-justice movements. From local meetups to grassroots political groups, dangerous exclusion comes with flattening *transgender* to identity. This flattening not only limits people's access to necessary resources, it also deepens a transgender/cisgender wedge between gender-nonconforming people based on who does or does not reject their original gender categorization. This wedge furthers the dangerous illusion—perpetuated by groups like so-called gender-critical feminists—that these groups (e.g., trans men and butch lesbians) have separate interests and goals.[21] Now, in particular, is not a time for unnecessary division. We perpetuate the war against self-directed gender nonconformity when we undermine political solidarity across gender-nonconforming people, whatever categories or words they use to describe themselves.[22] Our shared, defiant pursuit of happiness is what is truly at issue. With it, we collectively challenge the widely assumed narrative that someone's genital size dictates how their life is "supposed" to go.

Transgender Experience Is Not All Gender Nonconformity

My project of explicitly centering transgender experience within our picture of "transgender" is not entirely revisionary. "When it comes to gender and sexuality," Berlant writes, "there are no introductions . . . only reintroductions."[23] What I'm advocating actually is a return to the past—a recentering . . . with some clarification. The original meaning of *transgender* within theory and activism was not singularly focused on identity. It was understood in broader terms that emphasized a wide expanse of gender nonconformity. Far from trying to fit these experiences into a binary, early champions of the term *transgender* stressed that gender nonconformity comes in colorful and diverse shapes, and that it is a fool's errand to try to contain them within strictly delimited boundaries.

Jack Halberstam, commenting on this early meaning, writes that the term *transgender* originally arose in order to serve a particular need: the political need for a shared concept that would join together the "many lived forms" of gender variance.[24] Susan Stryker echoes this in *Transgender History*:

> The term *[transgender]* implies movement away from an initially assigned gender position. It most generally refers to any and all kinds of variation from gender norms and expectations. . . . What counts as *trans*gender varies as much as gender itself, and it always depends on historical and cultural context. It seems safe to say that the difference between gender and transgender in any given situation, however, involves the difference between the dominant or common construction of gender and a marginalized or infrequent one.[25]

The term *transgender,* Stryker tells us, points to the experience of diverging from assigned gender expectations, not from an assigned gender categorization. Her description, which emphasizes dynamicity, suggests that *transgender* is better understood as a process than as a feature or identity. *Transgender* is a doing—one that different individuals undertake to different degrees and in different ways. Along similar lines, Julia Serano writes that *transgender* captures a "broad coalition of gender diverse people (as originally intended)"; Leslie Feinberg takes it to encompass people who "traverse, bridge, or blur the boundary of the gender expression they were assigned at birth"; and in sweeping language, Riki Wilchins describes *transgender* as anyone who "transgresses gender."[26] These descriptions are not the same, but a clear theme runs through them: *transgender* has to do with not obeying entrenched rules of gender.

The meaning of *transgender* suggested by this theme is often called the "umbrella meaning." Although the identity-based meaning is common in the public sphere, the umbrella meaning prevails within trans and queer studies, particularly within humanistic disciplines. This meaning has its critics, in no small part because it can be easily interpreted as the idea that *transgender* covers the entire spectrum of gender nonconformity. Interpreted this way, *transgender* more or less applies to everyone. After all, no one perfectly obeys gender rules all the time. As boys/men and as girls/ women, people are told they ought to have bodies that look certain ways and do certain things but never others; that they should walk and talk in certain ways and not others; that they should love and desire certain people and be disgusted by others; that they should have certain emotions and never feel or express others; that they should enjoy certain foods and entertainment and mock others; and so on and so on. The rules of manhood and womanhood are gerrymandered and extensive, as well as fluctuating and contested. They are beyond anyone's perfect attainment. Rebecca Reilly-Cooper combines this observation with the umbrella meaning of *transgender* and concludes that *transgender* is meaningless. In that case, she writes, "every single one of us is transgender."[27]

Reilly-Cooper's argument rests on the hidden premise that, because the umbrella meaning points to a spectrum of gender nonconformity with no clear cutoff between "transgender" and "nontransgender," there is thereby no distinction between *transgender* and *nontransgender*. The premise harbors a fallacy (specifically, the "heap" or "sorites" fallacy). It's true: the umbrella meaning does not give us fixed or precise boundaries around *transgender*. That's fine with me—I think the project of trying to articulate such boundaries is pernicious. But this fluidity isn't unique to *transgender,* and it doesn't mean that everyone falls beneath this concept. *Disability,* for example, covers a continuous spectrum of embodied differences, but that doesn't mean that all bodies are disabled. The distinction between "disabled" and "nondisabled" is vague and contextual, but the distinction is nevertheless essential to the social and political work that we ask the term *disability* to do. In fact, it is because of this flexibility that *disability* can focus our attention on people who, in particular times and places, need care due to incapacities or impairments that bring serious costs or restrictions into their lives.[28] Similarly, just because "transgender" is a spectrum doesn't mean that everyone is transgender. The distinction between "transgender" and "nontransgender" is also vague and contextual, but it is still meaningful. And, too, its flexibility is essential to its communicative work.

That said, Reilly-Cooper's argument challenges us to say more about this distinction. What kind of gender nonconformity—if not all gender nonconformity—does *transgender* illuminate? As I see it, the answer breaks down into two parts: self-directedness and costliness.

There are many ways—costly ways—that people fail to conform to their society's gender norms. Many of these ways are outside of their control. For example, in societies that expect men to be physically fit and to be financial providers, men with physical disabilities and those who cannot find work do not conform to these gendered expectations. In societies that tell women they should have straight hair and light skin, many women of color do not conform to these gendered expectations. When gender norms embed prejudices of race, class, and disability—and they always do—there can be no practical separation of gender nonconformity from differences of race, class, and disability. But *transgender* does not primarily concern these differences. *Transgender,* I believe, illuminates nonconformity that is self-directed, or that is sourced in one's own will. *Transgender* involves transgression that flows from desire.[29] It appears when people choose gender nonconformity and not as an "effect of helplessness before [their] own sexual and gender orientation."[30] *Transgender* entails self-assertion.[31]

But self-directed nonconformity is not the whole of transgender experience.

I have yet to meet someone who has never—not once—chosen to break a gender rule. Maybe you're a man who occasionally paints his fingernails or a woman who stops shaving her legs in the winter. Maybe you explored queer sexual desires for a period during college or decided that marriage and children weren't for you. These actions, like all self-directed gender nonconformity, risk social penalties. That risk is highly contextual and variable; the penalties for self-directed gender nonconformity also are on a spectrum. But we do not ask *transgender* to draw attention to anyone who experiences any degree of penalty for self-directed gender nonconformity. Instead, we ask this term to help us see people who risk severe penalty for this nonconformity—the kinds of penalties that deeply harm or restrict life opportunities.[32]

All of this maintains that "transgender" is a spectrum. Gender nonconformity, self-directedness, and costliness all are relational notions that do not have fixed thresholds or forms. That's as it should be. How we use *transgender* is a contextual matter that depends on background assumptions about what is relevant to the conversation. We can recognize, at the same time, that certain rules of gender are more widespread and viciously enforced than others. Among the most ubiquitous and brutally enforced gender rules are: rules about the sexual body parts (especially genital size) men and women ought to have; rules about the sexual behavior men and women should engage in; and rules about how men and women should signal their genital size through clothing, hair, and comportment, or what Harold Garfinkel calls "cultural genitals."[33] True to this observation, stereotypes of transgender people typically imagine people who deviate from these central rules of gender: people who have modified their sexual body parts, people who diverge from heteronormativity, and people whose "cultural genitals" do not communicate their genital size. These are common forms of transgender experience, but they are not the only ones.

Not that I'm going to give you a list. My aim, in this essay, is not to provide a litmus test for being transgender. I do not think such a test is possible or desirable. By asking about the meaning suggested by the communicative labor we put to *transgender,* I am asking who should be centered within transgender politics, not who should be excluded from it.[34] The minute we start to question who "really" is transgender is the minute we turn away from this center to fixate instead on policing borders.

Final Thoughts

I've suggested that, given the work that we ask *transgender* to do, transgender experience lies at the heart of *transgender.* That experience is relational. It concerns not only a doing but also society's reaction to that doing. Its hallmark is self-directed gender nonconformity that risks severe penalty. The fact that this nonconformity is penalized does not mean that transgender people would be better off obeying the rules of gender. In my own experience, self-directed gender nonconformity was the only passage between the Scylla of dissociation and the Charybdis of self-destruction.[35] It brought social consequences, but the attempt to conform guaranteed existentially worse outcomes. I am not alone; the same is true for many others.

Transgender people are exponentially more likely to be victims of sexual and domestic abuse, to be marginalized from the work-force, to lack access to health care or social safety nets, and to be victims of violence.[36] But our pursuit of gender-nonconforming de-sire is not the pursuit of self-destruction. It is the pursuit of plea-sure, ease, and presence in our bodies and in our relationships. It is the pursuit of happiness. Far from a harbinger of woe, *transgen-der* is a testament to the magnetism of realizing desire and of the intimate connection between this realization and human flourish-ing. The desire to be what we know that we are is powerful. For some, it is more powerful than the most viciously enforced para-digms of who and what we ought to be.

Notes

I am especially grateful to M. J. Crockett, Michael Della Rocca, Alicia Fowler, Daniel Wodak, and the editors of *Trans Philosophy* for helpful feed-back during the development of this paper.

1. For example, Florida governor Ron DeSantis propagates rhetoric that equates transgender people with pedophilic "groomers" and gender-affirming health care with mutilation and "chemical castration." See "Ron DeSantis," GLAAD Accountability Project, updated 2022, https://www.glaad.org/gap/ron-desantis.
2. David Valentine, *Imagining Transgender: An Ethnography of a Category* (Durham, N.C.: Duke University Press, 2007).
3. Valentine, *Imagining Transgender,* 114–15.
4. Gayle Salamon, "Justification and Queer Method, or Leaving Philoso-phy," *Hypatia* 24, no. 1 (2009): 227.
5. Lauren Berlant, *Desire/Love* (Brooklyn, N.Y.: Dead Letter Office, BABEL Working Group, 2009), 44: "People are schooled to recognize as worthwhile only those desires that take shape within the institu-tions and narratives that bolster convention and traditions of propri-ety. They learn, further, to be afraid of the consequences when their desire attaches to too many objects or to objects deemed 'bad.'" See also Eve Kosofsky Sedgwick, *Epistemology of the Closet* (Berkeley: Uni-versity of California Press, 2008).
6. Céline Leboeuf uses this phrase to describe a parallel phenomenon surrounding racial ambiguity. The demand "What are you?" Leboeuf writes, indicates that the speaker will withhold recognition of your personhood until you conform to their "logic of . . . seeing." See Céline Leboeuf, "'What Are You?' Addressing Racial Ambiguity," *Critical Phi-losophy of Race* 8, no. 1 (2020): 299.
7. See Talia Mae Bettcher, "Trans Identities and First-Person Authority,"

in *"You've Changed": Sex Reassignment and Personal Identity,* ed. Laurie Shrage (Oxford: Oxford University Press, 2009), 110: "If [a trans woman] is not avowing genital status, [a non-trans-friendly person will wonder] what is she doing and why? Indeed, since gender presentation is no longer taken to communicate genital status, this ignorance does not merely concern what she is doing with words, it concerns all gendered behavior and self-presentation."

8. Andrea Long Chu, "On Liking Women," *N+1* 30 (Winter 2018).

9. Berlant, *Desire/Love,* 45.

10. Robin Dembroff, "Beyond Binary: Genderqueer as Critical Gender Kind," *Philosophers' Imprint* 20, no. 9 (2020): 12.

11. For further discussion of this methodology, see Sally Anne Haslanger, *Resisting Reality: Social Construction and Social Critique* (New York: Oxford University Press, 2012).

12. Joanne J. Meyerowitz, *How Sex Changed: A History of Transsexuality in the United States* (Cambridge, Mass.: Harvard University Press, 2004); Susan Stryker, *Transgender History* (Berkeley, Calif.: Seal Press, 2008); Jack Halberstam, *Trans*: A Quick and Quirky Account of Gender Variability* (Oakland: University of California Press, 2018); Leah DeVun, *The Shape of Sex: Nonbinary Gender from Genesis to the Renaissance* (New York: Columbia University Press, 2021).

13. Some insist that *gender* must be understood very locally, others believe it can be understood more broadly—even globally. I'll remain neutral on this here, but I want to note that the historical and cultural scope of *gender* has direct implications for the scope of *gender nonconformity.*

14. See Talia Mae Bettcher's argument that trans people have "first-person authority over their own gender" ("Trans Identities and First-Person Authority," 98). Our gender nonconformity is an expression of internal awareness about what is required for our personal health and well-being. We have first-person authority over this, despite whatever is considered "natural" and the "normal." See Douglas Baynton, "Disability as Justification for Inequality in American History," in *The New Disability History: American Perspectives,* ed. Paul Longmore and Lauri Umansky (New York: New York University Press, 2001).

15. Cailin O'Connor argues that binary taxonomies can make human coordination more efficient but quickly create entrenched and self-perpetuating social divides between the two groups. See Cailin O'Connor, *The Origins of Unfairness: Social Categories and Cultural Evolution* (New York: Oxford University Press, 2019). See also Helana Darwin, "Challenging the Cisgender/Transgender Binary: Nonbinary People and the Transgender Label," *Gender & Society* 34, no. 3 (2020): 358. I am not claiming that this is the only use of *transgender* that would create a transgender/cisgender binary; my point is that it is a widespread use that does create a binary.

16. Luce deLire, "Beyond Representational Justice," *Texte Zur Kunst,* March 2023, 58.

17. The basis for these categorizations changes over time and place. See Gilbert Herdt, *Third Sex, Third Gender: Beyond Sexual Dimorphism in Culture and History* (New York: Zone Books, 2020); Meyerowitz, *How Sex Changed.*

18. Bettcher has extensive discussion of the "evil deceiver or make-believer" trope about those with transgender identities. Talia Mae Bettcher, "Evil Deceivers and Make-Believers: On Transphobic Violence and the Politics of Illusion," *Hypatia* 22, no. 3 (2007): 43–65. This trope is actively weaponized within academic philosophy. See, for example, Kathleen Stock, "XIV–Sexual Orientation: What Is It?," *Proceedings of the Aristotelian Society* 119, no. 3 (2019): 295–319; Alex Byrne, "Are Women Adult Human Females?," *Philosophical Studies* 177, no. 12 (2020): 3, 783–803.

19. Dean Spade, *Normal Life: Administrative Violence, Critical Trans Politics, and the Limits of Law* (Durham, N.C.: Duke University Press, 2015); Valentine, *Imagining Transgender.*

20. Valentine, *Imagining Transgender.*

21. Jack Halberstam, "Transgender Butch: Butch/FTM Border Wars and the Masculine Continuum," *GLQ: A Journal of Lesbian and Gay Studies* 4, no. 2 (1998): 287–310, https://doi.org/10.1215/10642684-4-2-287.

22. Elizabeth S. Corredor, "Unpacking 'Gender Ideology' and the Global Right's Antigender Countermovement," *Signs: Journal of Women in Culture and Society* 44, no. 3 (2019): 613–38.

23. Berlant, *Desire/Love,* 3.

24. Halberstam, *Trans*,* 8.

25. Stryker, *Transgender History,* 19.

26. Julia Serano, *Whipping Girl: A Transsexual Woman on Sexism and the Scapegoating of Femininity* (Emeryville, Calif.: Seal Press, 2007), xii; Leslie Feinberg, *Transgender Warriors: Making History from Joan of Arc to Marsha P. Johnson and Beyond* (Boston: Beacon Press, 1997), x; Riki Wilchins, *Burn the Binary! Selected Writing on the Politics of Being Trans, Genderqueer and Nonbinary* (New York: Riverdale Avenue Books, 2017), 58.

27. Rebecca Reilly-Cooper, "Gender Is Not a Spectrum," *Aeon,* June 28, 2016, https://aeon.co/essays/the-idea-that-gender-is-a-spectrum-is-a-new-gender-prison.

28. Elizabeth Barnes, *The Minority Body: A Theory of Disability* (Oxford: Oxford University Press, 2016). Similarly for being old, being thin, being bald, etc. For an overview of the philosophical literature on vagueness, see Stanford Encyclopedia of Philosophy, s.v. "Vagueness," by Roy Sorensen, last modified June 16, 2022, https://plato.stanford.edu/entries/vagueness/. For a framework for ontic vagueness, see Elizabeth Barnes, "Ontic Vagueness: A Guide for the Perplexed," *Noûs* 44, no. 4 (2010): 601–27.

29. Judith Butler, *Gender Trouble: Feminism and the Subversion of Identity* (New York: Routledge, 1990); Louise Vasvári, "Queer Theory and Discourses of Desire," *CLCWeb: Comparative Literature and Culture* 8, no. 1 (2006): https://doi.org/10.7771/1481-4374.1290; Michel Foucault, *The History of Sexuality: An Introduction* (New York: Knopf Doubleday Publishing Group, 2012). What these transgressions look like and how they are received depends on factors like race, ability, and class. See C. Riley Snorton, *Black on Both Sides: A Racial History of Trans Identity* (Minneapolis: University of Minnesota Press, 2017); Bonnie Smith and Beth Hutchison, eds., *Gendering Disability* (New Brunswick, N.J.: Rutgers University Press, 2004); Cathy Cohen, "Punks, Bulldaggers, and Welfare Queens," *GLQ: A Journal of Lesbian and Gay Studies* 3 (1997): 437–65; Susan Stryker, Paisley Currah, and Lisa Jean Moore, "Introduction: Trans-, Trans, or Transgender?," *Women's Studies Quarterly* 36, no. 3/4 (2008): 12.

30. Wilchins, *Burn the Binary!*, 55.

31. Self-directed gender nonconformity is an example of what I call "agential identity" in work with Cat Saint-Croix, or externally actualized desires to relate to others in new ways. See Robin Dembroff and Cat Saint-Croix, "Yep, I'm Gay: Understanding Agential Identity," *Ergo: An Open Access Journal of Philosophy* 6, no. 20 (2019): 571–99.

32. Under what I hope are the more liberatory conditions of the future, *transgender* will not need to do this—or perhaps any?—conceptual labor.

33. Harold Garfinkel, *Studies in Ethnomethodology* (Cambridge: Polity, 1984).

34. Naomi Scheman, "Queering the Center by Centering the Queer: Reflections on Transsexuals and Secular Jews," in *Feminists Rethink the Self,* ed. Diana Meyers (Boulder, Colo.: Westview Press, 1997), 124–62.

35. Janet Mock, *Redefining Realness: My Path to Womanhood, Identity, Love & So Much More* (New York: Atria Books, 2014); Thomas Page McBee, *Man Alive: A True Story of Violence, Forgiveness and Becoming a Man* (San Francisco: City Lights Books, 2014); Jacob Tobia, *Sissy: A Coming-of-Gender Story* (New York: G. P. Putnam's Sons, 2019); Leslie Feinberg, *Stone Butch Blues* (Ithaca, N.Y.: Firebrand Books, 1993).

36. Sandy James, Jody Herman, Susan Rankin, Mara Keisling, Lisa Mottet, and Ma'ayan Anafi, *The Report of the 2015 U.S. Transgender Survey* (Washington, D.C.: National Center for Transgender Equality, 2016).

Replicating Gender
Reflections on Gender Concepts, Gender Kinds, and History
Stephanie Kapusta

Most trans and queer communities respect gender self-identifications. One's gender is based neither on biological characteristics nor on one's social role or the norms attached to the specific binary genders "man" or "woman." There are genders beyond the binary and between "man" and "woman." However, trans-critical or so-called gender-critical voices have questioned how gender identities can be about gender (the concept) at all. The concept of gender is tied to a person's biological features and the social expectations and norms that apply to them—that is, to objective, material realities. How can one determine one's own gender subjectively so that one's identity is a gender identity and not some other sort of subjective state? Wouldn't one be just "changing the subject" or "making things up"?[1]

A parallel challenge is addressed within philosophy to "ameliorated" or "new" accounts of gender concepts or gender kinds. Within ameliorative projects of gender concept construction, for example, arguments are presented as to why certain concepts should be used with an eye to furthering specific aims, like moral or political aims. More generally, there is a considerable effort on the part of analytic philosophers to present coherent accounts of gender language, concepts, and metaphysics that are more inclusive of trans and nonbinary people.[2] The amelioration, modification, or replacement of dominant (cisnormative) gender concepts and language, particularly when driven by a postulate of trans and nonbinary inclusion, has, in turn, spawned a philosophical reaction from some quarters of analytic philosophy that are undergirded by clearly trans-exclusionary ideas and aims.[3] Although these trans-exclusionary arguments differ in detail, they share a strictly binary view of sex and gender. They have this in common with other philosophical projects that, even if not so explicitly trans-exclusionary, end up excluding trans people from their accounts of gender.[4] And one of the arguments often encountered is that ameliorated or gender-inclusive accounts of gender do not conform with traditional, ordinary common sense or standard thought and talk about gender.

I do not intend to discuss all the different strands of this trans-exclusionary work. My focus here will be on select arguments from trans-exclusionary views that make historical continuity of some sort a criterion for dismissing identity claims by trans and nonbinary people. Two arguments that invoke historical continuity—one about gender concepts, the other about gender metaphysics—are explicitly formulated by their authors as critiques of efforts to change the landscape of the way we understand gender.[5] In contrast, my aim is to show that these arguments contain flaws that—once corrected in plausible ways—allow for a certain historical continuity between past and present gender concepts, as well as with past and present gender nonconformity or gender variance. I thus hope to make a modest philosophical contribution to ground the connections some queer and trans historians attempt to make between marginalized communities separated in history, while respecting historical differences.[6]

Bogardus: Conceptual and Semantic Continuity

Tomas Bogardus claims that ameliorative, trans-inclusive approaches to gender concepts are incoherent since they cannot reconcile two competing postulates. For, on the one hand, they seek to modify existing concepts without changing the subject. And, on the other hand, they produce "surprising" content for their proposed ameliorations, and so "*intentionally* depart from the way concepts are ordinarily used."[7] This approach is thus "apt to originate new concepts, rather than modify the conceptions of our existing concepts."[8] The question thus becomes: What individuates a concept—that is, what features or mechanisms make it *this* concept rather than a different one? How we understand these features will determine whether trans-inclusive gender concepts are still gender concepts.

Following R. M. Sainsbury and Michael Tye,[9] Bogardus suggests that concepts ("woman," for example) are individuated historically through their original use (concept "originalism") and passed down through ancestral relations of reproducing usages. Tokens (uses) of concepts are copied and preserved over time through the degree of deference that subjects have toward previous uses. Nonoriginating uses are marked by the feature that the use involves deference to other uses, by the same subject or another subject, and the use makes possible the accumulation of information from other uses, by the same subject or other subjects.[10]

For example, when Murray Gell-Mann introduced the concept "quark," he was originating it. Gell-Mann's first use of the concept was "not governed by any conformist norm" and did not involve any "informational accumulation."[11] Similarly, Tomas Bogardus claims that ameliorative projects with regard to the concept "woman" do not defer to the ordinary use of the concept (containing a conception of women as adult human females) and do not draw on that use in a cumulative way.[12] Using this argument (and some others), Bogardus concludes that the "inclusion problem"—expanding or modifying current gender concepts to encompass trans and nonbinary identities—"cannot be solved."[13] Attempting to do so, we simply end up with different concepts.

I think we need to look at this view of concept individuation a little more closely, as Sainsbury and Tye's account possesses several nuances. The historical concept-reproducing mechanism is deferential intention to use the concept in the same way as others have used it and to draw information from that use.[14] This view accommodates the fact that different subjects can, over time, use the same concept to refer to different referents; there can be "reference shift." For example, Sainsbury and Tye offer the example of the concept "meat," which, they claim, was used in the fifteenth century to refer to the property of "being edible"; as used today, its referent is the property of "being flesh." On the authors' theory of individuation through origination, we can say that either the same concept has changed its referent through some form of "gradual drift" or that, at some point, a new concept was introduced "expressed by a word spelled and pronounced the same way." Sainsbury and Tye opt for the first alternative since they find "no event that seems a good candidate for the introduction of a new concept."[15]

However, postulating this kind of reference shift creates problems of its own.[16] If, for example, I believe that broccoli is meat, and you believe that only animal flesh is meat, on what grounds is your belief the correct one? Why could I not simply be intentionally deferring to an earlier use of the concept? In fact, why should we not say that your concept is simply a different concept, since the first users who restricted the extension of the concept "meat" to animal flesh failed, in fact, to defer to the original use of the concept? Believing that broccoli is meat is a false belief. For this conclusion to go through, Sainsbury and Tye have to fall back on convention or standardization:

> Nowadays, the standard thinkers'-reference to the concept MEAT restricts it to flesh. It would clearly be wrong to say that those of us who now believe that spinach is not meat are mistaken. The standard thinkers'-referent of the concept MEAT excludes spinach.[17]

The idea, then, is that what thinkers standardly believe sediments the reference shift of a concept. Yet, it remains the same concept as before the shift due to the "smooth history" of concept token reproduction—that is, "the concept being handed on in ways that unquestionably make new users count as users of the concept, even if mistakes were made about its referent."[18] Effectively, Sainsbury and Tye are saying the use of the contemporary concept-community establishes the referent. Conceptual continuity with past use, however, is established by deferential intention to use the concept "in the same way" without this necessarily succeeding in employing the concept with exactly the same extension as earlier uses.

We can understand why the same concepts might change meaning if we distinguish the following questions:

Concept identity: What makes it the case that two token words or elements of thought express the same concept?

Metasemantics: What makes it the case that a token word or element of thought has the semantic value it does?[19]

For Sainsbury and Tye, the first question is answered by recourse to the intention of subjects to defer to the subjects' earlier uses. We can thus imagine a reproductive lineage of concept-copying uses from the originating use. The second question is answered by particular concepts' gradually becoming standardized as *the* extension of the concept. Of course, this does not exclude the possibility that, during some period before standardization of a univocal use, the same concept had two or more different referents (extensions) and/or throughout the concept's history of usage certain concept-subcommunities preserved the concept's referent or "shifted" it in a different direction. In a similar way to Sainsbury and Tye's concept ancestry, Laura Schroeter and François Schroeter speak of "representational traditions" in which token elements of thoughts (uses of a concept) stand in a historical/causal relationship *R*. Here, *R* does not have to necessarily involve intentions of deference but may happen even unintentionally, as people engage through linguistic and other practices with the concepts of others. It is distinct representational traditions that individuate concepts. The second question about the semantic value of token elements of thought (their "content" or referent) is, on this view, answered by the idea of "metasemantic coordination": words and thoughts that express or use a concept normally inherit their meanings (referents) from the representational tradition in which the concept stands through *R*. They write:

> The reference of a token element of thought *[x]* is determined on the basis of a set of properties *P* of the whole representational tradition demarcated by *R*: for example, patterns of attitudes and cognitive dispositions associated with the concept, history of how uses of the concept are causally triggered by features of the environment, causal feedback relations entrenching the use of the concept over time, shared practical and theoretical interests subserved by the tradition, principles of rationalizing interpretation.[20]

The emphasis, then, is on the fact that we need to take whole representational traditions in determining the content of our referential concepts. But the content (i.e., referent or extension) of our concepts is one thing; substantive conceptions or articulations of that content can differ widely. Ernest Rutherford's specific theoretical model articulating the concept "atom" is quite different from current theories of the atom. But the "shared practical and theoretical interests" of Rutherford and today's physicists justify the view that they all have a referential concept of the same thing.

The same idea holds for human category concepts like "race." Some hold that this is a biologically explanatory concept; others, that it captures social hierarchies.[21] These are quite different substantive articulations of the concept "race." The contention is, however, that they are articulations of the same concept. We can easily see how the idea extends to gender concepts, such as "woman" and "man." There is no reason to conclude, as Bogardus does, that ameliorative projects—or other projects for "alternative" gender understandings—"change the subject," at least not as long as the ameliorative projects' accounts mirror or explain to a significant degree the concept usages of extant gender concept-communities or subcommunities that stand in the same representational tradition.[22]

This is also a way of understanding Robin Dembroff's "imitation project" for gender concepts, in which dominant groups are urged to follow the concept and language use of alternative (trans and queer) groups.[23] Dembroff's account is broadly ameliorative. They present moral and political arguments for queer and trans concept and language use to be more broadly applied. In light of the ideas presented so far, we can understand this project as proposing that the dominant (cisnormative) group restandardize, or otherwise reformulate and repractice, the understandings and articulations of gender concepts by adopting the understandings and practices of alternative, subaltern branches of the concepts' historical development. Again, contra Bogardus, this doesn't need to involve changing the subject since, in light of concept originalism or representational traditions, the concepts in each community are the same. In this scenario, both dominant users and subaltern users belong to the same gender concept-community.[24] Trans-inclusive extensions of concepts such as "woman," "man," "girl," and "boy" may seem to some like different concepts. But, within a historical perspective—depending on the nature of the usage-reproducing mechanism—there is no reason to accept they are.

Let's now turn from gender concepts to historical gender kinds.

The Demand for Ontological Continuity: Bach's Historical Gender Kinds

A social kind is generally taken to be a collection of things exhibiting a relative unity in virtue of a characteristic or underlying property or feature that is mind-dependent or more broadly social in character; it might be based in commonly held beliefs and representations, in conventions and language, in social norms and expectations, or in institutions, for example. Examples of social kinds include money, race, gender, law, corporations, and artwork.[25] Some of the philosophers who consider the existence conditions, construction, structure, or causal effects of social kinds are interested in them from a methodological point of view: collections of entities that constitute social kinds as such—as opposed to random or gerrymandered collections of social objects—have predictive potential that allows social actors to measure, predict, and intervene in social processes.

For social kinds to provide a basis for explanation and prediction, they need to exhibit a significant degree of stable unity. Ruth Garrett Millikan, for example, suggests the mechanism by which the members of a category form a relatively stable and identifiable kind is that historical processes replicate tokens of the category because these tokens fulfill certain valuable functions.[26] Millikan initially had biological species in mind but extended the approach to social kinds.

Theodore Bach follows Millikan's approach.[27] But he justifies it in terms of the "responsible modeling" of social reality. Namely, Bach locates the challenge of projects of amelioration or modification of gender concepts in balancing two postulates of social modeling: the postulate to make our concepts and terms (taxonomy) responsive to social reality, on the one hand, and the postulate that we should shape them in light of moral and political considerations, on the other. The second postulate assumes that our terms and concepts—how we carve up the world—are not fully determined by the way that the social world is. But Bach criticizes some feminist authors for invoking "weak and vague" criteria for how our concepts should answer to social reality.[28] There is no specific determination of how our ameliorated social taxonomies relate to real social kinds. How is it that such projects don't simply make things up? Bach argues that authors such as Sally Haslanger "overplay the formless character of the empirical world."[29] By extension, this is potentially a criticism of trans-inclusive projects of concept or meaning modification.[30] We may—for political reasons—agree to call trans women "women." But this should not be confused with counting them as members of the real and inductively meaningful gender kind "woman."

Against John Locke's contention that there are few or no clear-cut boundaries in the natural world, Bach claims the opposite: the natural world clumps up into clearly discernible groupings of entities exhibiting common features. These are the natural kinds (like species or H_2O) that make up the world. But crucially, the same goes for the social world; there are also clotting mechanisms in the social world. It is in virtue of these mechanisms—mostly social institutions that wield significant causal influence—that specific sets of social properties are currently and mind-independently clustered together (as opposed to being disorganized jumbles).[31]

Social ontology should aim to describe and explain the mechanisms responsible for the clumping together of social reality. Gendered reality is, according to Bach, clumped together around the social kinds "woman" and "man." The responsible approach to social modeling would then first seek to determine how and why human social reality is dichotomously clumped together in this way. Even before we start thinking about ameliorated concepts and taxonomies of social reality with a view to influencing that reality, we should first focus on "identifying, tracking and accurately describing mind-independent social kinds of humans."[32]

Bach's Theory of Historical Gender Replication

Let's now look at Bach's own account of gender kinds and how they clump together. Bach argues that to belong to a gender kind, such as "woman," is to stand in a relation to ancestral women, replicated by relatively similar, and relatively stable, ontogenetic processes, principally, by various institutional and societal modes of socialization, combined with psychological processes of conformity bias and prestige bias. Membership of gender kinds is determined by being subject to these replicative social processes on the basis of perceived bodily sexual dimorphism.

One of Bach's central claims is that men and women are replicated through social processes in relation to their stabilizing roles regarding a more fundamental historical kind, the historical gender system. Bach makes use of an analogy with automobiles, an analogy originally employed by Millikan. The subsystems of an automobile—for example, the transmission—are replicated on a production line, and they fulfill their particular function within the more fundamental system that is the automobile. The design of the car itself has been selected for in the sense that the model of car satisfies the needs or preferences of a sufficiently large number of clients. Just as the other parts and subsystems of the car, the transmission subsystem is replicated from a master design to contribute to the car's functioning in a way that maintains the car model's selling power and attractiveness to potential clients.

Car transmissions in a particular model are replicated because they have proven successful in responding to selection pressures in the car market. The transmissions belong to historical kinds since they are replications from a lineage of transmissions, according to a template. Moreover, they possess a teleological function. That means that they perform a task that responds successfully to past selection pressures, such as changing gears. However, Bach insists that, in the case of such historical kinds, it is participation in the lineage of replicated tokens that determines historical kind membership, not how well or badly the replicated token fulfills its teleological function.

Bach claims that, analogously to the automobile transmission, "woman" and "man" are social roles that are subsystems or components of the binary gender system. The gender system consists of the following elements:

Binary sexual categories: male and female as defined by chromosomes, hormones, and reproductive organs

Conceptual gender dualism: the tendency for members of a society to think and categorize in terms of masculine or feminine

Gender identity or self-concept: the process by which one attains personal identification with a gender role, the understanding of oneself as gendered in a particular way, and the acknowledgment that certain gender norms apply to oneself

Binary gender socialization practices: here one could list a whole series of practices, such as any arrangements that facilitate or enforce gender segregation, the differential treatment of children depending on their gender classification, sexual objectification, and discrimination

Social and legal institutions: gender differences in the law and in institutions

Binary gendered artifacts: clothes, toys, accessories, rituals, and role models

Binary gender roles for individuals: social position, behaviors expected of women and men in various contexts, division of labor, and bodily presentation

The above components are causally dependent. For example, gender identity may be formed under the influence of socialization practices. Moreover, its expression may fulfill a gender role. The list of components is not meant to be exhaustive.

"Binary gender roles for individuals" is treated in more detail. These gender roles—"man" and "woman"—have a teleological function that can be identified by noting which behaviors maintain and stabilize the binary gender system in response to selective pressures. From various sources, Bach reconstructs an account of what those selective pressures were. The cultural selection pressures to which the traditional binary gender system responds are thus largely a question of securing material resources for individuals and for communities in circumstances of evolving environmental and technological conditions. The teleological gender functions are normative in the sense that they are "supposed to" stabilize the binary gender system.[33] They do not necessarily inform what we might take to be morally or politically normative.

Among the more specific gender functions considered, Bach lists status and power within gender hierarchy, the division of labor within family and in professional environments, personal and interpersonal characteristics (agency versus passivity, for example), and body management practices.[34] Sexed individuals who perform these functions or exemplify these properties "in conformity to the dualisms that structure a gender system acted to stabilize that system more than individuals who did not exemplify these properties."[35] The contribution of these functions to the stabilization of the gender system in turn favors the historical replication of women and men—that is, of gender roles assigned to and inculcated upon dichotomized biological embodiments of female and male.

The ontogenetic process proceeds mainly through socialization and gender-based classifications at various levels of society. For example, parents treat and talk to offspring differently depending on their biological sex assignment. Schooling further continues and reinforces this differential socialization. From a young age, individuals are molded to fulfill historical replications of typically feminine and masculine roles, and the differences are expressed in the law and in state policy.

Bach claims that not every individual need functionally resemble the other members of their gender. Of women, in particular, Bach states, "If a particular female has undergone the ontogenetic process through which one exemplifies a participatory relation to a lineage of women, then even if she fails to exemplify any of the properties of women's historical gender role, she is still a woman because she has the right history."[36]

Trans Exclusion and Insistence on Continuity of Gender Kinds

Let's now look at some reasons to doubt Bach's account of historical gender kinds. One of Bach's key assumptions is that *there exist clearly discernible processes of gender socialization corresponding to the dichotomous social roles "woman" and "man."* In making this assumption, Bach is dealing with an abstraction that is far from clearly delineated in many individual instances. In fact, it is fair to say that Bach does not solve the challenges involved with giving accurate, clearly delineated philosophical accounts of "woman" and "man" but simply shifts those challenges onto the task of giving accurate, clearly delineated philosophical accounts of "female" or "male" processes of gender socialization/replication.

The employment of words, artifacts, differential treatment based on physiology, segregated activities, and labeled spaces all seem central to processes of gendered socialization on Bach's account. For Bach, it is essential that one be the object of such processes, that one is worked upon by these traditional processes of socialization and social categorization, not whether one fulfills certain gender roles or identifies in a certain way. However, if we look at the level of individuals, it is far from clear that any of us are exclusively subject to female or male socialization conceived in this way. Here are some considerations why.

Sandra Lipsitz Bem's early contention that a degree of felt other-gender typicality as well as felt same-gender typicality (i.e., a degree of psychological "androgyny") produces better psychosocial outcomes within gender development seems to be a fruitful notion in later research.[37] In light of Bach's account of gender replication, this finding would be quite significant. It could suggest that the effects of gender socialization (and self-socialization—a point I return to) are not either-or processes, organized around a female/male dichotomy, but that many of us may be subject to different types of socialization to varying degrees, and our self-socialization (for example, learning from modeled behavior, adaptation under the influence of social sanction) may proceed at least in a partially androgynous, nonbinary way.[38] This would certainly cast doubt on claims made by Bach that women (resp. men) are those who are subject to the correspondingly "female" (resp. "male") ontogenetic processes of replication. It is more accurate to say that many people are subject to various types of processes of socialization and self-socialization (and not necessarily directly related to gender) in varying degrees.[39] Some react with resistance to gender socialization and attempt to influence it, further complicating the neat binary delimitations Bach makes into "female" or "male" socialization.[40]

It is plausible to conjecture that many transgender people who were assigned a man's gender role at birth but who, from a certain age, possess a psychological sense of being a woman were not subject to the ontogenetic processes that replicate historical lineages of women—namely, female socialization. On Bach's account, they are simply not women.[41] Bach claims that those transgender women who exemplify all or most "of the historical properties of women's gender role" can become women later in life if their appearance makes them objects of the replicative machinery that produces historical women, either on the basis of acquired physiology or gender role (including, presumably, typically feminine body management practices).[42] In short, instead of a sufficient threshold of features we require women to possess in order to attain membership in the kind "woman," we now must decide which features of socialization processes, and how many of them, determine membership in the historical kind "woman." However, as I argue above, which gender people have been socialized into may, in many cases, be indeterminate.

But there is another important aspect of the binary gender system that Bach does not mention. We know that in various sociohistorical contexts, the binary-structured system of gender has been coercively imposed on non-Western cultural gender systems and traditions through colonial violence.[43] The insistence on a smooth, continuous history of social replication elides the fact that there are gender systems whose supposed discontinuity has been coerced through attempts at assimilation and cultural genocide. We can legitimately ask whether the insistence on historical continuity for gender kinds—intentionally or unintentionally—proposes a normalization of past historical disruptions of a colonizing nature.

Trans-exclusionary accounts of gender concepts and kinds can, no doubt, be refuted in various ways. I have indicated some ways to do so in this chapter. There is, however, no need to reject the historical approach to gender concepts and gender kinds. It is of particular interest and importance how mechanisms of conceptual continuity, as well as reaction and resistance, play a key role in the formation of evolving trans and nonconforming gender kinds and concepts.[44] In fact, philosophers' accounts can ground historians' reclamation of the past for various gender communities as not completely "other" while avoiding anachronous claims to continuity in understandings. To conclude, I will briefly sketch how.

One way philosophical accounts can contribute to understanding history is to take gender concepts as a philosophical anchor—an anchor that would allow historians to speak of the same gender concepts (such as "woman," "man," and "two-spirit") while respecting different languages and specific articulations, as well as to investigate whether, or to what extent, gender concepts branch into different concept-subcommunities and how concepts undergo reference shift.

Historical studies needn't assume continuity and linearity. Understanding historical gender kinds as subject to more nonlinear disruption, resistance, and breakdown, as well as being coercively imposed, historians can investigate forms of gender variance, conceived as disruption and as resistance to dominant social gender replication. Importantly, oral and written traditions can perhaps show researchers that the gender binary has not been so ontologically clumped together by causal mechanisms as is often assumed.

Notes

Earlier versions of this paper were presented at the Canadian Society for Women in Philosophy meeting in October 2017, at the Aristotelian Society/Mind Association Open Session in July 2018, and at the Minds of Our Own Workshop in October 2018. I thank the various respondents for their critical remarks and feedback.

1. For a clear statement of the problem, see B. R. George and R. A. Briggs, "Science Fiction Double Feature: Trans Liberation on Twin Earth," hosted on PhilPapers, last modified March 25, 2019, https://philpapers.org/archive/GEOSFD.pdf. Several of the ideas in this chapter build on what B. R. George and R. A. Briggs have to say about the historical continuity of gender concepts ("categories" in their nomenclature).

2. Talia Mae Bettcher, "Trans Women and the Meaning of 'Woman,'" in *The Philosophy of Sex: Contemporary Readings,* ed. Nicholas Power, Raja Halwani, and Alan Soble (Lanham, Md.: Rowman & Littlefield, 2013), 233–58; Talia Mae Bettcher, "Through the Looking Glass: Trans Theory Meets Feminist Philosophy," in *The Routledge Companion to Feminist Philosophy,* ed. Ann Garry, Serene Khader, and Alison Stone (New York: Routledge, 2017), 393–404; Katharine Jenkins, "Amelioration and Inclusion: Gender Identity and the Concept of *Woman,*" *Ethics* 126 (2016): 394–421; Katharine Jenkins, "Toward an Account of Gender

Identity," *Ergo: An Open Access Journal of Philosophy* 5, no. 27 (2018): 713–44; Robin Dembroff, "Real Talk on the Metaphysics of Gender," *Philosophical Topics* 46, no. 2 (2018): 21–50; Robin Dembroff, "Beyond Binary: Genderqueer as Critical Gender Kind," *Philosophers' Imprint* 20, no. 9 (2020): 1–23, http://hdl.handle.net/2027/spo.3521354.0020.009; Michael Rea, "Gender as Self-Conferred Identity," *Feminist Philosophical Quarterly* 8, no. 2 (2022): art. 3.

3. Rebecca Reilly-Cooper, "Gender Is Not a Spectrum," *Aeon,* June 28, 2016, https://aeon.co/essays/the-idea-that-gender-is-a-spectrum-is-a-new-gender-prison; Tomas Bogardus, "Some Internal Problems with Revisionary Gender Concepts," *Philosophia* 48 (2020): 55–75; Tomas Bogardus, "Why the Inclusion Problem Cannot Be Solved," *Philosophia* 50 (2022): https://doi.org/10.1007/s11406-022-00525-9; Alex Byrne, "Are Women Adult Human Females?," *Philosophical Studies* 177 (2020): 3,783–803; Kathleen Stock, *Material Girls* (London: Fleet, 2021); Holly Lawford Smith, *Gender-Critical Feminism* (Oxford: Oxford University Press, 2022).

4. Theodore Bach, "Gender Is a Natural Kind with a Historical Essence," *Ethics* 122 (2012): 231–72.

5. On gender concepts, see Bogardus, "Why the Inclusion Problem Cannot Be Solved"; Bogardus, "Some Internal Problems." On gender metaphysics, see Bach, "Gender Is a Natural Kind"; Theodore Bach, "Real Kinds in Real Time: On Responsible Social Modelling," *Monist* 102, no. 2 (2019): 236–58.

6. On trans history and historicity, see Leah Devun and Zeb Tortorici, "Trans, Time, and History," *TSQ: Transgender Studies Quarterly* 5, no. 4 (2018): 518–39; on making transhistorical connections in queer theory, see Carolyn Dinshaw et al., "Theorizing Queer Temporalities: A Roundtable Discussion," *GLQ: A Journal of Lesbian and Gay Studies* 13, no. 2–3 (2007): 177–95.

7. Bogardus, "Some Internal Problems," 67.

8. Bogardus, 71.

9. R. M. Sainsbury and Michael Tye, *Seven Puzzles of Thought and How to Solve Them: An Originalist Theory of Concepts* (Oxford: Oxford University Press, 2012).

10. Sainsbury and Tye, *Seven Puzzles of Thought,* 42; Bogardus, "Some Internal Problems," 68.

11. Sainsbury and Tye, 43.

12. Bogardus, "Some Internal Problems," 69–71. Sally Haslanger's ameliorated definition of *woman* is that women are those subordinated on the basis of real or imagined adult femalehood. But Bogardus argues that being an adult female is not a cumulative part of the definition in the right way. For example, once women's subordination ceases, so do women. Yet, in such a scenario, there are presumably still adult human females. Haslanger's amelioration thus changes the subject.

13. Bogardus, "Why the Inclusion Problem Cannot Be Solved." I do not discuss Bogardus's other arguments here. In this essay, I am interested in historical understandings of concept and kind individuation.
14. Sainsbury and Tye speak of "C-reproducing mechanisms" where C is a concept. *Seven Puzzles of Thought,* 60.
15. Sainsbury and Tye, 46.
16. Paul Horwich, "Critical Notice of *Seven Puzzles of Thought and How to Solve Them: An Originalist Theory of Concepts,* by R. M. Sainsbury and Michael Tye," *Mind* 123, no. 492 (2014): 1,123–39.
17. Sainsbury and Tye, *Seven Puzzles of Thought,* 72.
18. Sainsbury and Tye, 72.
19. Laura Schroeter and François Schroeter, "Semantic Deference versus Semantic Coordination," *American Philosophical Quarterly* 53, no. 2 (2016): 193–210.
20. Schroeter and Schroeter, "Semantic Deference," 202.
21. François Schroeter, Laura Schroeter, and Kevin Toh, "A New Interpretivist Metasemantics for Fundamental Legal Disagreements," *Legal Theory* 26 (2020): 84.
22. Evidently, there are also other ways to refute Bogardus's charge that ameliorative projects "change the subject." For different approaches, see Derek Ball, "Revisionary Analysis without Meaning Change (Or, Could Women Be Analytically Oppressed?)," in *Conceptual Engineering and Conceptual Ethics,* ed. Alexis Burgess, Herman Cappelen, and David Plunkett (New York: Oxford University Press, 2020), 35–58; Sally Haslanger, "Going On, Not in the Same Way," in Burgess, Cappelen, and Plunkett, *Conceptual Engineering and Conceptual Ethics,* 230–60. Haslanger also employs the Schroeters' notion of "representational tradition" but sees the main representational interest as consisting less in something epistemic agents interpret and more in a general, practice-based coordination (Haslanger, "Going On," 249). Without providing as much detail, B. R. George and R. A. Briggs also argue that "the genders *woman* and *man* are individuated . . . by their historical continuity with categories that were originally closely connected to sex biology." George and Briggs, "Science Fiction Double Feature," 2.
23. Dembroff, "Real Talk," 36–38.
24. This is also why their disputes about concept meaning are substantive and not merely verbal: they are not simply talking past one another. See Ball, "Revisionary Analysis without Meaning Change." Sainsbury and Tye insightfully note: "In taking someone to have wrongly applied a concept . . . one still aims to use the very concept she used, and in that manner one defers to her usage." Sainsbury and Tye, *Seven Puzzles of Thought,* 42.
25. Stanford Encyclopedia of Philosophy, s.v. "Social Ontology," by Brian Epstein, last modified winter 2021, https://plato.stanford.edu/archives/win2021/entries/social-ontology/.

26. Ruth Garrett Millikan, "Historical Kinds and the 'Special Sciences,'" *Philosophical Studies* 95, nos. 1–2 (1999): 45–65.

27. Mari Mikkola notes and briefly discusses the trans-exclusionary implications of Bach's account. See Mari Mikkola, *The Wrong of Injustice: The Role of Dehumanization in Feminist Philosophy* (Oxford: Oxford University Press, 2016), 101–2. Marion Godman brings some interesting criticisms against Bach's theory from a more cultural evolutionary perspective. See Marion Godman, "Gender as a Historical Kind: A Tale of Two Genders?," *Biology and Philosophy* 33, no. 21 (2018): https://doi.org/10.1007/s10539-018-9619-1. See also George and Briggs, "Science Fiction Double Feature," 17–20.

28. Bach, "Real Kinds in Real Time," 240

29. Bach, 244.

30. Bach, 254–55.

31. Bach, 243.

32. Bach, 245.

33. Bach, "Gender Is a Natural Kind," 251.

34. Bach, 254–55.

35. Bach, 255.

36. Bach, 261.

37. Sandra Lipsitz Bem, "Gender Schema Theory: A Cognitive Account of Sex Typing," *Psychological Review* 88 (1981): 354–64; Carol Lynn Martin, Diane N. Ruble, Naomi C. Z. Andrews, Dawn E. England, and Kristina Zosuls, "A Dual Identity Approach for Conceptualizing and Measuring Children's Gender Identity," *Child Development* 88, no. 1 (2017): 167–82.

38. Desiree D. Tobin, Meenakshi Menon, Madhavi Menon, Brook C. Spatta, Ernest V. E. Hodges, and David G. Perry, "The Intrapsychics of Gender: A Model of Self-Socialization," *Psychological Review* 117, no. 2 (2010): 601–22.

39. Lynn S. Liben, "Gender Development: A Constructivist-Ecological Perspective," in *New Perspectives on Human Development,* ed. Nancy Budwig, Elliot Turiel, and Philip David Zelazo (Cambridge: Cambridge University Press, 2016), 145–64.

40. Leon Kuczynski and Jan De Mol adopt a dialectical account of socialization in which both children and parents encounter relations of contradiction and contestation within their interactions. See Leon Kuczynski and Jan De Mol, "Dialectical Models of Socialization," in *Theory and Method,* vol. 1 of *The Handbook of Child Psychology and Developmental Science,* 7th ed., ed. W. F. Overton and P. C. M. Molenaar (New Jersey: John Wiley and Sons, 2015), 323–68.

41. In *The Wrong of Injustice,* Mikkola makes a similar observation (100). The same can, presumably, be said of men who are also defined by their participation in historic replicating lineages.

42. Bach, "Gender Is a Natural Kind," 261.

43. See, for example, Kai Pyle, "Naming and Claiming: Recovering Ojibwe and Plains Cree Two-Spirit Language," *TSQ: Transgender Studies Quarterly* 5, no. 4 (2018): 574–88.

44. See Heidi Levitt, "A Psychosocial Genealogy of LGBTQ Gender: An Empirically Based Theory of Gender and Gender Identity Cultures," *Psychology of Women Quarterly* 43, no. 3 (2019): 275–97; Heidi Levitt, "Applications of a Functionalist Theory of Gender: A Response to Reflections and a Research Agenda," *Psychology of Women Quarterly* 43, no. 3 (2019): 309–16.

Laughing at Trans Women
A Theory of Transmisogyny
Amy Marvin

A Laughable Trans Woman

In 2013, videographer Alli Coates recorded performance artist Signe Pierce walking around Myrtle Beach, South Carolina, at night for their short film *American Reflexxx*.[1] Surrounded by crowds and neon lights, Pierce moves from place to place as the night progresses, occasionally stopping to strike a pose for the camera and nearby gawkers as the evening reaches a state of sensory overload. Pierce repeatedly stands out, wearing a reflective silver mask to obscure her face, a short blue dress, and lime green high heels. Standing out soon leads to insult and violence, as Pierce experiences derisive laughter, dehumanizing speech, sexual harassment, and a sudden shove that causes her to fall on the concrete sidewalk while jeered at by a curious mob. And yet, she is also able to harness the affects that coalesced around her that evening to dispel the crowd, picking up her heels and clacking them together as the crowd runs away. The concluding scene plays a slowed down and distorted clip of Robin Thicke's hit creeper anthem "Blurred Lines," panning up to show Pierce covered in bruises and bleeding cuts about an hour into her evening walk. Recounting her experience in a later interview, Pierce reflects, "People were hurling bottles at my head and throwing slurs left and right on the streets. It went beyond bullying, it was assault."[2] Pierce's embodiment as curious spectacle for a crowd in public space thus fed a violent combination of attention and indifference.

Originally, Pierce and Coates planned the art piece to engage with hypersexuality, pornography, and femininity through the lens of cyborg feminism. In an interview, Pierce explains:

> In regards to the character, I'd been inspired by portraying the hyper-sexualized "ideal girls" you see on TV/online/in porn: blonde, sexy, and silent without any signified sense of purpose or identity, other than the inherent condition of being observed. I'm interested in what happens when you take that girl out of the screen and drop her into reality.[3]

Pierce expected this character to receive catcalling and curious attention but did not anticipate the size of the mob and the violence they brought in practice.[4] She also did not anticipate the degree to which her character was read as trans and responded to through transphobia. Throughout the evening Pierce was frequently insulted and exposed as a trans woman, with members of the crowd yelling "It's a shim!" or suggesting that she was "really a man." Later Pierce reflects, "We expected there would be catcalling and general playfulness, but the violence was absolutely shocking and the questions about my gender were unexpected. My perceived gender ambiguity ended up becoming a major part of this piece."[5] Finding herself on the receiving end of transphobia was particularly surprising for Pierce because she is a cis woman, not a trans woman, and she had not intended for her art to engage with transphobia.

The context of a cis woman being read as a trans woman is interesting because it highlights the social meanings and reactions of transphobia beyond a naturalized matter of fact. How might a cis woman unintentionally become trans in public space, and what does this mean about the combination of laughter and violence that she was met with? Rather than focus on the empirical question of whether people tend to find trans women funny, I instead look at the philosophical meaning of transmisogyny as a way of encountering trans women in the world as laughable. To further pin down the conditions that socially mediate this laugh, I proceed by breaking down the dimensions of transphobia that construct trans women as laughable. As with transphobia, transmisogyny is a multidimensional process, and part of what I am up to in this essay is arguing for an approach that brings together work on transphobic ideology, institutions, and cultural emotions or affect. Specifically, I will argue that trans women are socially positioned as laughable through ideologies of transphobia, the gendered construction of public space, and the circulated emotion of disgust, thus empowering social isolation and subjugation through transmisogyny. I will conclude by drawing from these dynamics to argue that transmisogyny involves positioning trans women as abject givers rather than as human givers. In what follows, I begin by bringing together work on transphobia by Talia Mae Bettcher and Viviane Namaste. I then link the politics of transphobic laughter with Sara Ahmed's analysis of cultural emotions in circulation, specifically disgust. Finally, I draw from Kate Manne's work to link transphobic laughter against trans women with misogyny, which reinforces both the expulsion and subjugation of trans women.

Bettcher and the Revealing Laugh

In her essay "Evil Deceivers and Make-Believers," Talia Mae Bettcher focuses on the centrality of costumes, make believe, and suspicions of deception to operations of transphobia. She describes the double bind through which the gender presentation of trans women is constructed as mere appearance in contrast to the reality of genitalia as the sole determinant of identity, such that trans people get framed as a masquerader or a deceiver.[6] Either position places trans people in a double bind since they are framed as living a lie, constructed as "both fictitious and morally suspect."[7] Beyond the various personal and social consequences of having one's identity cast as an immoral lie, Bettcher is primarily interested in the ways that this construction of trans people fuels and legitimizes violence against trans people, who under this framework of transphobia must be exposed or punished through violence.[8]

Through her analysis of transphobia, Bettcher is also engaging in the philosophy of fashion and clothing, pointing to a specific irony enacted by clothing in contemporary ideologies of gender presentation. Though much of gender presentation is assigned the function through clothing and attire of concealing inappropriate exposure to sexed bodies through an essential link with genitals, Bettcher points out that such gendered presentations of clothing are taken to communicate the sexed bodies and genitalia so concealed. That is, by concealing an uncomplicatedly sexed body, gendered clothing works to communicate and expose a truth within, such that under the ideology of the "natural attitude" gender presentation is assumed to correspond with a particular sexed, genital configuration. The gender presentation of trans people is in part so challenging to such "systematic symbolic genital disclosures" because the signs of gender presentation no longer align with an expected, unmediated, and self-evident truth.[9] Trans people thus become forced into the role of "evil deceiver or make-believer" in part due to the simultaneous concealing and exposing function of clothing in gender presentation.

Bettcher's analysis helps to explain how a cis woman performance artist unintentionally became a trans woman in public space. Pierce comments on her reflective mask:

> There's something scary because you see this robot woman who is commanding her own identity, but she's in this sexy feminine form that we associate with hyper-sexualized woman all the time on TV, in porn. The cyborg has a certain strength to transcend biology. People saw this porn star walking down the street, but she's wearing this cold austere shield. You can't read her expression, and this created a fear of the "other."[10]

If Pierce is correct that her performance caused a stir through the combination of feminine hypersexualization, defiance, strength to transcend biology, and the "cold austere shield" of her face mask, then Bettcher's analysis adds another dimension to explain why her appearance unexpectedly also came to be interpreted as transfeminine.

First, Pierce performed specifically as hypersexualized and as feminine. This performance aligned with mass media assumptions that all trans people are trans women and that trans women cultivate sexualized hyperfemininity as a costume or deception.[11] Second, Pierce's face-obscuring mirror mask signaled to the crowd that she was not only dressed up in a costume but also potentially enacting a contrast between her gendered appearance and an assumed sexed reality. Pierce's character of a cyborg porn star thus unwittingly became a trans character. Her mode of being in public space is that of someone whose gender is seen to be masquerade or artifice, like a trans woman, and reactions to her presence in public space were caused by trans readings of her gendered style.

When Pierce's character became trans, she also became distinctly laughable, subject to ridicule, jeers, mockery, and harsh laughter that often coincided with pushing, bottle throwing, and shoving. Julia Serano points out several precedents to the laughability of trans women in media as concealed and exposed spectacle, linked back to the construction of trans women as either dangerously deceptive or laughably pathetic. On one side of the bind, films such as *A Mighty Wind* frame trans women as comically pathetic, highlighting their inability to successfully embody womanhood beyond its appearance.[12] On the other side, shows such as *The Jerry Springer Show, There's Something about Miriam,* and the film *Ace Ventura: Pet Detective* focus on trans women through a sensational moment of exposing their deception, eliciting laughter at the trans woman herself, at the unwitting man, and at the overall situation of exposure.[13]

The 2003 reality TV show *There's Something about Miriam* in particular requires some direct attention to the laughter it elicited. The show was built as a longer setup for the classic *Jerry Springer* trans episode: producers pay a trans woman to reveal a secret, either staged or through an elaborate setup, that she had been keeping from a cis man. The reveal moment is usually framed with language such as "I was born a man" or "I am a man," to which the unwitting cis man responds in shock, horror, disgust, or anger. *There's Something about Miriam* extends this formula by combining it with the reality TV dating show format where a group of suitors compete to be chosen in a series of romantic and physical challenges, popularized by 2000s shows such as *The Bachelor.* Model Miriam Rivera, who at the time was just twenty-one years old, reveals at the end that she is a trans woman, causing the winning man to become stunned and uncomfortable. Meanwhile, the losing men are unable to contain the laughter that had been brewing in the background during the entire reveal moment, some exclaiming to the others with glee that they already knew "that's a man." In an individual interview, one of the losers alternates between giggling and growing visibly distressed while explaining, "You either laugh or cry, so I think I just laugh. You have to laugh didn't you."[14]

The example of *There's Something about Miriam* brings up further intersections between gender and race, including the interplay between the sexualized framing of trans women as a deceptive danger and cultural scripts that frame Latina femininity as hypersexual, exotic, and consumable.[15] Despite these complexities and the inclusion of an actual trans woman, the setup of the show shares an affinity with *American Reflexxx*'s social experiment presentation. The camera that Coates brought to the scene magnified through the setup of an exploitative and sensationalist reality television apparatus, further encouraging Coates's audience to see her as a trans woman.

Referring back to Bettcher's work helps to unpack the response to Rivera's reveal, beyond an unfortunate combination of sensationalism and interpersonal stereotypes, by connecting such reactions to a broader social and political situation. Bettcher's link between transphobia, forced reveals, and sexual violence also helps to explain moments when the *There's Something about Miriam* contestants not only laugh to refrain from crying but also fixate on Rivera's body, mentioning getting a peek at what's underneath or making childish references to sausages and balls. Considering this aspect also indicates an affective dimension to their humor beyond mirth, inclusive of feelings such as shock and disgust. Similar affects are circulated in films such as *Ace Ventura* and allegedly funny television shows such as *Family Guy* when, in reference to *The Crying Game,* the exposure of a trans woman leads to a cascading effect of vomiting cis men for the amusement of the viewer.[16]

Turning to Bettcher's account of transphobia explains why Pierce came to be constructed as a trans woman in public space and why this coincided with sexual attention and violence. In the next section, I continue to analyze these relationships between transphobia, laughter, and violence by focusing on the relationship between these and the construction of public space itself through Namaste's account of transphobia as genderbashing.

Namaste and the Repelling Laugh

A long-standing fear and experience among trans people is getting laughed at while trying to access services or otherwise moving through public space. A 1995 essay by Taylor Priest in *Chrysalis*

Quarterly described growing up with a fear of being made fun of for questioning gender. Priest writes:

> A child who does not feel secure will not venture out into the world, will not try new things, will be afraid to fail. To cope with the world the child learns to avoid things and people: "They can't laugh if they can't see me." This child learns not to invest too much effort: "If I never try, I never fail."[17]

In a 2002 issue of *Transgender Tapestry,* Nancy E. Wilson also reflects on the impact of the laughter and mockery directed by peers and popular television shows against "men who dressed as women" and "men in dresses," noting that she never understood why they were supposed to be funny. She continues:

> I finally concluded it indeed wasn't inherently funny, and probably was never really intended to be so. What it is indeed is a twisted form of intimidation, usually a crude attempt at what some sort of "majority" considers "correct" behavior. The laughter isn't directed toward something that amuses, but toward a group of people in order to intimidate them, in hopes of changing their social behavior.[18]

Priest and Wilson, writing almost a decade apart, acknowledge the prevalence of derisive attitudes toward trans and gender-nonconforming people while they were growing up and its regulatory effect on their navigation of public space.

In addition to childhood fears and representations, derisive laughter has been a frequent factor when trans people attempt to access more formalized institutional spaces. A news article in *Renaissance* reports on an attempt by one hundred transgendered people, their partners, and their children in October 1995 to participate in the first annual Transgender Lobby Days at the U.S. capitol.[19] Alongside praise for the event's general success is a brief paragraph about less successful moments, including both ghosting and laughter as a form of refusal. The report mentions, "In the office of an Oklahoma congressman, staffers laughed at the delegates and stated there are no transgendered people in Oklahoma."[20] Beyond the U.S. political apparatus, in 2000 Phyllis Randolph Frye wrote on discrimination against underemployed and homeless trans people in medical clinics, explaining:

> The unemployed homeless or the underemployed transgen-
> ders get little help from public medical clinics. They are often
> ridiculed by staff in the waiting rooms and do not come back.
> I know of FTM's [trans men] who could not afford male hor-
> mones after being fired. . . . They could not get help because
> they were laughed at or refused.[21]

Laughter thus combines with transphobia and economic precarity
to discourage trans people from accessing public space and services, including necessary medical care. Dismissive and derisive
treatments of trans people also have a long-standing presence in
media and journalism. While looking through archives, C. Riley
Snorton notes that much coverage of Black trans and gender-
nonconforming people was "framed as jokes, as indications of
their supposedly essential disposability."[22] Beyond Pierce's one
night of unwittingly performing as trans, derisive laughter and
mockery have had a long-standing impact on trans people's access
to public space.

This combination of laughter and transphobia in public space
can turn deadly. Both trans magazines and trans studies in the
1990s and first decade of the 2000s often discuss the death of Tyra
Hunter as a shocking instance of transphobia in public space.[23] On
August 7, 1995, Hunter, a twenty-four-year-old Black trans woman,
was in the passenger seat of a car on her way to her hairdresser job
when the car was involved in an accident. Instead of giving Hunter
emergency medical care, after discovering that Hunter did not
have the body expected of a cis woman, the responding firefighter
EMTs instead exchanged laughter and disparaging jokes about
her trans body.[24] When she was finally taken to the emergency
room, a doctor refused to treat her, and she died from her already
neglected injuries. Afterward, Hunter's mother sued the city and
won on the basis of neglect and malpractice.[25] Though it was responded to through community reporting and activism, Hunter's
death remains one of the deadliest recorded instances of connections between laughter, transphobia, anti-Blackness, and violence
as they meet in public space.

To better understand these intersections between transphobia, laughter, and violence, I find it helpful to turn to Viviane K.
Namaste's discussion of genderbashing in *Invisible Lives,* as she fo-

cuses specifically on gender, policing, and violence in public (and private) space. Namaste builds upon discussions of queerbashing to argue that violence against sexual and gender minorities is often a matter of "policing gender presentation through private and public space."[26] Namaste notes that because sexuality is frequently fused with and read off of gender presentation, situations of violence and harassment frequently are based on normative assumptions about gender expression, including the use of pejorative names and slurs that are used to justify an attack.[27] Because public space is regulated based on gender norms and a compulsion to present as both properly gendered and heterosexual, Namaste asserts that trans people (and especially trans women) have a higher risk of being violently put in check for daring to enter public spaces.[28] She links the exclusion of trans women from public space with the specific spaces associated with trans people, usually visible at night for socialization and work by sex workers while also heavily policed.[29]

Namaste's analysis is helpful for understanding both the violent reactions to Pierce's costumed presence in public space and its relationship with the collective laughter, mockery, and humormaking among the crowd. If Pierce is experiencing, as Namaste suggests, a reaction to her presence as someone perceived to be a trans woman in public space, then gender norms also bring Pierce into contact with violence and other forms of expulsion. Namaste focuses specifically on violence and genderbashing as a parallel to queerbashing, but this expulsion need not reach the level of the person who pushed Pierce onto the sidewalk and injured her leg. Instead, laughter and jeers serve as part of a spectrum of responding to a body marked as having an abnormal gender when daring to enter policed sites of gender normativity. Namaste's analysis thus usefully bridges with Bettcher's to explain how the communicative norms of gender can lead to both interpersonal transphobia and the organization of public space as it intersects with transphobic ideology and policing.

Returning to Hunter, her death was part of a larger situation of oppression in which people engage with trans lives through derision and ridicule as a common collective practice in public and private space. Humor is thus not just a matter of individuals causing harm but also a larger network of people engaging in complicity with systematic norms that mark some lives as threatening and not worthy of care. Hunter was laughed at not merely due to the isolated unethical actions of two EMTs but instead because of culturally mediated reactions to bodies that do not fit transphobic, racist, and sexist norms.

Continuing from the discussion in the previous section of reactions to the reveal moment of Rivera in *There's Something about Miriam,* Hunter's death at the hands of laughing EMTs also implicates the emotional life of laughter and particularly disgust as it connects with oppression and violence. In the next section, I will turn to these specifically emotional aspects of transphobia to draw out the attracting and repelling force of its laughter.[30]

Ahmed and the Disgusted Laugh

In *The Cultural Politics of Emotion,* Sara Ahmed emphasizes that disgust is frequently mediated through cultural circulations of emotions that stick to some objects and people to signify them as dangerous, polluting, sickening, contaminating, and too close for comfort. This circulation then leads to reactions such as expulsion. Ahmed writes:

> To name something as disgusting—typically, in the speech act, "That's disgusting!"—is performative. It relies on previous norms and conventions of speech, and it generates the object that it names (the disgusting object/event). To name something as disgusting is not to make something out of nothing. But to say something is disgusting is still to "make something"; it generates a set of effects, which *then adhere as a disgusting object.*[31]

Ahmed emphasizes that although disgust does not attach to just any object or person, it arises from a fertile ground of norms to performatively name the object or person as disgusting. In this context, disgust relies on a "historicity of signification," accrued through history and culture rather than naturally.[32] People and bodies become threatening not in and of themselves but through "an effect of the histories of contact between bodies, objects, and signs."[33] The circulation of emotions such as disgust and their stickiness to specific objects and people are thus a social relationship requiring political analysis rather than simply attributed to unmediated natural causes, habits, or dispositions.

Ahmed notes that in some instances, the object or person associated with disgust is experienced as too close, threatening, and beneath the disgusted. Ahmed writes:

> The bodies of others become the salient object; they are constructed as being hateful and sickening only insofar as they have got too close. They are constructed as non-human, *as beneath and below the bodies of the disgusted.* Indeed, through the disgust reaction, "belowness" and "beneathness" become properties of their bodies. They embody that which is lower than human or civil life.[34]

Mediated through disgust, people may be encountered not only as outside the bounds of human life and its polities but also as below these, framed through a threatening close contact that must be expelled. It is thus not a surprise that the circulation of disgust is also frequently a circulation of dehumanization, neglect, and violence.

The social and political circulation of disgust explains not only the sexualized disgust directed at Pierce and Rivera but also the laughing response used by the EMTs against Hunter. The realization that someone is a trans woman, whether mistaken or otherwise, carries with it not just shock but also the danger of having been attracted to her or having shared a world with her. This potential reaction of shock and danger also extends to people who may unexpectedly be required to provide intimate care to a trans woman, such as EMTs. Ahmed emphasizes that disgust involves not only a contact between the disgusted and the object or person circulated as disgusting but also a reaction of pushing away. Ahmed writes:

> Disgust is clearly dependent upon contact: it involves a relationship of touch and proximity between the surfaces of bodies and objects. That contact is felt as an unpleasant intensity: it is not that the object, apart from the body, has the quality of "being offensive," but the proximity of the object to the body is felt as offensive. The object must have got close enough to

make us feel disgusted. As a result, while disgust *over takes* the body, it also *takes over* the object that apparently gives rise to it.[35]

In addition to this relationship of contact and closeness, Ahmed emphasizes that disgust motivates a relationship of pushing away, following the work of Julia Kristeva on abjection.[36] An encounter with a person who has been sedimented with disgust threatens the stable, walled-off self of the disgusted subject through a threatening permeability and thus must be pushed away as abject.[37] Returning to the EMTs, laughter serves the emotion of disgust by distorting a living Black trans woman in need of care into a figure of too-close-and-must-be-pushed-away. Transphobia thus short-circuits life-saving care due to the necessity of intimacy, proximity, touch, and skill directed toward a life considered unworthy or dangerously false.

When disgust mediates a situation where one party is constructed as threatening, too close, and outside the scope of care while simultaneously in need of care, laughter serves as a potentially powerful antidote to the abject encounter. The EMTs, in contact with a Black trans woman not experienced as a person but instead as a repelling presence, were able to change the terms of this contact through the collective response of laughter and its accompanying mirth and relief. In response to Pierce, Rivera, and Hunter, laughing at trans women becomes a license to shove away a mere sexualized costume, a refusal of love after a staged reveal, and a disintegration of necessary intimate care.

This is not to argue that such laughter is the same across differences. As a white cis woman, Pierce could have potentially opted out of the situation by removing her mask and appealing to the crowd with her normative status. This reflects Deirdre Davis's insight that street harassment against African American women has an intensified relationship with othering, disenfranchisement, and frequent microaggressions.[38] Laughter as street harassment thus plays into the differential effects of laughter as described by Ahmed, since racist and sexist laughter in public space can saturate a social space as a means of exclusion.[39] It is notable that Pierce's experience with transphobic laughter led to interviews about her art, whereas laughter targeted at trans women of color is not typically responded to with broader care, social recognition, and material support.

The Laugh of Transmisogyny

So far, I have argued that trans women are frequently constructed as laughable. Through Bettcher, this laughableness is influenced by a gender ideology that associates trans people with costuming and inauthenticity, fueling intimate sexualized violence. Through Namaste, this laughter is also a means of pushing trans people out of public space. Through Ahmed, this laughter simultaneously works upon the push and pull of expulsion and attraction through disgust. Taken together, the ideology of gender combined with the circulation of emotions makes laughter a force of violence in many trans women's lives. To finalize the relationship between these dynamics and transmisogyny, I will now sketch the function of transmisogynistic laughter for this conclusion.

In *Down Girl,* Kate Manne sets out to define misogyny as distinct from sexism, objectification, and patriarchy. Specifically, Manne describes sexism as a branch of justification for the oppression of women, misogyny as a branch that enforces the oppression of women, and patriarchal ideology as the underlying systematic ideology of male dominance over women that utilizes both sexism and misogyny.[40] Manne explains:

> Misogyny . . . functions to enforce and police women's subordination and to uphold male dominance, against the backdrop of other intersecting systems of oppression and vulnerability, dominance and disadvantage, as well as disparate material resources, enabling and constraining social structures, institutions, bureaucratic mechanisms, and so on.[41]

Misogyny is thus the "law enforcement branch" responding to potential threats for the norms of patriarchy.[42] In addition to including violence and threats, Manne associates with misogyny a long list of actions aiming to punish, deter, or warn, including "ridiculing, humiliating, [and] mocking," indicating that practices related to laughter are used for misogyny.[43] Furthermore,

Manne envisions her account as compatible with understanding misogyny against trans women, also called transmisogyny, though she explicitly takes a step back from drawing out this connection further.[44]

Continuing her analysis, Manne argues that a key aspect of the patriarchal dominance fueling misogyny is the differential norm of giving between (cis) men and (cis) women. Specifically, women are expected to be "human givers" and provide "moral goods and resources" to men as part of their moral and social role in society.[45] Manne emphasizes, "Women are tasked not only with performing certain forms of emotional, social, domestic, sexual, and reproductive labor but are also supposed to do so in a loving and caring manner or enthusiastic spirit."[46] Additionally, gender norms also often impose expectations that men are entitled to and owed attention, favor, and care from women.[47] Manne provides an analogy between men and a restaurant customer "who expects to not only be treated deferentially—the customer is always right— but also to be served . . . attentively with a smile."[48] When not met with the deference and enthusiasm owed to his position, and even more so when expected to give nonsexual attention and service to women, Manne argues that men often behave like an angry customer who has not been given the service they expect from their server.[49] Manne thus emphasizes that when women do not fulfill their role as "human giver," men often react with overblown frustration, anger, or even heightened violence to reimpose the gendered norms of domination that supposedly entitle them to special services.

Looking at the collective sexualization, attention, disgust, and repulsion involved in laughing at trans women complicates this arrangement of intended givers in relation to intended receivers. If misogyny, as explained by Manne, frames women as human givers owing services to men, then transmisogyny also frames trans women in relation to their utility to men and to the larger situation of gender domination. However, through gender ideology, the arrangement of public space, and the emotional life of transphobia, trans women are considered either improper vessels for this arrangement or at the very best conditional, only suitable for relationships that are fleeting or secret. As Bettcher argues, this subordination occurs at the level of ideology with the "natural attitude" that either trivializes all bodies falling outside nontrans norms or casts them as inherently threatening or violent. As Namaste argues, the regulation of trans bodies is also institutionalized in the construction and policing of public space. As indicated by the prevalence with which they are consumed within pornography, pushed into sex work amid mass culture marginalization, and denied material subsistence through expulsion from the labor force, the bodies of trans women are frequently tethered to this structure in which women are punished for not serving the desires of men as human givers. But due to their deviation from norms about women's bodies and from expectations about the ideal role of women in relationships, trans women are also frequently not granted a culturally legitimized "human giver" role described by Manne as a key factor of misogyny. Rather, through the distortions highlighted by Bettcher that enact transphobia as a reductive trivialization and sexualization of the other, trans women can be appropriated into this role but also easily thrown away as mere refuse, capable of satisfying the needs of the individual man but also not considered an appropriate choice for the human giver role. Relegated to a status outside relationality and community through ideology and institutions, the bodies and lives of trans women are thus frequently used or expunged from civil society as is convenient for effecting and maintaining dominant gendered power relationships.

The encounter with Hunter's body by the EMTs is thus not merely shock but also a reaction fueled through a specific imbalanced gendered economy that centers some gender roles (cis men) as receiving attention and care in relation to other gender roles (cis women) that are expected to serve as human givers (via Manne's analysis), with the bodies of trans women frequently recruited on an as-needed or as-wanted basis for more underground forms of cis men's desire. An unwanted trans woman, and especially an unexpected and unwanted trans woman's body, thus circulates through emotions such as disgust, through which any contact with a trans woman might be experienced as dangerously close such that she must be pushed away as a dangerous outlier to gendered norms. As Namaste emphasizes, this emotional encounter is often not solely about gender, as it may also circulate histories of disgust around Black people's bodies under racism, women's bodies under patriarchy, and sex workers' bodies under sexualized and racialized capitalism.[50] Disgust thus frequently characterizes the cultural circulation of emotions around trans women's bodies, further distributed by productions of mass culture such as *The Jerry Springer Show* that frame the revelation of an unwanted or unknown trans woman as a scene of spectacle and disgust, revealed not to be a human giver but instead an abject fantasy-gender masked through deception. Hence the ritual of collective vomiting and the inevitable laugh is a means of turning away through cruel mirth. Intimacy with trans women is presented first as horror, then as comedy.

   In conclusion, the construction of trans women as laughable in ideology, public space, and mass media cultural production is likely to influence what it means for us to inhabit, comport ourselves within, and retreat from public space. Recall Priest and Wilson discussing the isolating effects of growing up in a world where gender variance is responded to primarily through jest. Trans risibility is political, and the ethics of trans humor cannot be reduced to an interpersonal deployment of harmful stereotypes.

   Trans laughter is not fully determined here. Given the many potential modalities of trans laughter, it would be incorrect to assume that the only laughter Hunter or Rivera knew while they were alive was a cruel laughter. Calling for an attentiveness to situation comedy over reductive seriousness, Jules Gill-Peterson writes:

> I think trans people are really fucking funny, especially when we are being bimbos. Trans women are the best situation comedians I have ever met. Especially if they are supercharged with the frisson of other comedic traditions, like camp, being Jewish, or being brown. I loathe the intense sincerity of much trans political speech today and the moral frameworks used to enforce it.[51]

Gill-Peterson calls attention to the importance of not treating studies of transphobia, transmisogyny, and violence as the end of trans studies, since this frequently reduces trans women of color to mere symbols of violence to be traded around for ungrounded theory or activism points. In this context, we might consider the common practice of making fun of the tendency of academics and nonprofits to mention trans violence and then shallowly throw in the phrase "especially trans women of color" as a form of looking inclusive. Likewise, trans philosophy of humor cannot be reduced to a philosophy of transphobic humor. I thus hope to see further work on laughing *with* trans women as this project continues.

Notes

1. *"American Reflexxx,"* Alli Coates + Signe Pierce, April 7, 2015, YouTube video, 14:02, https://www.youtube.com/watch?v=bXn1xavynj8.
2. Signe Pierce, "Interview: American Reflexxx," interview by Alexis Anais Avedisian, *Rhizome,* August 19, 2015, https://rhizome.org/editorial/2015/aug/19/interview-american-reflexxx/.
3. Alli Coates and Signe Pierce, "'We Didn't Set Out to Make a Piece about Dehumanization, Mob Mentality, or Violence': Alli Coates and Signe Pierce Talk 'American Reflexxx,'" interview by John Chiaverina, *ARTnews,* May 4, 2015, https://www.artnews.com/art-news/artists/we-didnt-set-out-to-make-a-piece-about-dehumanization-mob-mentality-or-violence-alli-coates-and-signe-pierce-talk-american-reflexxx-4056/.
4. Coates and Pierce, "'We Didn't Set Out.'"
5. Signe Pierce, "A Dangerous Walk: Interview with Signe Pierce," interview by Lara Pan, *Musée Magazine,* June 2019, https://museemagazine.com/features/2019/4/24/a-dangerous-walk-interview-with-signe-pierce.
6. Talia Mae Bettcher, "Evil Deceivers and Make-Believers: On Transphobic Violence and the Politics of Illusion," *Hypatia* 22, no. 3 (2007): 50.
7. Bettcher, "Evil Deceivers and Make-Believers," 50.
8. Bettcher, 47.
9. Bettcher, 54–55.
10. Pierce, "Dangerous Walk."
11. Julia Serano, *Whipping Girl: A Transsexual Woman on Sexism and the Scapegoating of Femininity* (Berkeley: Seal Press, 2007), 229.
12. Serano, *Whipping Girl,* 38.
13. Serano, 37–39.
14. *There's Something about Miriam,* episode 6, aired March 4, 2004, on Sky1.
15. Juana María Rodríguez, *Sexual Futures, Queer Gestures, and Other Latina Longings* (New York: New York University Press, 2014), 170–71.
16. *Family Guy,* season 8, episode 18, "Quagmire's Dad," aired May 9, 2010, on Fox.

17. Taylor Priest, "Between Worlds," *Chrysalis Quarterly* 2, no. 2 (Summer 1995): 51, archived by the Digital Transgender Archive at https://www .digitaltransgenderarchive.net/files/q524jn79p.
18. Nancy E. Wilson, "'Officially' Transgendered," *Transgender Tapestry* 100 (Winter 2002): 46, archived by the Digital Transgender Archive at https://www.digitaltransgenderarchive.net/files/8g84mm35j.
19. I have kept the terms used in archives largely intact rather than alter them to fit conventional usage.
20. "TG Lobby Days a Huge Success! Transgendered Activists Visit Capitol Hill," *Renaissance News & Views* 9, no. 11 (November 1995): 6, archived by the Digital Transgender Archive at https://www .digitaltransgenderarchive.net/files/r781wg03d.
21. Phyllis Randolph Frye, "Facing Discrimination, Organizing for Freedom: The Transgender Community," in *Creating Change: Sexuality, Public Policy, and Civil Rights,* ed. John D'Emilio, William B. Turner, and Urvashi Vaid (New York: St. Martin's Press, 2000), 455, archived by the Digital Transgender Archive at https://www.digitaltransgenderarchive .net/files/0k225b10t.
22. C. Riley Snorton, *Black on Both Sides: A Racial History of Trans Identity* (Minneapolis: University of Minnesota Press, 2017), 145.
23. Richard Juang, "Transgendering the Politics of Recognition," in *The Transgender Studies Reader,* ed. Susan Stryker and Stephen Whittle (New York: Routledge, 2006), 706–19.
24. Monica Roberts, "Tyra Hunter Anniversary," *TransGriot* (blog), August 7, 2007, https://transgriot.blogspot.com/2007/08/trya-hunter-anniversary .html.
25. Maria Elena Fern, "Death Suit Costs City $2.9 Million," *Washington Post,* August 7, 1998, https://www.washingtonpost.com/archive/local /1998/12/12/death-suit-costs-city-29-million/b8ab4d34-1907-463c-b5d5 -64ec00dee2a1/.
26. Viviane K. Namaste, *Invisible Lives: The Erasure of Transsexual and Transgendered People* (Chicago: University of Chicago Press, 2000), 135–36.
27. Namaste, *Invisible Lives,* 140.
28. Namaste, 145.
29. Namaste, 147.
30. There is a larger context of writing about violence that work in trans philosophy should address. As Jin Haritaworn and C. Riley Snorton argue in their now classic essay on trans necropolitics, there is a metapolitics of using examples of trans women of color as a means for making a philosophical argument about trans violence. Initially I had avoided referring to Tyra Hunter as an example in the version of this essay that landed in my dissertation because her death has been mobilized for various projects that are only tenuously connected with improving the lives of trans women of color. However, after further discussion, I am not convinced that it would be better to simply not

discuss relevant examples of violent laughter as directed at trans women of color. It may be that another metacritique is required: What kind of value is produced by trans scholarship and who (e.g., publishers) are the ones that make a profit from these trans archive-graves? An intervention might require something more radical than intra-essay commentary and, hence, seems to be beyond the scope of this practice. The conclusion of the essay is inspired by these considerations. See C. Riley Snorton and Jin Haritaworn, "Trans Necropolitics: A Transnational Reflection on Violence, Death, and the Trans of Color Afterlife," in *The Transgender Studies Reader 2,* ed. Susan Stryker and Aren Z. Aizura (New York: Routledge, 2010), 70–71.

31. Sara Ahmed, *The Cultural Politics of Emotion* (New York: Routledge, 2004), 93.
32. Ahmed, *Cultural Politics of Emotion,* 92–93.
33. Ahmed, 90.
34. Ahmed, 97.
35. Ahmed, 85.
36. Julia Kristeva, *Powers of Horror: An Essay on Abjection,* trans. Leon Roudiez (New York: Columbia University Press, 1982).
37. Ahmed, 86.
38. Deirdre Davis, "The Harm That Has No Name: Street Harassment, Embodiment, and African American Women," *UCLA Women's Law Journal* 4, no. 2 (1994): 175–77.
39. Sara Ahmed, *What's the Use? On the Uses of Use* (Durham, N.C.: Duke University Press, 2019), 175–76.
40. Kate Manne, *Down Girl: The Logic of Misogyny* (New York: Oxford University Press, 2018), 20.
41. Manne, *Down Girl,* 19.
42. Manne, 63.
43. Manne, 68.
44. Manne, 24–25.
45. Manne, 175.
46. Manne, 46.
47. Manne, 117, 130.
48. Manne, 50.
49. Manne, 50.
50. Viviane Namaste, "Undoing Theory: The 'Transgender Question' and the Epistemic Violence of Anglo-American Feminist Theory," *Hypatia* 24, no. 3 (2009): 20, 23.
51. Jules Gill-Peterson, "Paranoia as a Trans Style: The Situation Comedy of Trans Life," *Sad Brown Girl,* Substack, February 2, 2021, https://sadbrowngirl.substack.com/p/paranoia-as-a-trans-style.

PART II
Embodiment, Materiality, and Phenomenologies of Flesh

Thinking Trans Embodiment
On Contingent "Home" and Trans Fatigue
Ryan Gustafsson

Trans bodies are often imagined as on the move—crossing borders, journeying *from* and *to*—or as supposedly stuck, desirous of movement but unable to escape.[1] The idea of being in the "wrong body" is key to this figure, as "wrongness" serves as the impetus for this movement and the obstacle to be overcome. According to Talia Mae Bettcher, there are two variations of the wrong body model. The strong view holds that "inner gender identity determines one's sex/gender," and hence surgery "simply changes the wrong body into the right body."[2] The weaker view holds that "one begins as a transsexual" and through sex-change surgery subsequently becomes a woman or a man.[3] In both, transition requires surgery, which would enable movement from the so-called wrong body to the putative right one—the "right" body being, as Sandy Stone points out, unambiguously male or female. The wrong body as a "correctable problem,"[4] which has come to dominate Western understandings of trans lives and desires, positions the trans body as tragically incomplete and trapped, while the normative transgender subject is cast as a redemptive figure capable of finally arriving at "proper embodied belonging."[5] This arrival, if late, is "often framed as a 'coming home' to one's new body."[6]

The pressure on trans people to articulate their needs, desires, and life histories in clinical settings, in ways that resonate with dominant social and medical understandings of what being trans looks and feels like, cannot be understated. As Jay Prosser argues, "Being trapped in the wrong body has become the crux of an authenticating transsexual 'rhetoric': language, narrative, and figures that the subject deploys to obtain access to hormones and surgery."[7] The imperative to recite this authenticating rhetoric in order to render intelligible one's transness not only perpetuates the notion of "wrongness" as intrinsic to trans embodiment, it also reinforces the construct of a knowing, authorial subject who knows their "wrongness" in the right way and from the right time. Yet, Prosser continues, "being trapped in the wrong body is simply what transsexuality feels like."[8] The notion of wrongness remains prevalent, according to Prosser, because it effectively articulates "the experience of pre-transition (dis)embodiment" and the subjective experience of dysphoria.[9]

This commitment to understanding lived experience is crucial for trans phenomenology and trans theory, and this is precisely why, building on work in trans studies by thinkers such as Talia Mae Bettcher, Jack Halberstam, Gayle Salamon, and Sandy Stone, I suggest that we ought to think trans embodiment in more capacious ways than that offered by the wrong body idea. If, as Maurice Merleau-Ponty contends, the body is the "vehicle of being in the world" and mediates all experience, then whose, what, or which body is being trapped by the "wrong" body?[10] Andrea Long Chu points out the central issue here: "Isn't the whole point of the naked phenomenality of 'felt sense' that the very thing that feels itself to be trapped in the wrong body *is nothing other than the wrong body itself?*"[11] The wrong body is the object and the "site" of disclosure in its *"already being there."*[12] Deploying a static, deterministic account of trans embodiment as either pre- or post-surgery, the idea of the wrong body and its continued dominance occludes the temporal dimensions of trans identifications and concrete lived experiences.

In this chapter, I argue that what I call "contingent home" and the lived habitual body are productive concepts for thinking trans embodiment that complicate notions of wrong-bodiedness. The impetus behind this theorization, and my stake in problematizing notions of "home," is worth foregrounding here. As a nonbinary Korean transnational adoptee whose identity, nationality, location, language, etc., are an outcome of mass out-migration and displacement due to developmentalism, militarism, and stigma surrounding single motherhood, "home" and embodied belonging are complicated and enduring questions. Where "home" can be said to be, who you were or might have been "back" there, to where is a "return" imagined (even as impossible), when does one "arrive" after having always already departed: the magnitude and inexhaustibility of these questions can sometimes feel overwhelming—but they must also be concretely situated. I am a settler who currently lives and works in so-called Australia, on the stolen land of the Wurundjeri people of the Kulin nation; my attempts at homemaking must always be situated in relation to Australia's history of settler colonialism and the ongoing impacts of dispossession. A call for a theorization of "contingent home" that remains closer to concrete experience does not entail eradicating these questions but rather seeks to understand how they are lived and grappled with.

I start by outlining how the notion of wrong-bodiedness is tied to "home" conceived as proper and authentic belonging. This notion of "destinational" home, which has been the subject of Latina feminist and queer critique, can be traced to everyday experiences of home as providing refuge, orientation, and a place for the self.[13] However, a phenomenology of home also reveals a more everyday sense of home as intersubjective and historically emergent, developed via everyday practices that Mariana Ortega calls "home-tactics": "meanwhile" home as a privileged but contingent place of rest.[14] I then turn to the lived habitual body, which I differentiate from the body "at home" in the world. Both contingent home and the habitual body express how familiarity and (im)mobility are developed over time in dialogue with the external world and the conditions it offers. Finally, to demonstrate the uses of thinking trans embodiment through the prism of home, I end with a discussion of trans fatigue. In offering this analysis, the chapter aims to contribute to a growing body of work broadly described as trans phenomenology.[15]

The Wrong Body and Authentic Home

Aren Z. Aizura's and Nael Bhanji's work on trans citizenship pose trenchant critiques of narratives that position transgression "as a necessary but momentary lapse on the way to proper embodied belonging, a proper home and full social inclusion."[16] According to Aizura, such narratives, discernible in Prosser's account of wrong-bodiedness and gender transition, frame transgression as redeemable via its inclusion "under the aegis of normality or ordinariness."[17] The "liminality of transgender" is replaced or overcome through a "restorative" individualistic politics of home.[18] The wrong body, within which one is trapped or ensnared, is the preoperative body, defined vis-à-vis what it is not or, more precisely, what is not yet: the right body, the futural body-to-come. This sense of home as full and proper inclusion is tied, as Aizura argues, to national citizenship and its mandates to productivity, reproduction, property ownership, and wealth accumulation. The extent to which one's claim to home achieves social recognition is of course dependent on relations of power, as home in this sense is constantly (re)made via processes of exclusion. This is demonstrated in the common xenophobic refrain that racialized bodies ought to "go home" because they threaten the homeliness of those with a sense of entitlement over territory. As Aizura and Jack Halberstam point out, the degree to which one achieves "homeliness" or "rightness" is largely dependent on race, class, gender presentation, and privilege.[19]

In this linear trajectory of coming home as triumph over liminality or bodily alienation, home is imagined as a site of and for authenticity.[20] As Bhanji writes, for Prosser "to feel 'at home in one's skin' is to be taken in the world for who one feels oneself to be."[21] The proper or authentic home is an idealized place of supposedly true belonging—it is where one can finally be who they really are, unconditionally included. It is a futural, static home to which we are oriented and for which we strive. For some, this futural home— the "right" body—is also the home that has been lost and to which we long to return. In Henry Rubin's study of self-identified FTMs in San Francisco, Boston, and New York, for example, his participants describe the "unparalleled act of treachery" whereby, upon adolescence, "they had lost their androgynous, prepubescent bodies" and were "no longer recognizable to others (or even sometimes to themselves) as boys or men."[22]

In what follows, I discuss how a phenomenology of home offers a way of accounting for these idealized notions of home mobilized in the idea of wrong-bodiedness as liminality geared toward its own erasure and the right body as destination. The desire to come, go, arrive at, and feel at home can be gleaned in everyday practices and meanings of what it means to be in the world. These need not, however, lead to the formulation of proper, authentic, or destinational home. Indeed, we can invoke a more everyday rendering of "home"—contingent or "meanwhile" home—that affirms the body–world nexus and the inseparability of homeliness and conditions of livability.

Orientation and a Place for the Self: Mobilizing "Home" as Destinational

Home, which occupies a privileged position in classical phenomenology, is often distinguished from physical shelter or built environment.[23] Exceeding or transcending a house, home is accomplished through prolonged inhabitation and cultivated familiarity. Yet its privilege, according to Emmanuel Levinas, stems from its being the condition of human activity. For Levinas, to dwell entails a break from the anonymity of the natural world, "a coming to oneself, a retreat home with oneself as in a land of refuge."[24] As Kirsten Jacobson writes, home is a place for both "*self*-nourishment and *self*-development," where "one feels sheltered from outside intrusions" and demands.[25] As an essential dimension of how we inhabit the world and understand ourselves within it, it is unsurprising that *home* is a complex and emotionally charged term that recurs in discussions of—and contestations over—place, belonging, and identity. In its everyday usage, *home* is "overburdened" with meanings and imbued with sentimentality, such that "it seems to resist a concerted and systematic analysis."[26]

We may consider the home as a particular intimate and familiar place, a place we start from and to which we return. In this sense home fulfills an orienting function, allowing one to find one's bearings in space and determine where one is; it serves as a privileged point according to which something or somewhere is near or far. It provides a sense of direction, giving us somewhere to come from and a place to go to. In turn, home allows us to situate others in space and to give directions. It provides a kind of footing or steadiness in the world, a hold on it—a relative stability that enables movement and that permits us to pursue our daily activities and projects. In other words, the steadiness in the world that home affords is tied to the steadiness *of* the world. Functioning as an affective and material anchor, home allows for journeying.[27] We can venture away with the conviction that we may come back to it; we hold the expectation that it will retain its familiarity for us, that insofar as it is "our" place, it will remain poised for our return.

Indeed, as a retreat or refuge, home is conceived as a familiar place *for* the individual self. In this conception, home provides orientation and is also where I am oriented well: things are within my reach and remain where they have been placed. Social interactions are relatively consistent, and there is a sense of familiarity and security, "even if this security is one of being comfortable in relationships and ways of behaving" that are dangerous or unstable.[28] It is where we have our ways of doing things—a place for, and cultivated by, the rhythms of daily life.

This conventional sense of home as a stable refuge we may return to that orients us (well) in the world, and that is experienced as our own, can be mobilized in a nostalgic and exclusionary sense: home is where we long to be, it is where we once were, it is the place we are trying to get back to. It is what we have lost and, with it, our sense of belonging and orientation in the world. Here, the one who roams and journeys for the lost home is often an individualized masculine figure; the maternal as the "place which did not change," generative in its atemporality.[29] As the exemplar place of our own, a place that belongs and "responds" to us, this home is always potentially under threat—a sanctuary in need of defending and fortification.[30] This romanticized sense of home is often thrust into the future as something to attain and is tied to an uncomplicated, particular kind of belonging Ortega calls "authentic belonging."[31] As futural, home cannot be returned to because it is a destination at which one is always yet to arrive. It is deployed as an imagined, ideal place that requires production or building and that would put an end to the desire for movement. Here, home is a kind of promise as well as an activity with an imagined end point. This destinational sense of home, I suggest, is aligned with the idea of the right body as full, proper, embodied belonging. It positions, as Bhanji argues, "the in-between space of gender transition" as "a site of *future* homely possibility."[32]

Toward Contingent, "Meanwhile" Home

Yet key to home is repetition (or repeatability): coming and going, arriving and departing, leaving and staying in. Home is porous, and this porosity is necessary for its functioning and sustainability.[33] In *Home and Beyond,* Anthony J. Steinbock describes Husserl's use of the German expression *Stamm* in his later writings. *Stamm,* which can mean "stem," "trunk," "root," or "lineage," has the sense of an origin that is not primordial beginning *(Ur)* and that involves repeated generation, intersubjectivity, and participation.[34] According to Steinbock:

> Unlike origin *[Ursprung],* stamm is not unidirectional. A phenomenology of origins or of *primordial* constitution *[Ur-konstitution]* traces a movement that goes out from an origin; it is a genesis of self-temporalization, from past to future, as it were. A stamm, however, is not only a past "from which," but a "from which" that bears *repeating* in the form of a "toward which." *Stamm* entails a normal familiarity that is built up by actively repeating as appropriating and coming back to.[35]

Returning and circling back to, appropriation and participation are central to the generation of home as the place of generationality. Home is, according to Steinbock, "where we generationally repeat ourselves," taking up and activating inherited norms and traditions and participating in the generation of future ones.[36] Of course, to say that home is always already relational, that it is where we participate in the generation of the social and historical world, is not to suggest that the experience of home is positive or harmonious. Home is the site "through which basic forms of social relations and social institutions are constituted and reproduced,"[37] and it can be a place of transphobia, oppression, alienation, and violence.[38] As Sara Ahmed argues, disorientation and estrangement are often experienced by those whose bodies are "out of place"—one can "feel oblique" and assailed at home or while pursuing inhabitance as a goal.[39] Yet we participate in its making because we are ineluctably engaged in the world, whether this takes the form of critique, resistance, indifference, and so on—and when we leave particular homes and make home and homeliness elsewhere.

Ortega's concept of "hometactics," which is mobilized against the myth of home and authentic belonging—the destinational home I have been trying to problematize—is particularly instructive here. Drawing on the work of María Lugones, for whom "home" is inseparable from violence, what Ortega calls "hometactics" involves the making do via everyday practices that leads not to the fortification of idealized home but to a "sense of familiarity" and ease cultivated by marginalized folks in the midst of unhomely, disruptive conditions and worlds.[40] The concept of "hometactics" affirms both the mundane, everyday ways in which "multiplicitous selves" have and continue to "make do" and the "desire to return to a place called home" while being "perfectly aware of its traps."[41] Building on Ortega's account, what I call "contingent home" is always in process, historically situated, porous, and (re)made in relation with others and the norms of the social world in which it is located. In understanding home not as primordial origin but as emergent and generational—as generated, and as generative of a future—we see that home is an intersubjective project always already underway. It is "a type of genesis *within* historicity, and not abstracted from it."[42] Contingent home is a more quotidian, temporal, and relational understanding of home: home as the place of the everyday existence, which can sometimes feel frustrating, inadequate, or boring in its familiarity. This home is not necessarily the home one yearns to return to, and it may not be the home to which one feels one properly or unconditionally belongs. One may not know how one ended up here; one may be here due to a host of losses. This home is not the romanticized home of the past, but neither is it the idealized home-to-come: it is not necessarily where one wishes to end up or the home one consciously strives toward. It does not presuppose a sovereign, individual subject with a clear sense of where they want to go (e.g., the right body or embodied belonging) or even where they have come from. Rather, contingent home is the concrete home of the now or the "meanwhile." *Meanwhile* refers to an intervening period of time; the term *while*, signifying "space of time," can be traced back to the root *kweie-*, "to rest, to be quiet."[43] Contingent or meanwhile home is a place of relative or temporary comfort, ease, and rest—a place generated via hometactics, everyday intersubjective practices of making do, and relations of interdependency that support livability in the now of our concrete situations.

Contingent or meanwhile home is what is negated in futural, destinational home, and yet it is the vehicle through which the latter is striven for. Understanding home as contingent draws attention to the ways in which our concrete possibilities and imagined collective futures are developed through our lived situations as these unfold. Again, as Ortega reminds us, this is not to deny that one may be oriented toward idealized, futural home and invested in arriving/coming home—but it is to situate this desire and how it is grappled with in the space and time of concrete, existent home.

Habituation and Conditions of Homeliness

I have noted the intersubjective, processual, and ambiguous nature of contingent home—which is eclipsed in the conception of destinational home and the linearity it imposes on trans narratives. If, as I have been suggesting, the wrong body is aligned with idealized, destinational home, is there a way of thinking embodiment in terms of contingent home? As a privileged sphere of relative or temporary rest, which is historically situated and supports livability in our concrete situations, contingent home is linked to the lived, habitual body. The habitual body, in turn, reflects and is expressive of conditions of (un)homeliness that are afforded to it and that it finds in the world. Importantly, I wish to distinguish between the lived habitual body and the body at home in the world; the latter is one that experiences a relatively seamless "body-world compatibility," as Corinne Lajoie points out in her analysis of disorientation in illness.[44] This phenomenological understanding helps to clarify the privileges afforded to the body at home in the world when it comes to energy expenditure and time, which will be key to my discussion of trans fatigue.

Philosophers note how home and body "co-define" or co-support one another.[45] Home affords a level of comfort and mineness, but this is developed through sustained embodied existence and interaction. As Iris Marion Young puts it, "The home is an extension of and mirror for the living body in its everyday activity" and is hence not simply linked to personal identity but is its very "materialization" and endurance over time.[46] For Jacobson, "home is phenomenologically akin to our body" insofar as both constitute "the base of our action," providing "a place of initial stability and a foundation for the self."[47] According to Merleau-Ponty, my body is "a permanence on my side" and always "on the margins of all of my perceptions."[48] As "the vehicle of being in the world," the body mediates all experience.[49] My body "is not primarily in space, but is rather of space," and it is through it that I have a perspective and a hold on the world.[50] Indeed, "place" relies on our embodied existence and is first of all a "relation of self and the world through my body" rather than an objective location.[51]

Many scholars working in disability studies and philosophy of race point out that classical phenomenology has assumed and privileged a universal, normative subject—the anonymous and normate "body"—and upheld the integration between self and world as optimal.[52] As Lajoie argues, this "ideal of a seamless fit" between body and world excludes a vast array of lived experiences, as well as "claims to alternative forms of bodily dwelling."[53] Phenomenology's emphasis on the temporal and intersubjective dimensions of embodied existence, however, allows us to focus on ways of experiencing one's body in the world other than that of seamless integration.

In Merleau-Ponty's philosophy, body develops a sense of familiarity in the world through habituation. Habit is not a form of knowledge, nor is it an automatic reflex. It is an embodied implicit knowledge; if we had to locate where it "resides," Merleau-Ponty writes, we would find it not "in thought nor in the objective body, but rather in the body as the mediator of a world."[54] It demonstrates, as David Morris writes, "the temporal depth of the body."[55] Through the continuous acquisition of habit, the body achieves a kind of prereflective understanding that allows one to engage in unthinking ways. The lived habitual body is hence expressive of the environments it has navigated and the experiences—disruptive, alienating, joyful, and otherwise—that it has undergone; it is deep, historical, and subjectively felt. This does not mean that one's developed habits are not unsettled or rendered no longer operative; it is to emphasize the temporality of the lived body, which is ineluctably enmeshed in the world, always in an embodied circuit with its environments and with others. This lived habitual body, inseparable from the social, can be gleaned in Eli Clare's powerful invocation of his body as home—as involving other bodies, histories, and communities, the acknowledgment of violence and shame, and the impetus for a "refiguring" of the world.[56] The lived body may not find in the world conditions of homeliness.

Merleau-Ponty's account of habit, further developed by Helen Ngo, also helps to clarify the particular privileges afforded to the body at home in the world. For Merleau-Ponty, habit expresses a power or capacity to develop a kind of bodily know-how in order to better—and more quickly and creatively—meet the demands of concrete situations. It allows one to move through the world with more ease, with a kind of embodied understanding and prereflective readiness for situations one is familiar with or that have familiar aspects or general "feels" to them. Allowing one to gloss over certain details, habit allows for the expansion and extension of the body in space. Importantly, while habit may take time to develop, it also saves time. It saves energy. As Ngo argues, "The relationship between habit and rest is . . . codependent and cogenerative"; habituation "opens up the possibility of restfulness."[57]

The body at home in the world, then, is the body that moves with relative ease, that expends less energy when engaging with the world, and is hence afforded rest and respite. The body at home in the world finds most situations familiar and manageable and is able to realize their intentions quickly and without significant disruption. In this sense, the body at home in the world moves out of the way, retreating in order to engage. In short, the body at home in the world is the body that finds home in the world—that finds more of the world homely, because they are anticipated and supported by their environment. Consequently, the body at home in the world is the body that has to expend less energy and time navigating a world that is homely for it. It is more effective and mobile, more comfortable and seemingly independent, because it finds in the world conditions of homeliness. And because of this homeliness and relative ease, this body finds more occasions for rest.

Trans Fatigue

Contingent home and the lived habitual body express the achievement of familiarity over time, which develops in dialogue with the social world and its conditions of livability. As I note above, phenomenology demonstrates how home and body co-define one another. It also helps to clarify why and how certain bodies find ease in the world and when pursuing their projects. This account is crucial for understanding trans fatigue.

By *trans fatigue* I have in mind the generalized depletion experienced by trans subjects navigating (un)homeliness in the world. It is important to note here that depletion is experienced more or less acutely depending on whether one faces other forms of oppression, as well as one's level of familiarity within given social environments. What I aim to offer here is one way of conceptualizing the exhausting impacts of being what Dean Spade calls "impossible." As Spade argues, "Trans people are told by legal systems, state agencies, employers, schools, and our families that we are impossible people who are not who we say we are, cannot exist, cannot be classified, and cannot fit anywhere."[58] Impossibility is also discernible in Bettcher's account of the "basic denial of authenticity,"[59] a key form of transphobia that immobilizes trans people in what she calls a "double bind"—whereby they are represented as either deceivers or pretenders and subject to ridicule, condescension, fear of exposure, violence, and murder.[60] This is due to an entrenched and naturalized "appearance-reality contrast between gender presentation and sexed body."[61] The stakes of being an impossible person are high.

Trans fatigue is an outcome of being a body that is not at home, but this is not a private, individual experience of wrongness in one's body but rather an experience that arises out of the interaction between body and world. This is not to say that one does not experience gender discomfort; moreover, access to trans health care is absolutely necessary. However, fatigue cannot be alleviated by transitioning insofar as the body cannot individually upend transphobia. It is because the trans person is navigating a world that is unhomely—sometimes too a home that is unhomely—that energy has to be expended. To be a body at home is to have know-how, ease of mobility, and familiarity, the ability to not have to calculate, acquaint oneself with, and worry about one's body and position in space precisely because it is not space, in the strict sense, but familiar, homely, place. Possibilities for homeliness are differentially distributed, as our social contexts anticipate certain bodies, pathways, and orientations.[62] The body at home follows pathways with relative ease and tends not to be stopped and interrogated, surveilled, ridiculed, misgendered, or subject to harm—or hypervigilant regarding the ever-present possibility of encountering such situations. In other words, it is tiring to not be at home. It is exhausting to be unable to rely on habit and know-how, to lack the support of tacit knowledge. To be at home is to have a developed, supported, cultivated familiarity—and this means that one is more free and able to direct one's energies elsewhere. The trans person, as a body that is not at home, is exhausted or depleted because the world is not homely for them, because the world is, precisely, exhausting.

Here we may draw on Gilles Deleuze's insight that one is "tired by something, but exhausted by nothing."[63] Trans fatigue is not the outcome of anything one has done or said. As a supposedly impossible individual, the trans person is assailed at the level of who they are. This is why it is the world that is experienced as exhausting, not a set of discrete tasks. Tiredness relates to feeling spent or depleted due to activity, whereas fatigue is a generalized feeling of depletion or being worn down accumulated over time. Yet, and importantly, fatigue arises not solely from this wearing down but also in and through pressing on. It arises because of the energy expended in navigating transphobic society while also living one's projects and commitments, continuing in the face of it. In this sense, it can be said to be properly located not in an individual body but rather in the relation between embodied existence and the social world.

This living on or through is supported by contingent, meanwhile home, which is why cultivating these spaces is so crucial. We may then ask: If meanwhile home is a place of relative comfort, retreat, and rest, what does rest involve for the body that is not at home in the world? Merleau-Ponty provides a useful starting point for a phenomenology of rest in his description of how the "muscular tensions" of the body indicate a "normal position of rest, [a] position where nothing would be felt as figure, where the body would return to its background, and in relation to which any other [position] is [an] expressly perceived divergence or anomaly."[64] This description provides a key insight for an account of rest, which must also be concretely situated. Restfulness involves a particular lived body returning to its own tendencies for comportment, a normal position that this body has developed over time. While it may not always be possible to achieve a position "where nothing would be felt as figure," the lived (subjectively felt) and relative aspect of rest that Merleau-Ponty puts forward is striking—it is dynamic and open to change, as it shifts depending on one's lived situation. Rest is hence something that must be learned and experimented with, something we must constantly feel into—as possibilities for rest arise out of the interplay among one's lived embodiment, relations with others, and the social, legal, and material conditions one navigates. Hence, restfulness is a product of sedimentation, and like habit, it too expresses a relation between body and world. Furthermore, this notion of bodily rest can be applied to the rest afforded at home, as the abiding structure is similar: contingent home provides the possibility for the body not at home in the world to achieve and experiment with rest, because it is a place where, relatively speaking, one no longer stands out or is on guard and one's identity ceases to be questioned. In a world that is experienced as unhomely, and where one is immobilized by the double bind, contingent home offers a place for rest, if only temporarily. Home is where, as Max J. Andrucki and Dana J. Kaplan claim, trans people may "experience themselves as subjects and not objects."[65]

As Susan Stryker and Paisley Currah write, "Transgender bodies are always somewhere" despite "the transgender body" serving as "an avatar of its age: an elastic, recategorizable body for an era of flexible accumulation."[66] Indeed, to say that the trans person—as impossible—is a body that is not at home does not mean they do not have home, that they do not dwell with others or participate in the generation of social and historical worlds. To claim as such would be to capitulate to a politics of idealized, futural home, which is precisely what the idea of contingent home resists. Trans homeliness already exists as a collective endeavor; it has and continues to generate more just ways of being in the world and being with others. It does not necessitate moving from the so-called wrong to the right body, and it may not involve medical transitioning at all.

The work of home is always ongoing, in process, and a fundamentally intersubjective project. It is this dimension that risks foreclosure in accounts of trans embodiment that throw homeliness squarely into the future: that home is always to come, not now. As I have tried to show in this essay, approaching trans embodiment through the prism of home offers a framework for analyzing the temporal and relational dimensions of trans experiences. How might we account for the time of experimentation, hesitation, the process of transitioning in its myriad of forms, waiting, and pressing on? How does transitioning become not just an abstract possibility but one of *my* concrete possibilities? How are our horizons of viability imagined, inhabited, and grown into—despite, and hence in relation to, what can feel at times exhausting or even unbearable? These are just a few of the questions posed by trans experiences that trans phenomenology, in shifting the focus away from right- or wrong-bodiedness, might consider.

Notes

1. Despite this association of trans embodiment with mobility, it should be noted that trans migrants have rarely been centrally positioned within trans studies. The collections *Transgender Migrations: The Bodies, Borders, and Politics of Transition* (New York: Routledge, 2011), edited by Trystan T. Cotten, and *Queer and Trans Migrations: Dynamics of Illegalization, Detention, and Deportation* (Urbana: University of Illinois Press, 2020), edited by Eithne Luibhéid and Karma R. Chávez, are noteworthy in this regard. I thank the editors for drawing my attention to this point, among others, and thank both the editors and the anonymous reviewer for their generous feedback and comments.
2. Talia Mae Bettcher, "Intersexuality, Transgender, and Transsexuality," in *The Oxford Handbook of Feminist Theory*, ed. Lisa Disch and Mary Hawkesworth (New York: Oxford University Press, 2016), 418.
3. Bettcher, "Intersexuality, Transgender, and Transsexuality," 418.
4. Sandy Stone, "The *Empire* Strikes Back: A Posttranssexual Manifesto," in *The Transgender Studies Reader*, ed. Susan Stryker and Stephen Whittle (New York: Routledge, 2006), 227.
5. Aren Z. Aizura, "Of Borders and Homes: The Imaginary Community of (Trans)sexual Citizenship," *Inter-Asia Cultural Studies* 7, no. 2 (2006): 290; Ulrica Engdahl, "Wrong Body," *TSQ: Transgender Studies Quarterly* 1, no. 1–2 (2014): 267–69; Cael Keegan, "Moving Bodies: Sympathetic Migrations in Transgender Narrativity," *Genders* 57 (2013):

https://www.colorado.edu/gendersarchive1998-2013/2013/06/01/moving
-bodies-sympathetic-migrations-transgender-narrativity.

6. Aren Z. Aizura, "The Persistence of Transgender Travel Narratives," in *Transgender Migration: The Bodies, Borders, and Politics of Transition,* ed. Trystan T. Cotten (New York: Routledge, 2011), 142.

7. Jay Prosser, *Second Skins: The Body Narratives of Transsexuality* (New York: Columbia University Press, 1998), 69.

8. Prosser, *Second Skins,* 69.

9. Prosser, 69.

10. Maurice Merleau-Ponty, *The Phenomenology of Perception,* trans. Donald Landes (New York: Routledge, 2012), 84.

11. Andrea Long Chu, "The Wrong Wrong Body: Notes on Trans Phenomenology," *TSQ: Transgender Studies Quarterly* 4, no. 1 (2017): 149.

12. Chu, "Wrong Wrong Body," 149.

13. Gloria Anzaldúa, *The Gloria Anzaldúa Reader* (Durham, N.C.: Duke University Press, 2009); Mariana Ortega, *In-Between: Latina Feminist Phenomenology, Multiplicity, and the Self* (New York: State University of New York Press, 2016).

14. Ortega, *In-Between,* 193.

15. N. F. Baldino, "Trans Phenomenology: A Merleau-Pontian Reclamation of the Trans Narrative," *Res Cogitans* 6 (2015): 162–70; Talia Mae Bettcher, "Trans Phenomena," in *50 Concepts for a Critical Phenomenology,* ed. Gail Weiss, Ann V. Murphy, and Gayle Salamon (Evanston, Ill.: Northwestern University Press, 2020), 329–35; Henry Rubin, "Phenomenology as Method in Trans Studies," *GLQ: A Journal of Lesbian and Gay Studies* 4, no. 2 (1998): 263–81; Henry Rubin, *Self-Made Men: Identity and Embodiment among Transsexual Men* (Nashville: Vanderbilt University Press, 2003); Gayle Salamon, *Assuming a Body: Transgender and the Rhetorics of Materiality* (New York: Columbia University Press, 2010); Gayle Salamon, *The Life and Death of Latisha King: A Critical Phenomenology of Transphobia* (New York: New York University Press, 2018).

16. Aizura, "Of Borders and Homes," 293.

17. Aizura, 294.

18. Aizura, 295.

19. Aizura; Jack Halberstam, *Female Masculinity* (Durham, N.C.: Duke University Press, 2018).

20. Nael Bhanji, "Trans/scriptions: Homing Desires, (Trans)sexual Citizenship and Racialized Bodies," in *The Transgender Studies Reader 2,* ed. Susan Stryker and Aren Z. Aizura (New York: Routledge, 2013), 512–26.

21. Bhanji, "Trans/scriptions," 516.

22. Rubin, *Self-Made Men,* 10–11.

23. Gaston Bachelard, *The Poetics of Space* (Boston: Beacon Press, 1964); Emmanuel Levinas, *Totality and Infinity: An Essay on Exteriority* (Pitts-

burgh, Penn.: Duquesne University Press, 1969); Anthony J. Steinbock, *Home and Beyond: Generative Phenomenology after Husserl* (Evanston, Ill.: Northwestern University Press, 1995).

24. Levinas, *Totality and Infinity,* 156.
25. Kirsten Jacobson, "A Developed Nature: A Phenomenological Account of the Experience of Home," *Continental Philosophy Review* 42 (2009): 359, 358.
26. Steinbock, *Home and Beyond,* 187.
27. Jacobson, "Developed Nature."
28. Jacobson, 356.
29. Doreen Massey, *Space, Place, and Gender* (Minneapolis: University of Minnesota Press, 1994), 167; Simone de Beauvoir, *The Second Sex* (Harmondsworth: Penguin Books, 1983).
30. Jacobson, "Developed Nature."
31. Ortega, *In-Between,* 196.
32. Bhanji, "Trans/scriptions," 517.
33. Helen Ngo, *The Habits of Racism: A Phenomenology of Racism and Racialized Embodiment* (Lanham, Md.: Lexington Books, 2017).
34. Steinbock, *Home and Beyond,* 194.
35. Steinbock, 194–95.
36. Steinbock, 195.
37. Peter Saunders and Peter Williams, "The Constitution of the Home: Towards a Research Agenda," *Housing Studies* 3, no. 2 (1998): 82.
38. Shelley Mallett, "Understanding Home: A Critical Review of the Literature," *Sociological Review* 52, no. 1 (2004): 62–89.
39. Sara Ahmed, *Queer Phenomenology: Orientations, Objects, Others* (Durham, N.C.: Duke University Press, 2006), 170.
40. Ortega, *In-Between,* 203.
41. Ortega, 193.
42. Steinbock, *Home and Beyond,* 196.
43. Online Etymology Dictionary, s.v. "while," accessed January 22, 2024, https://www.etymonline.com/word/while.
44. Corinne Lajoie, "Being at Home: A Feminist Phenomenology of Disorientation in Illness," *Hypatia* 34, no. 3 (2019): 557.
45. Jacobson, "Developed Nature," 268; Edward Casey, *Getting Back into Place: Toward a Renewed Understanding of the Place-World* (Bloomington: Indiana University Press, 1993); Ngo, *Habits of Racism*; Iris Marion Young, *On Female Body Experience: "Throwing Like a Girl" and Other Essays* (New York: Oxford University Press, 2005).
46. Young, *On Female Body Experience,* 140. See also Casey, *Getting Back into Place.*
47. Jacobson, "Developed Nature," 359–61.
48. Merleau-Ponty, *Phenomenology of Perception,* 93.
49. Merleau-Ponty, 84.
50. Merleau-Ponty, 149.

51. Merleau-Ponty, 149.
52. Ahmed, *Queer Phenomenology*; Eli Clare, *Exile and Pride: Disability, Queerness, and Liberation* (Durham, N.C.: Duke University Press, 2015); Frantz Fanon, *Black Skin, White Masks* (New York: Grove Press, 2008); Kim Q. Hall, "Limping Along: Toward a Crip Phenomenology," *Journal of Philosophy of Disability* 1 (2021): 11–33, https://doi.org/10.5840/jpd20218275; Lajoie, "Being at Home"; Ngo, *Habits of Racism*.
53. Lajoie, "Being at Home," 556.
54. Merleau-Ponty, *Phenomenology of Perception*, 146.
55. David Morris, *The Sense of Space* (Albany: State University of New York Press, 2004), 91.
56. Clare, *Exile and Pride*, 13.
57. Ngo, *Habits of Racism*, 101.
58. Dean Spade, *Normal Life: Administrative Violence, Critical Trans Politics, and the Limits of Law* (Durham, N.C.: Duke University Press, 2015), 120.
59. Talia Mae Bettcher, "Appearance, Reality, and Gender Deception: Reflections on Transphobic Violence and the Politics of Pretence," in *Violence, Victims, Justifications: Philosophical Approaches,* ed. Felix Ó Murchadha (Oxford: Peter Lang, 2006), 175–200; Talia Mae Bettcher, "Understanding Transphobia: Authenticity and Sexual Abuse," in *Trans/forming Feminisms: Transfeminist Voices Speak Out,* ed. Krista Scott-Dixon (Toronto: Sumach, 2006), 203–10.
60. Talia Mae Bettcher, "Evil Deceivers and Make-Believers: On Transphobic Violence and the Politics of Illusion," *Hypatia* 22, no. 3 (2007): 43–65.
61. Bettcher, "Evil Deceivers and Make-Believers," 48.
62. Ahmed, *Queer Phenomenology*.
63. Gilles Deleuze, "The Exhausted," *SubStance* 24, no. 3 (78) (1995): 4.
64. Maurice Merleau-Ponty, *The Sensible World and the World of Expression,* trans. Bryan Smyth (Evanston, Ill.: Northwestern University Press, 2020), 103.
65. Max J. Andrucki and Dana J. Kaplan, "Trans Objects: Materializing Queer Time in US Transmasculine Homes," *Gender, Place & Cultures* 25, no. 6 (2018): 794.
66. Susan Stryker and Paisley Currah, "General Editors' Introduction," *TSQ: Transgender Studies Quarterly* 2, no. 4 (2015): 540.

"I Look Too Good Not to Be Seen"
Multiple Meaning Realism and Sociosomatics
PJ DiPietro

Living at the brink of dispossession refocuses the meaning of life and embodiment for trans of color communities. Specifically, because embodied differences emerge through social formation, including the formation of the human against the reduction of matter to a nonhuman condition. Social constructivism and new materialism offer complexity to the study of nonhuman conditions, the stations of thinghood, and animality. Reality is disorienting for trans of color communities because of the multiplicity of our embodiments. If we seek legibility through gender transition, we encounter the genre of the human in all its enticing might. Yet, at once, we remain stuck in the prehuman stage of nonwhiteness. Furthermore, the genre of the human extracts its power from the very material production of thinghood. This experience of bodily distinctions and differences, simultaneously fluid and stagnant, shapes our intuition about the reality of embodiment.

It may feel counterintuitive to talk about alternatives to the human in terms of the reality of embodiments. Often, claims about what reality is have a bad rap in feminist circles. Particularly, because dominant views conflate reality and nature. Feminism dislikes an inquiry whose claim to certainty rests on the idea that the natural world has an order outside the realm of social construction and that is, therefore, independent of oppression and ideology. For trans of color communities, multiplicity leads into an examination of reality that reframes the link between humanity and thinghood.

This chapter pursues three interrelated inquiries about multiple realities and embodiments. First, I engage the often-intractable divide between culture and nature in Sally Haslanger's metaphysics of gender. In so doing, I sketch an account of embodiment as an entangling entanglement, a sociosomatic assembling of adulterated biomaterial worlds and impure biosocial domains. More than the interweaving of nature and culture, I understand that the notion of sociosomatics captures a realist and materialist ecology of always already biophilic←→always already sociogenic entangling. I focus on the notion of stabilization in Haslanger's metaphysics and pinpoint evidence that shows thoroughly social yet not only social entanglements as they concern gendered and sexed distinctions. Second, I draw on Talia Mae Bettcher's multiple meaning realism to underscore the role that stabilization plays in the demarcation of sex/gender distinctions within oppositional realities. Finally, I turn to histories of Black and Brown ballroom cultures to investigate the process of sex/gender stabilization and its shaping of multiple, including antistructure, realities.

Objectivism, Realism, Embodiment

Feminist philosophers continue to be puzzled by what looks like an intractable tension between gender (as sexed subjectivities that become varied and multiple) and sex (as an ineradicable rift between male and female).[1] The idea that biology determines an absolute binary between cisgender man and woman, combined with the idea that bodily differences proliferate without a predetermined end, supposedly explains major contemporary accounts of the reality of embodiment. The former account accommodates a tradition that is known in Western philosophy as the metaphysics of substance— that is, the idea that the world consists of entities defined by essential characteristics and that they unequivocally exclude any ambiguity between one thing and another. According to the essentialist view, biology marks bodies as either male or female. The latter account accommodates a tradition that, by contrast, is known as the metaphysics of events. That is, the notion that the world consists of processes whose dynamic creates constant change and, hence, supports a world of ambiguity. An essentialist view considers that gender underlies ideologies about the hierarchical order of differences between cisgender men and women. Sexist and patriarchal hegemonies rest on constructing biology-based differences as clearcut and absolute. Subsequently, they justify a culture that subordinates anything that falls beneath the male/masculine station. Conversely, a process-centered view of gender underpins antisexist and antipatriarchal counterhegemonies that support the notion of performance-based differences. As performative, they unfold in shifting fashion and, consequently, have the potential of affirming a culture of insubordination against male/female hierarchies.

Feminist scholarship and political work contends with the complexities of sexed and gendered embodiments. Yet, it often operates under the belief that reality is one and its interpretation is multiple. In fact, biology-based, culture-based, and performativity-based approaches may align with the gravitational force of this monism. Not only essentialist but also social constructionist and performative accounts of sex and gender may recapitulate claims against ontological pluralism.[2] As I shall demonstrate later in this chapter, I embrace ontological pluralism since it is true to the experience of social groups who lack autonomy in the colonial/modern ordering of the world. I feel deflated when some feminist theorists demand that nonconforming embodiments materialize critical, queer, deconstructive viewpoints about sex and gender. My realism tells me that resistance ongoingly repurposes the *how* or the many modes with which it meets domination and oppression. In fact, minoritized individuals and collectives engage with essentialist and constructivist views according to context or at once within the same context. Moreover, what is typically understood as a context may prove insufficient to capture complexities that arise from the contradictions of oppressing←→being oppressed←→resisting. Thus, subjectivities who lack autonomy in the neocolonial order of the world do not become empowered just because some contexts create legal, institutional, or market conditions that favor self-realization as expression of free will. Social backing of resistant intentions for minoritized selves may stem from marginal, oppositional, and alternative realities regardless of whether the self finds themself within a context overriding dominant or nondominant relations and arrangements.

I seek to retain a realist emphasis in the metaphysics of sex/ gender that I review next. I converse with Sally Haslanger's model mainly because of its commitment to a critical version of realism.[3] I also seek to trouble some of her metaphysical commitments since they often lead feminist practitioners to align with the least inclusive implications of her proposal. I put aside the ascriptivist and conferralist approaches to gender metaphysics of the last decade, which offer bold accounts of gender as a social unifying role or as an individual and communal social property, respectively.[4] Both provide novel ways of thinking about social kinds. My interest, however, doesn't lie with revisiting if sex/gender is a social kind or what kind of social kind it is. Instead, I proceed with an account that, stemming from Black feminist studies, women of color feminism, and their praxes, supports decolonial versions of objectivism.

Haslanger's feminist metaphysics speaks to the materialist turn that sees in everything that lives the outward-looking orientation of relations while they connect a changing whole. The material world, according to this view, is enmeshed in social formation as much as social construction is interwoven in the biophysical realm. No longer is the supremacy of perception or the mind taken for granted. Her proposal condemns post-structuralist accounts of sex and gender for their underlying theory of reference. Favoring discourse, she argues, preemptively limits what we may know about the reality of sex/gender. She challenges poststructuralist ideas that link the very act of naming what lies beyond discourse with understanding it. That is, Haslanger's realism questions the belief that discourse always already prefigures and, thus, constitutes an extradiscursive realm. By supporting the belief that the world includes some pregiven objects, critiques such as Haslanger's lead feminist philosophy to metaphysical inquiries about the nature of sexed bodies.[5]

Concerning sexed distinctions, Haslanger refers to *nature* as an infrastructure that, regardless of the sociopolitical regime, neatly determines in causally significant manner an effective way of relating to the bodies we are given. Clearly, her metaphysics combines a version of essentialism—that there is a something that makes something the thing it is—with a version of constructivism—that there are schemas with which we make sense of things, such as bodies, according to political and social contexts. An objective type or infrastructure, which stands independent of human perception, prompts grouping of things. Grouping functions by convention, of course, but also, Haslanger argues, by the mere ontology of the world, by properties that are structurally more relevant to what the world is. These properties "play a fundamental role in determining what the world (as a whole) looks like and how it evolves" regardless of what conventions we hold about it.[6] Instead of relying on the putative force of nature to dictate what bodies can be or do, her metaphysics seeks to identify properties that are ontologically fundamental and that relate to bodily distinctions in a nontrivial and causally meaningful way.

Haslanger's model makes room for a contextual account of objective types as she claims that "one's gender may not be entirely stable, and that other systems of oppression may disrupt gender in particular contexts: a woman may not always function socially as a woman; a man may not always function socially as a man."[7] At least in certain contexts, she argues, an objective type compels the stabilization of sex/gender and allows a woman thereby to socially function as woman. A person is observed or imagined, she says, within a context that stabilizes gender whenever a person is said to have "the bodily features presumed to be evidence of a female's biological role in reproduction."[8] The capacity for pregnancy and, as such, the chromosomal distinction between female and male is the objective type that Haslanger offers.[9] Primarily, she refers to "endosex," or sex characteristics that physically match what is expected for female or male bodies.[10] In her own words, the subordinate positions that women occupy as a group are "marked and justified by reference to (female) sex."[11]

In the most politically salient read of Haslanger's metaphysics, strands of the feminist movement find responses to their concerns about the flattening of sexual distinction and its epistemic and ontological valence. For example, Monique Wittig's works, embraced in the 1970s by radical lesbian feminists, examine both the state of being born a woman and the process of becoming one. Wittig describes a phallocentric economy that consigns femininity to the anomalous mark of nature, a "physical defect" of sorts.[12]

She makes evident that "female," or "woman," follows the political ideology, the straight mind, that renders the negative inscription of the body (that which is not male) into a natural kind.[13] While at times Haslanger's proposal approximates Wittig's, the former reserves references to sex, such as chromosomal distinctions, to an objective, experience-independent reality. In other words, she contributes to the normative sociosomatic association between XX-bodies and cisgender women.[14]

Contextual and social constructivist aspects of Haslanger's account correspond to the process of stabilization. By this process, she means normative assignation. Because of the type of realism that she espouses, I am inclined to think that *normativity* doesn't translate into heteronormativity, homonormativity, or transnormativity. Instead, I understand that she refers to two interconnected processes of normativity. First, the most realist normativity, which entails the ascription of a certain unity to a set of features. Let's say that we are not compelled by the reality of our bodies to ascribe a core place to kidneys in the unity that we call sex/gender. We are likely to be compelled by the reality of our bodies to ascribe a core place to ovaries in the unity that we call sex/gender. We could refer to this process in Haslanger's model as first-order ascription. Second, the way in which ascription operates makes room for contexts in which ovaries cohere with the unity that we call sex/gender. Yet, it also makes room for contexts in which they do not cohere with such a unity.[15] This normative coherence is what we could call second-order ascription.

In her latest work, María Lugones claims that coloniality entails reconceiving sex as nonambiguous and dimorphic.[16] White and Euro-American colonizers established a hegemonic order within which gender functions as a bodily trait of humans. As such, it stands opposite other bodily projects that colonization subjugated. She highlights that coloniality shapes the link between first-order and second-order ascriptions. I understand Haslanger's model to function within the bounds of coloniality's reconceiving of sex/gender as dimorphic.[17]

The unity of "gender," or "woman," involves two modes of attribution. Firstly, it entails features that compel us to ascribe them a core role with regard to that unity. Secondly, it encompasses contexts in which these features, those that elicit the presumption of evidence of female sex, may or may not cohere according to first-order ascription. Lugones claims that coloniality reserves the role of reproduction of the species for Euro-American women while colonized "women" became various versions of not-women and, thus, automata or reproducers of unwaged labor force.[18] I am not sure whether, in Haslanger's argument, *contexts* and *systems of oppression* are interchangeable. I assume that they are not. However, it seems that systems of oppression do create various contexts, such as those that Lugones describes within coloniality.

In the United States, a dominant patriarchal order marginalizes and discriminates against women across various contexts, including contexts in which sex/gender tracks incompatible features (for instance, endosex, secondary sex characteristics, self-identification, legal designation, and societal perception). Out of the interplay of systems and contexts, restricting and enabling arrangements codetermine realities. Incompatible realities may coexist as a trait of ontological pluralism. That is, contexts bear on the mattering, the sociosomatic entangling, that gender and sex designate. I must note that contradictions may arise among second-order ascriptions, from one context to another. Stabilization performs a socio-ontological looping between contradictions. Their tenor may bring into question first-order ascription. Let me provide an example regarding sexual and reproductive rights across two contexts.

In context A, the state of Texas's S.B. 8 prohibits access to abortion procedures as soon as a heartbeat can be detected in the fetus.[19] Within context A, *abortion* refers to procedures that bodies perceived to have certain features—sexual resources capable of attaining pregnancy—may access as long as available technology does not detect a beating heart other than the pregnant person's. According to S.B. 8, pregnancy is a "human female reproductive condition" with the following features: it begins with fertilization, it is carried out by a "woman," and it must be calculated from "the first day of the woman's last menstrual period."[20] Basically, by the time the pregnant person becomes aware of the interruption of the menstrual cycle, which amounts to a potential pregnancy, there is no time to seek an abortion procedure. Notice that the bill refers indistinctly to "human female" and "woman." It should also be noted that, at least as an implied reality, S.B. 8 remains silent about pregnancies carried to term by bodies other than women's or by technologies replacing the gestational sac.[21]

Within context B, New York State's Reproductive Health Act permits access to abortion care for any person aged eighteen or older prior to week twenty-four of pregnancy.[22] After week twenty-four, the Reproductive Health Act names the fetus's viability, as well as the gestating person's health and life risks, as factors to be considered, between care providers and the gestating person, to reach a decision about abortion. Within context B, *abortion* refers to procedures that bodies perceived to have certain features—sexual resources capable of attaining pregnancy—may access at age eighteen and for twenty-four weeks if the gestating person arrives at such a decision autonomously.

Discrepancies between context A and context B are compatible with the system of oppression that we call patriarchy or, more specifically, heterocisnormative patriarchy. These discrepancies between contexts also point to something being amiss in Haslanger's objectivism. I am thinking about first-order ascription in her proposal. Within context A, the bodily features that matter as core for first-order ascription—the unit that may seek abortion procedures—remits to the presence of certain reproductive resources but also to the undifferentiation between technology and nature and between gestating person and fetus. While antirights language in S.B. 8 is effectively an assault on cisgender women's reproductive autonomy, the ban clearly targets more than just "human females'" or "women's" bodies. Ironically, this is the unintended sex/gender inclusivity of the state's abortion law. It also targets trans, gender-nonconforming, and nonbinary-gender bodies if they were to seek abortion procedures. Within S.B. 8, the context targets both cis and noncis bodies. It doesn't differentiate between technology that provides ultrasound detection of a heartbeat and technology that provides chromosomal designation of a gestating person or between nature as encoded by chromosomal information and as capacity of a gestating person to house a second heartbeat. It does not follow that S.B. 8 only targets "female" bodies since the context, according to glaring evidence, implicates the use of technology, medical criterion that reads technology as nature's truth, and both legislative and medical practice that regards physiological differentiation as matters of state's prerogative and not of personal autonomy.

Undifferentiation between technology and nature within S.B. 8 may lead us to infer that certain intersex individuals count as gestating persons.[23] Available genetic technology tells us that some intersex people can potentially get pregnant. Thus, if the bill doesn't differentiate between technology and nature's truth when it comes to the fetus's heartbeat, it follows that it must agree with the genetic truth when it comes to intersex bodies' capacity for pregnancy.[24] As it concerns gestating person and fetus, it's the presence of the fetus's heartbeat that defines the existence of a gestating person in the letter of the bill. It doesn't matter what the exact chromosomal variant of the pregnant carrier is; what matters is whether that body could grow and house a second heartbeat within it. Thus, the bill includes intersex bodies among those that could potentially carry a second heartbeat within them.[25] S.B. 8 advocates would be hard-pressed to explain why intersex individuals pose an exemption to the bill unless they sought to clarify the social role that technology plays in the demarcation of pregnancy as a condition that pertains only to a "woman [who] is carrying the developing human offspring."[26] Moreover, due to its archaic understanding of gender, S.B. 8 conflates intersex, nonbinary, and even trans bodies into the legal and medical category "woman."

In conclusion, context A consists of medicolegal enablements and constraints, as well as heterocissexist oppression, that seek yet fail to stabilize first-order ascription. Our analysis reveals that reconceiving sex—only females possess the objective infrastructure to get pregnant—is always already materially transformed by second-order ascription—only women menstruate, house a second heartbeat within them, and are responsible for carrying to term a developing human offspring. Second-order ascription bears on the stabilizing looping to the extent that a realist feminist metaphysics reveals the sociosomatic entangling at work under sex/gender distinctions. If, according to Haslanger, a woman is a person said to have, within a stabilizing context, "the bodily features presumed to be evidence of a female's biological role in reproduction," S.B. 8 shows that bodily features that provide evidence of such a role in reproduction undergo a thoroughly social, yet not merely social, constitution process.[27] Bodily features are much more socially produced than originally imagined by Haslanger's metaphysics.[28] S.B. 8 helps shape an entangling of technology, chromosomal information, reproductive tissue behavior, expert knowledge, legal definition, and decision-making as they codetermine bodily features.

My contention about Haslanger's objectivism is twofold. Discrepancy between contexts A and B tells us something about first-order and second-order ascriptions and the ways that second-order ascription, fully contextual for Haslanger, bears on first-order ascription, thoroughly ontological in her proposal. Attending to the significance of language use for metaphysics, and following second-order ascription, I don't deny the importance of exposing the myriad ways in which antirights state laws target cisgender women and, specifically, pregnant cisgender women. I seek, however, to underscore that second-order ascription—the fact that we typically read abortion-restricting laws as concerned mainly with (cisgender) women—may narrow the terms in which metaphysics makes sense of first-order ascription. This complicated looping between first-order and second-order ascriptions allows us to state that embodiments may in fact present and be perceived as, or be legislated into or out of, playing the female role in biological reproduction. As a sociosomatic entanglement, this role provides evidence of the thoroughly yet not only social mattering of gendered and sexed distinctions. By now, it should be clear that I seek a realist materialism that is less hung up on sorting what infrastructure is truly causally significant in the demarcation of sex/gender and more engaged with the ways that sociosomatic entangling bears on what makes certain infrastructures, and what disqualifies others from being, causally significant.

I mentioned that my contention about Haslanger's objectivism is twofold. The second contention that I have in mind is the discrepancy between contexts A and B. This discrepancy tells us something about the explanatory accuracy of the notion of "system of oppression." If systems of oppression operate as thoroughly social yet matter-altering relations, it follows that our account of them should give uptake to sociosomatic complexity. If we understood systems of power as assemblages, or as intermeshing, interlocking, fusing, compounding, entangling entanglements, or as codetermining, implicating both discursive and extradiscursive domains, contending with variability, indeterminacy, and position-relative agencies both biophilic and not, the metaphysical valence of systems of oppression would greatly vary. It would allow us to comprehend the mutual implication of an adulterated biomaterial world and an impure biosocial domain. Thus, the discrepancies between Texas and New York with respect to abortion law would lead us to navigate the ongoing loop between first-order and second-order ascriptions and, simultaneously, to hold on to the conflicting, multiple mattering of sociosomatics.

Multiple Meaning Realism

The multiple meaning position of sex/gender that philosopher Talia Mae Bettcher proposes offers a realist account of the meaning of *woman*.[29] Her metaphysics retains the realism of facts that obtain within specific contexts. At the same time, building on ontological pluralism, Bettcher pushes beyond contextualism. As I mentioned in the prior section, oppressing←→being oppressed←→resisting shape subjectivities and intentions in contradictory ways. While some contexts may temporarily halt or boost dominant or resistant logics, they do not necessarily offer counterstructures or anti-structures.[30] There are contexts that, in fact, shift specific normative ascriptions. For example, a gender studies classroom where all participants respect each other's "preferred" gender pronouns challenges second-order ascriptions. However, this classroom context rarely transforms social structures that inform multi- or supracontextual ascription.[31] In that sense, contexts may allow contradictory enablements and restrictions. Such is the case of Texas's S.B. 8 and its unexpected sex/gender inclusivity.

The multiple meaning position brings together two critical feminist insights: first, members of marginalized communities face conditions that are likely to enhance our perception of reality, including the fact that we experience oppressing←→being oppressed←→resistant realities, and second, resistant realities alter and broaden the meanings, including distinction and differences, that mainstream realities uphold. For Bettcher, *woman* is not a term whose meaning depends on mainstream assumptions about sex/ gender distinctions and differences. It is a term whose meaning is multiple, but not necessarily as a matter of political or moral facts. Such would be the case of the gender studies classroom in which participants agree to make a moral or political statement by choosing to use and respect "preferred" gender pronouns. This is happening on college campuses regardless of whether students weigh sex/gender distinctions in their assessment of what it means to respect "preferred" gender pronouns.[32] Rather, in Bettcher's proposal, *woman* obtains its meaning through and across practices in accordance with the ways that nonmainstream, marginal, and resistant cultures and groups deploy the distinction/difference *woman*. The notion of stabilization that I previously explained can help us further Bettcher's argument.

I assume that I have effectively expanded the notion of stabilization in Haslanger's model. Bettcher's insights help us understand that stabilization operates in counterhegemonic, antistructure, and oppositional realities. Engaging with and committed to trans subcultures, Bettcher focuses on antistructural arrangements that obtain within and across both dominant and nondominant contexts. In the context of trans subcultures, specifically in Los Angeles, Bettcher pays attention precisely to what I call "sociosomatic looping." She provides glaring evidence of trans woman as a paradigm and not a borderline case of the sex/gender distinction *woman*. In such an ontological web, subcultural entangling entanglements permeate, rearrange, and infuse sex/gender distinctions. This oppositional, antistructure web displaces origin stories that typically stabilize cis as core and trans as peripheral.

Bettcher rejects the conflation of the multiple meaning position with perspectivism and semantic contextualism. To put it bluntly, a trans woman, within Haslanger's model, lies in the outskirts of the reconceiving of sex/gender as dimorphic within what Lugones understands to be the light side of the colonial/modern gender system.[33] Cissexism and heterosexualism, and their role in biological reproduction, stabilize "woman" within some or various contexts because colonial/modern structures inform the looping between second- and first-order ascriptions. Thus, within this colonial/modern stabilizing web, a trans woman could only marginally count as a person whose bodily features are presumed to be evidence of a female's biological role in reproduction. Proponents of semantic contextualism would be content with this view since it makes room for trans subcultures to emerge as parallel, yet marginal, contexts. The semantic contextualist also aligns with the idea that multiple meanings respond to political and moral facts and not necessarily to multiple realities or ontological facts. There is yet another limiting aspect to semantic contextualism. A relativist could reasonably claim that, as a matter of moral facts, there are contexts within which trans women are either delusional or deceitful.[34] Moreover, as Haslanger's view infers, a trans woman is semantically within her right to launch a moral fact claim about the reality of her embodiment but plain wrong if she seeks to launch an ontological claim about it. Ontologically speaking, trans women are not women but "evil deceivers."[35] Unlike perspectivism, or semantic contextualism, I read Bettcher as positing that oppression brings about ontological distinctions and differentiations and that, in response to or despite them, antistructural trans subcultures participate in informing realities where harm subsides or ceases to inflict pain.

Realness, Black and Brown Ontologies

Black and Brown urban communities fashion gender-nonconforming realities. They engage embodiment through realness. For Black and Brown trans women who face racist policing and misogynistic violence, among other harms, realness is a matter of both critiquing violent structures and affirming self and collective care.[36] The FX show *Pose* (2018–21) put this practice on blast for the twentieth-first century. *Pose* takes audiences back to the voguing and ballroom cultures within the Black, AfroLatinx, and Latinx underground of New York City's 1980s. This show examines responses to a society of full-blown hostility toward racialized trans, queer, nonbinary, and gender-nonconforming lives and embodiments.

Ballroom culture consists of bodily practices as they enact attributes that dominant culture denies to queer, trans, and nonbinary people of color. Performers at a ball compete in different categories that seek to measure "realness." According to

Marlon M. Bailey, being "a Ballroom-created standard," realness operates as criterion gauging the level of "adherence to certain performances, self-presentations, and embodiments that are believed to capture the authenticity of particular gender and sexual identities."[37] It is of importance to note that Bailey acknowledges the insiders' perspective over the ballroom culture, where femme queens and butch queens differentiate between drag and ball performance. While both may coexist within ballroom venues, femme queens fashion their self-presentation by living as women. Butch queens instead typically identify as gay men who perform in drag at the balls. When they participate in realness categories, they both seek to create the appearance of gender and sexual normativity, blending thereby into broader societal norms, including those that underwrite homophobic and transphobic violence. Femme and butch queens are deeply aware of what Bettcher describes as the rejection of dominant realities' divide between noncis and cis women. This division is oppressive and painful, and they experience it as such. In the context of ballroom, the term *woman* obtains within a set of practices that alter not just the perception of sex/gender, second-order ascription, but the very ontology of embodiment. Furthermore, queens also criticize the mainstream's tendency to conflate ballroom culture, where realness is emphasized to deflect discrimination and violence, with drag and costume balls. For them, as for Bettcher, reality presents at least as double if not multiple, a world where resistance meets domination, where realness contends with spectacle, and where subversion imports possibilities often erased by the hegemon.

Bailey expands on the realities that ballroom performers navigate as they home in on their competence to present realness. Indeed, they develop a "visual epistemology" based on the codes that society at large deploys.[38] They usurp the stabilizing looping through which *woman* obtains. In *Pose*'s first episode, Elektra, the mother of the House of Abundance, takes her children to the Museum of Fashion and Design. Modeled after the Museum at FIT (Fashion Institute of Technology), the House of Abundance hides in storage rooms and under display platforms until closing hours. The coveted prizes are the garments of an exhibit about royals. In ballroom culture, a house is a family-like structure whose members foster a sense of kinship born out of a shared experience of racial, class, and gender exclusion. The museum's exhibit puts on display the regime of visuality that governs monarchy, the epitome of aesthetic and material hierarchies. In a piercing scene, the queens first encounter a section of the exhibit with the busts of members of ancient Egyptian dynasties. Elektra, Blanca, and Angel stand before three different statues cast in clay and stone. They stare at the busts with an almost surprising look of recognition, as if they finally had confirmation of the existence of a royal lineage of Blackness. The House of Abundance sneaks out of the museum carrying a selection of royal wardrobe, which they will be donning hours later as they walk the "royalty" category. Pressed to exit as the alarm soars in the background, they shatter one of the glass windows of the building's facade. This exit strategy could also be read as the intentional act with which they condemn the orientation of the societal gaze. They are sick and tired of being placed on an exoticizing pedestal. They no longer consent to the visual regime of the museum. They reject it by affirming an otherwise reality.

Museums manifest the perverse fascination of white subjectivity with its appropriation of what it often fears but whose appeal it cannot refuse.[39] Shattering the glass through which the public consumes Black, AfroLatinx, and Latinx cultural production seeks to subvert the visual regime of normalized and passing gender expressions. When they realize that they are "locked in," Elektra states, "I look too good not to be seen." Hers is a reference to the puncturing force of resistant realities. Stabilization according to Haslanger's model doesn't account for realness and its royal stance. It leaves intact typical boundaries that shelter the seer and its arrogation of dominant views. It does so to the extent that the seer masks ontological anxieties under the crude divide between ontological, first-order ascription, and epistemic, second-order ascription. Multiple meaning realism defies the idea that first-order ascription locks in ontology. In the transition scene from the museum to the ballroom contexts, police officers chase down the queens across the city. Cops ride in their patrol car, following the masterful grid that surveillance affords them. Sirens wail as the queens strut concealed alleys on the way to the ball. An officer tells another over the radio, "Spotted them. Got a pretty good idea where they're headed." To spot them, lock them in, may align with the single-sided, carceral reality that Haslanger supports.[40]

Ballrooms, More Than Contexts

Bettcher's focus on subcultures of trans activism reminds us that excluded social groups do not always assume that the terms by which we live obtain within dominant views. Moreover, I have thus far claimed that systems of oppression and contexts are not one and the same, that systems of oppression may create various (in/compatible) contexts, and that contexts may halt or boost oppressive configurations. As it concerns sex/gender distinctions and differences, I posit that coloniality/modernity reconceives sex/gender as dimorphic, that there are contexts in which dimorphism wanes down, and that certain contexts may halt or boost heterocissexist dimorphism. I also claim that expanding the notion of stabilization allows us to pick up on more than contexts in which dominant views are bent. Indeed, multiple meaning realism builds on ontological pluralism as a philosophical interrogation of antistructures.

In what remains of this essay, I attempt to shift from a dominant and oppressive structure framework to another with multiple structures, including resistant, oppositional, and antistructures. Instead of foregrounding contexts in which dominant sex/gender distinctions wane down, I turn to contexts that on the surface align with dominant oppressive systems. However, by showing that oppositional structures underwrite such contexts, I arrive at an account of stabilizing looping wherein sex/gender distinctions refute and reject dominant realities.

According to queer of color geographers, ballroom culture offers countergeographies.[41] Its radical potential does not lie with claiming places for marginalized others. Rather, it affirms itself among lifeworlds without which kinship—proximity, intimacy, well-being—dries out for lack of conviviality. Ballroom culture remits back to other slices of space-time. It expands an archive of conviviality against the grain of dispossession. Novelist, playwright, and poet Langston Hughes examines this repository among the attendants at the Hamilton Club Lodge Ball of the New Negro era. The "strangest and gaudiest of all Harlem spectacles in the '20s," he describes.[42] Disorienting as it may be for a figure who has been reclaimed as a Black queer ancestor, Hughes adds layers of unbecoming contempt toward the ballroom's attendants.[43] He pays incisive attention to "the queerly assorted throng on the dancing floor, males in flowing gowns and feathered headdresses and females in tuxedoes and box-back suits."[44] Hughes is concerned with details—accoutrements, self-presentation, and style, among others—that thwart a positive queer reading. On the surface, he comes across as bothered by these attendants' lack of game. Almost in a satirical fashion, Hughes concedes that the many "social leaders of both Harlem and the downtown area" found the queer throng alluring because great distance separates the upper box and the ballroom floor.[45]

Hughes doubles up, "most of them [the throng of queens] look as if they need a shave, and some of their evening gowns, cut too low, show hair on the chest."[46] His slaying commentary casts him in an unforgiving light, his tone perhaps too critical and far from any contemporary redemption in the age of gender inclusivity. He ups the ante when he claims how pathetic he finds the presence "of many former 'queens' of the ball [who] . . . still wearing the costumes that won for them a fleeting fame in years gone by, stand on the sidelines now in their same old clothes—wide picture hats with plumes, and out-of-style dresses with sweeping velvet trains."[47] Whoever was at the receiving end of Hughes's words had to have felt a piercing wound. Sam See argues that Hughes considers drag culture's visual practices and affective products as Harlem's "most representative metonym."[48] Hughes relies on drag not as a universalizing grammar but rather as generic performativity whose appeal to emotion often undermines racial and sexual boundaries. That Hughes takes issue with performances that have lost their luster is another way of affirming this generic appeal to emotion and affect, compelling performers to confront contradictions between word and reality. Drag that doesn't deepen tensions across realness and reality falls prey to the visual regime of exoticizing and carceral ontologies.

If we relied on the notion that reality is single-sided and yet consisting of various contexts, we would understand the reality that Hughes describes as anti-Black and antiqueer, the context of the ballroom as restricting since the queer game of the attendants doesn't amount to realness. Conversely, if we followed multiple meaning realism and found that Hughes inhabits a Black and queer affirmation by undermining its positive slant, then the contexts would give way to enhancing antistructures. Among them, we find Hughes's throwing shade at his queer, gender-nonconforming contemporaries.[49] His slaying tongue pivots on the resistant realities of queer Harlem, those that occupy usual taxonomies of race, class, and gender to undermine them from within.

In his assessment of a voguing archive, however anachronistic this may sound, Hughes expects as a matter of fact a supreme dare of balance, choreography, and flexibility. He gets it. He trusts the pedagogy of Black kinship and its intergenerational practical wisdom on affect and style. Kinship is learned through the pedagogy of both home and ballroom (such as the House of Abundance's). Members yearn to ace the categories they walk. If you don't show initiative, your house members will get testy with you. You are not born cuntie, you strut your way into becoming it. Finessing the art of voguing entails sharpening one's tongue, for without it you lack fluency in the affective appeal of Black and Brown nonconforming and disidentifying ontologies. Ultimately, Hughes seems to have embraced the shadiest grammar of the 1920s Harlem balls, an antistructure sociosomatic entangling, an otherwise stabilization of an anticarceral throng.

Notes

1. Linda Martín Alcoff, *Visible Identities: Race, Gender, and the Self* (New York: Oxford University Press, 2005); Elizabeth Grosz, *Volatile Bodies: Toward a Corporeal Feminism* (Bloomington: Indiana University Press, 1994). María Lugones sees the enmeshment of sex/gender as one with the logic of coloniality. Thus, I refer to "sex" as "sexed distinctions." Gender, in her view, entails reconceiving sex as binary and absolute. She doesn't mean that decolonization would disentangle sex/gender. Rather, it would unravel those operations that gender certain populations at the expense of sexualizing nonwhite individuals and communities.
2. On ontological pluralism, see María Lugones, "Playfulness, 'World'-

Traveling, and Loving Perception" (1987), in *Pilgrimages/Peregrinajes: Theorizing Coalition against Multiple Oppressions* (Lanham, Md.: Rowman & Littlefield Publishers, 2003), 77–100; Kris F. Sealey, *Creolizing the Nation* (Evanston, Ill.: Northwestern University Press, 2020); PJ DiPietro, Jennifer McWeeny, and Shireen Roshanravan, *Speaking Face to Face: The Visionary Philosophy of María Lugones* (Albany: State University of New York Press, 2019); Sarah Hoagland, "Walking Together Illegitimately," *off our backs: the feminist newsjournal* 34, no. 7–8 (July–August 2004): 38–47; Liza Taylor, "Coalition from the Inside Out: Struggling toward Coalitional Identity and Developing a Coalitional Consciousness with Lorde, Anzaldúa, Sandoval, and Pratt," in *Feminism in Coalition: Thinking with U.S. Women of Color Feminism* (Durham, N.C.: Duke University Press, 2022), 106–49; Robin Dembroff, "Real Talk on the Metaphysics of Gender," *Philosophical Topics* 46, no. 2 (2018): 21–50.

3. Sally Haslanger, "What Good Are Our Intuitions: Philosophical Analysis and Social Kinds," *Proceedings of the Aristotelian Society Supplementary* 80 (2006): 89–118; Sally Haslanger, *Resisting Reality: Social Construction and Social Critique* (New York: Oxford University Press, 2012).
4. Charlotte Witt, *The Metaphysics of Gender* (New York: Oxford University Press, 2011); Ásta, *Categories We Live By: The Construction of Sex, Gender, Race, and Other Social Categories* (New York: Oxford University Press, 2018).
5. See also Alcoff, *Visible Identities*; Grosz, *Volatile Bodies*; Monique Wittig, *The Straight Mind and Other Essays* (Boston: Beacon Press, 1992).
6. Haslanger, "What Good Are Our Intuitions," 122.
7. Haslanger, *Resisting Reality*, 234.
8. Haslanger, 235.
9. As I will show shortly, chromosomal distinction is always already sociosomatic.
10. Feminisms are committed to the business of examining whose expectations these are.
11. Haslanger, *Resisting Reality*, 230.
12. Anja Heisler Weiser Flower, "Cosmos against Nature in the Class Struggle of Proletarian Trans Women," in *Transgender Marxism*, ed. Jules Joanne Gleeson and Elle O'Rourke (London: Pluto Press, 2021), 241.
13. Wittig, "The Straight Mind" in *The Straight Mind and Other Essays*, 27–28.
14. I understand that Haslanger refers to distinctions between egg-bearing and sperm-bearing human animals. Typically, human animals present with XX and XY chromosomes. The gender function of such a distinction may align with contexts that either stabilize or disrupt that function. The objective reality of XX does not change, as she would have it, but its function does due to the interaction of

systemic oppression and context. First-order ascription occurs at the level of distinction, while second-order ascription occurs at the level of difference.

15. In his study of the galenic unisex body, Thomas Laqueur argues that sex remained an epiphenomenon of gender hierarchies for Western societies until at least the seventeenth century. See Thomas Laqueur, *Making Sex: Body and Gender from the Greeks to Freud* (Cambridge, Mass.: Harvard University Press, 1992).

16. María Lugones, "Gender and Universality in Colonial Methodology," *Critical Philosophy of Race* 8, no. 1–2 (2020): 25–47.

17. Ethnohistories document multiple gender systems. Lugones works with a schematic approach through which she examines the introduction of racial classification, in the long sixteenth century, to extract human differences and distinctions out of colonized bodies. Gender dimorphism and sexualization have an axial role in coloniality's extractive mode.

18. María Lugones, "Heterosexualism and the Colonial/Modern Gender System," *Hypatia* 22, no. 1 (2007): 203.

19. See An Act Relating to Abortion, Including Abortions after Detection of an Unborn Child's Heartbeat; Authorizing a Private Civil Right of Action, Tex. S.B. 8, 87th Leg. (2021–2022), available at https://capitol.texas.gov/tlodocs/87R/billtext/pdf/SB00008F.pdf.

20. Act Relating to Abortion, 2.

21. It is not far-fetched to anticipate a near future when reproductive and cloning technologies will at least partially replace the gestational sac. Whose last menstruation would S.B. 8 refer to? Zygotes are in fact placed in the gestational sac of people who do not provide eggs for in-vitro fertilization. How to determine, in such cases, the carrier's last menstruation with respect to S.B. 8's construction of pregnancy?

22. New York Reproductive Health Act, S.B. S240, available at https://legislation.nysenate.gov/pdf/bills/2019/S240.

23. I am aware that the category "intersex" is often imposed upon people who do not identify as such.

24. See, for example, Brett A. H. Schultz, Soldrea Roberts, Allison Rodgers, and Khalid Ataya, "Pregnancy in True Hermaphrodites and All Male Offspring to Date," *Obstetrics & Gynecology* 113, no. 2, pt. 2 (2009): 534–36.

25. It matters that I show the way that second-order ascription (normative coherence) bears on first-order ascription (normative assignation or assessment). Ultimately, I am aware the political salience of these bills is that they typically (though not always) target self-identified cisgender women more than anybody else. I mean to show that even an incendiary bill such as S.B. 8 can mobilize metaphysical ascriptions that other social groups, or actors, would effectively and effervescently mobilize with feminist ends. I thank Rowan Bell for their invitation to engage metaphysical reflection on gender.

26. Act Relating to Abortion, 2.
27. Haslanger, *Resisting Reality,* 235.
28. I appreciate and retain the realist vein of Haslanger's approach. I don't mean to flatten the political valence of the subject "woman" as intrinsic to sexual and reproductive rights struggles. However, I do mean to point out that "woman" is a narrow category for antiracist, intersectional, and transnational feminist struggles, including sexual and reproductive rights struggles. I am not jumping from an ontological to a political analysis. I am claiming that they inform and implicate each other.
29. Talia Mae Bettcher, "Trans Women and the Meaning of 'Woman,'" in *The Philosophy of Sex: Contemporary Readings,* ed. Nicholas Power, Raja Halwani, and Alan Soble (Lanham, Md.: Rowman & Littlefield, 2012), 233–50.
30. See María Lugones, "Structure/Anti-structure and Agency under Oppression," in *Pilgrimages/Peregrinajes,* 53–63.
31. In such an example, the supracontextual or multicontextual ascription refers to the higher ed institution's data systems, which feed the gender designation given at birth into all contact points between students and institution (ID card, library card, library account, dining account, and registrar's office, among so many others).
32. Rarely do faculty initiate their semester by asking students to share, if they so desire, their gender pronouns. Instead, electronic self-identification is becoming increasingly common. Data systems that allow students to choose their gender pronouns have profound effects on self-care and self-esteem. Yet, electronic self-identification results in fewer opportunities to have significant conversations about institutional cultures and heterocissexism. It doesn't lead those who occupy cisgender positions to question their implication in heterocissexism. See Jae M. Sevelius, Deepalika Chakravarty, Samantha E. Dilworth, Greg Rebchook, and Torsten B. Neilands, "Gender Affirmation through Correct Pronoun Usage: Development and Validation of the Transgender Women's Importance of Pronouns (TW-IP) Scale," *International Journal of Environmental Research and Public Health* 17, no. 24 (2020): 9, 525.
33. Lugones, "Heterosexualism and the Colonial/Modern Gender System."
34. On October 31, 2022, Justice Clarence Thomas made the following statement during opening arguments about two major affirmative action cases before the United States Supreme Court: "I've heard the word diversity quite a few times and I don't have a clue what it means. It seems to mean everything for everyone." A relativist would be content with Clarence's reasonable line of questioning. Relativism leaves us hanging without an antidote against spurious denial of sociosomatic demarcations. Thomas's alleged ignorance denies the ontological valence of both sex/gender and race within ruling deviation theories and practices. Jelani Cobb, "The End of Affirmative Action,"

New Yorker, June 29, 2023, https://www.newyorker.com/magazine/2023/07/10/the-end-of-affirmative-action.

35. Talia Mae Bettcher, "Evil Deceivers and Make-Believers: On Transphobic Violence and the Politics of Illusion," *Hypatia* 22, no. 3 (2007): 43–65.

36. Gregory Samantha Rosenthal and Iris Gottlieb, "How to Become a Woman," *Southern Cultures* 26, no. 3 (Fall 2020): 122–37.

37. Marlon M. Bailey, *Butch Queens Up in Pumps: Gender, Performance, and Ballroom Culture in Detroit* (Ann Arbor: University of Michigan Press, 2013), 55.

38. Bailey, *Butch Queens Up in Pumps,* 65.

39. Laura Pérez, *Eros Ideologies: Writings on Art, Spirituality, and the Decolonial* (Durham, N.C.: Duke University Press, 2019).

40. I thank Perry Zurn for suggesting that my rendering of Haslanger's approach unveils its carceral logic.

41. Marlon M. Bailey and Rashad Shabazz, "Editorial: Gender and Sexual Geographies of Blackness: Anti-black Heterotopias (Part 1)," *Gender, Place and Culture* 21, no. 3 (2014): 316–21.

42. Langston Hughes, *The Collected Works of Langston Hughes,* vol. 13, *Autobiography: "The Big Sea,"* ed. Joseph McLaren (Columbia: University of Missouri Press, 2002), 208.

43. Dorothea Löbberman, "Richard Bruce Nugent and the Queer Memory of Harlem," in *Race Capital? Harlem as Setting and Symbol,* eds. Andrew M. Fearnley and Daniel Matlin (New York: Columbia University Press, 2019), 221–40.

44. Hughes, *Collected Works of Langston Hughes,* 208.

45. Hughes, 208. See also George Chauncey on heterosexist passing conventions that differentiate between middle-class and working-class men at the Hamilton Lodge in *Gay New York: Gender, Urban Culture, and the Making of the Gay Male World, 1890–1940* (New York: Basic Books, 1994), 266.

46. Hughes, Hubbard, and Sanders, *Collected Works of Langston Hughes,* 208.

47. Hughes, Hubbard, and Sanders, 209.

48. Sam See, "'Spectacles in Color': The Primitive Drag of Langston Hughes," *PMLA* 124, no. 3 (2009): 799.

49. *Throwing shade* is a vernacular through which ballroom scene members demonstrate "authority and superiority by teasing another queen about some aspect of her appearance or behavior." Lisa Weems, "The Quare Agenda of 'RuPaul's Drag U,'" *Counterpoints* 437 (2014): 94.

The Art(s) of Ecstasy
Black Trans Art in the Afterlife of Slavery
Che Gossett

> The afterlife of slavery is not only a political and social
> problem but an aesthetic one as well.
>
> —*Saidiya Hartman, "Saidiya Hartman*
> *on Working with Archives"*

If the afterlife of slavery, as Saidiya Hartman argues, is an aesthetic problem, what, then, is the relationship between abolition
and aesthetics? How might the analytics of blackness, feminist
theory, and trans studies, in their coimplicacy (in the sense of
being folded together) and entanglement, prompt a rethinking of
aesthetics—both its limits and possibilities? Abolitionist iconography shows the tensions and incommensurability between white
abolitionist designs for Black emancipation and Black political and
aesthetic imaginings of freedom. My critical ambition is to intervene in art-historical, museological, and visual studies discourses
and bring to bear methodologies of queer theory, gender studies,
African American studies, and art history to conjugate abolition
and aesthetics in contemporary Black art. My work traces how
abolition—not (only) as a juridical and legal event but as an incomplete grammar of futurity—is activated in contemporary Black art.
My work is in concert and conversation with scholars working at
the nexus of African American, visual, and media studies, scholars such as Nicole R. Fleetwood, Kara Keeling, David Marriott,
Rizvana Bradley, Kobena Mercer, and Tina M. Campt.[1] Frank B.
Wilderson III's interrogation of the capacity for any art form, but

especially cinema and film, to serve as a visual grammar of Black suffering (and, for that matter, Black reverie and joy), is also an open question that contours my work.[2] Wilderson's question is indebted to and following the groundbreaking path forged by Saidiya Hartman's work wherein she enunciates slavery's afterlife—the entanglement of slavery and putative freedom—as not only a social and political but an aesthetic problematic as well.[3] I focus on the visual as a register for blackness. Against "carceral aesthetics" as a disciplinary regime—which is one way to read the polysemic and capacious concept offered by Nicole R. Fleetwood—Black aesthetics have always sought to interrogate the visual as a grammar of capture and to create fugitive forms of aesthetic practice and art.[4] Hortense J. Spillers's concept of the "grammars of capture" argue that these are the political, aesthetic, social, and ontological vernaculars and regimes through which the afterlife of slavery and its entanglement(s) are reproduced and maintained.[5]

As a concept, abolition grows out of the Black radical tradition, which remade the grammar and praxis of abolition, stealing it away from its white abolitionist historicity and activating it anew. Blackness aims to abolish the constraints of putative freedom as well as slavery, which are entangled in an ontological deadlock. I posit abolition, then, as an open invitation into a radicalizing fold dedicated to ending the grammars of capture, which necessarily entails ending antiblackness and settler colonialism and capitalism. The contemporary political grammar of abolition has been reenergized by antiprison organizing, in particular the work of the academic and activist collective Critical Resistance and its founding members, the work of Mariame Kaba, and scholars in American, African American, and critical ethnic studies and gender and sexuality who focus on resistance to the expanding carceral state. The version of abolition offered by prison abolitionists locates the temporal coordinates of abolition in the present—as critically urgent and unfinished—as opposed to abolition as an already actualized event within the temporal register of racial liberalism. This very register entraps abolition in the temporality of the event itself. I argue that abolition can never be merely an event, it can only be a perennial and durational struggle the morphology of which changes the stakes and throws into question the very anchors of the social, the political, and the ontology of the subject. Abolition undermines what I term the "carceral metaphysics" of the subject, its claims to sovereign bodily self-possession and the notion of the body as property—not as a commodity. In this sense, abolition is an anti- and ante-normative ethical project as well as a philosophical project. Black freedom requires the abolition of the racial liberal figuration of freedom, freedom from freedom itself. The duration of the horizon of abolition is best described by Angela Y. Davis's statement that "freedom is a constant struggle."[6]

How to think the inseparability of blackness and abolition? Or, what if abolition is another name for blackness's radicality? On the one hand, blackness ruptures the historicity of abolition, activating its perennial potential and endless pursuit. On the other hand, blackness, as an insurgent force that both evades and challenges grammars of capture, is inherently abolitionist. The formalization of abolition (as historical waves), the periodization of abolition, and its reduction to an activist enterprise against the prison as the sole form of capture hazard a theoretical liability. This theoretical liability is the downplaying of antiblackness and the evacuation of Black radicality from and as abolitionist animacy. Following Saidiya Hartman's incisive observation that the afterlife of slavery is an aesthetic as well as a social problem, my work theorizes abolitionist aesthetics and blackness as an aesthetics of existence as a response to the ongoing crisis of the afterlife of slavery.[7] Blackness and the aesthetic figure as antagonistic, aporetic, and incommensurable. Further, as Marcus Wood demonstrates in *Blind Memory: Visual Representations of Slavery in England and America, 1780–1865,* the art historiography and iconography of the aesthetic is anti-black in that white abolitionists created abolitionist paraphernalia that reinforced the figuration of the enslaved as abject objects, raw material, in need of white redemption, and produced a whole visual arsenal of paraphernalia to this effect— from the emblematizing of Josiah Wedgwood's "Am I Not a Man and a Brother?," which was worn as fashion, from broaches to snuff boxes—that discloses how abolition was part of the visual and material culture of commodification under the aesthetic regime not just of racial slavery but of the anti-black aesthetic regime of emancipation as well. Blackness figures not only, as Wood (following Henry Louis Gates Jr.) argues, as an absent presence shaping, or as the empty signifier of, abolitionist aesthetics but rather as the hydraulic fueling the political and libidinal economy of what Anna Arabindan-Kesson terms "market aesthetics."[8] What, then, is salvageable or recuperable about the category of the aesthetic? Against the fungibility that underwrites the regimes of emancipation and slavery, abolitionist aesthetics, blackness's aesthetic radicality, refuses the double bind of the liberal humanist coordinates of the aesthetics of emancipation, as well as those of slavery. Abolition, then, is irreducible to the liberal-capitalist or jurisprudential temporalization of emancipation and, rather, is always emergent, capacious, and perennial. Freedom is never possessed, only constantly distributed. Freedom is a doing, not a property. The notion of abolition as a horizon is both temporal and spatial. Abolitionist temporality rejects the antiblackness of putatively postracial time and its attendant progress narratives. Fred Moten asks, "What is it to be an irreducibly disordering and deformational force while at the same time being absolutely indispensable to normative order, normative form?"[9] Here, Moten zeroes in on blackness's ontological double bind, which also characterizes its positionality in relation to the aesthetic, the social, and the political. While blackness, to use Nahum Dimitri Chandler's grammar, is "exorbitant" to the governing norms of the aesthetic even as it underpins it as a racial regime, Black art confronts the history of constitutive exclusion.[10] What will it take to radically upend a world that is rooted in an aesthetic-political and psychic life of antiblackness?

How do Black trans artists offer cinematic and abolitionist resistance to the anti-black violence of the afterlife of slavery and its corollary of Black trans archival effacement? Artist Tourmaline intervenes in the political genealogy of abolitionist aesthetics, moving with and through what Saidiya Hartman terms "critical fabulation" and exceeding the historicism of the archive itself.[11] The archive encases slavery in the past, whether museological, as in the exhibition and display of the relics of slavery figured as past, or through state or university institutionalization via historicization and documentation. Slavery as an ontological condition means that the status of the archive as a historical object is troubled and its logics of telos undermined. Dislocated from the archive as a purely historical grammar of capture, Tourmaline shows, in her historically informed and archivally informed cinematic and artistic work, how an engagement with the ecstatic temporality of blackness exceeds the register of the historical and moves in transit and interplay with the present and the future to come (in the sense of both unprovoked contingencies and freedom desires).[12]

Black trans historical figures are fugitive to the terms of the official archive, except in moments of criminalization wherein they appear through the register of the police record or court transcript—as in the 1836 case wherein Mary Jones enters the realm of archival legibility and visibility within the historical record. I first encountered the Mary Jones case in performance and Black studies scholar Tavia Nyong'o's *The Amalgamation Waltz,* and I rushed to order the court transcript.[13]

In his canonical essay on media aesthetics and technology "The Work of Art in the Age of Mechanical Reproduction," Walter Benjamin argues that the invention of lithography equates to an epistemic break for technologies of reproduction.[14] Benjamin traces the larger shift of the technologies of production and reproduction of art—from prehistoric ritual and cult formations to the advent of the lithograph, photograph, and film—and the ways in which artworks become detached from their religious milieu and inherit new meaning. Benjamin amends the history of technology by demonstrating that, prior to the invention of writing machines, graphic art was mechanized. For Benjamin, the lithograph is the transitory node between artistic craft, with its attendant closed circuit of reproduction that hinges on the figure of the individual artist hand-making the replica, and the larger technological infrastructure of the aesthetic form (drawing and illustration and movement) of photography and cinematography. It is via the lithograph as well as the court transcript that Mary Jones enters into the historical record.

Mary Jones, a Black trans woman, must have been full of what Ralph Lemon calls "shaky elegance" when she stood before the court room and was asked to justify her existence and her aesthetic and Black trans fugitive sociality before the judge and angry audience.[15] From the court transcript: "What induced you to dress yourself in women's clothes?"[16] A juridical interrogation of the legitimacy of Black trans aesthetics as against the sovereign law of white patriarchy. This juridical interrogation was redoubled by the parajudicial interrogation, the courtroom as a political and aesthetic theater, a scene of subjection, wherein Jones not only was forced to answer the judge's questions but also was subjected to the violent pathos of the white cis audience, who attempted to tear her clothing off. What is being interrogated is also what is being policed. Here the proper aesthetic subject is a properly gendered subject—which can only be a white subject—possessor of gender rather than dispossessed by gender. Aesthetically fugitive, on the run from gender's jurisdiction, Jones's Black transness figures her as outlaw. Jones's response: "I have always dressed this way amongst people of my own colour."[17] Always as "temporal drag."[18] Jones—criminalized as a Black trans sex worker—at once violates the terms of the gender binary, of sexual normativity, and of white heteropatriarchy and is punished and sentenced to Sing Sing penitentiary. Jones's aesthetic fugitivity is reimagined through Tourmaline's work.

> My work is about time travel. I'm trying to tune in to the dreams of freedom of those who came before and feel how they're still shaping this moment, and also into future versions of myself ushering in what's possible. Because of that, I think of legacy in a nonlinear way, like time folding in on itself.[19]

Tourmaline's film *Salacia* (2019) is a cinematic meditation on and critical fabulation of Mary Jones's biography.[20] Mary Jones is played by Rowin Amone, and the cast of the film is replete with Black trans actors; in this way, Tourmaline not only challenges the historical erasure of Black trans life but also puts into praxis the Black trans sociality of making the film itself. Tourmaline moves in the interstice between the historical record of Black trans life and the realm of the energetic and kinetic—tracing echoes and reverberations across time and space. For Tourmaline's cinematic and Black trans radical artistic imaginary, time and space are folded—they are shaped through their malleability and plasticity. There is an inherent resistance to revolutionary messianic and secular temporality, as well as to the conception of the revolutionary event as a secular miracle. Mary Jones employs spiritual, cosmological, and "para-theological" (to extend J. Kameron Carter's grammar) devices in order to move diagonally through time and space, to fold time and space.[21] Instead of these coordinates as fixed—time, space, the event as firmly hypostasized in both—rather, events and figures echo, reverberate across time and space in their vibrancy, aliveness, and amplification. Stonewall, by this reading and for example, never ended and the constellation of figures that orbit it and both potentialized and actualized it are still animating the radical horizon. The Black trans revolutionary event, like the Black trans revolutionary subject that Tourmaline activates, is not confined within the coordinates of historical and linear time and space but rather traverses time and space. Stonewall, rather than operating exclusively in the register of the event and its periodization, is an expression of kinetic energy and force. The grammar of the event as a singular, unrepeatable happening—one of the signatures of historical teleology and its corollaries of both progress and declension narratives—is left aside for another framework that includes but also does not remain only within the logic of speculation or futurism. Speculation and futurism make possible life and futurity.

While Black queer and trans speculation contours the work and is part of the theoretical and creative edifice—moving in the Black radical legacy and Black queer and feminist tradition of Octavia E. Butler and Samuel R. Delany and also in the milieu of films such as *Born in Flames* (1983)—so clearly recognizable in the optics of *Salacia,* there is also another formulation that shapes the work. Tourmaline's cinematic vision is conceptualized as the actualization of a manifestation and a theory of surplus—abundance—versus tragedy, lack, and negation. (In)famous for her transgressions—of the racialized gender binary and of the legal protocols regulating sexual difference and the criminalization of transness. As Kyla Schuller argues in *Biopolitics of Feeling,* "Binary sex does not exist in a parallel or intersecting dimension with race. . . . Rather the rhetoric of distinct sexes of male and female consolidated as a function of race."[22] Much of *Salacia* takes place in Seneca Village, a putatively free Black enclave founded in 1825 that was eventually destroyed through the use of eminent domain—showing the ruse of Black ownership (property in self or of objects)—to erect Central

Park in 1857. Little Africa, established through land grants by the Dutch East India Company in the 1640s was the other—and first—nominally "free" Black community in New York. Jones lived on Greene Street, in one of the many brothels in the area now known as SoHo and then known as Hell's Hundred Acres.[23] Jones and others at Seneca Village are neither free nor enslaved but are in a temporal and spatial interval of unfreedom, an ontological hold that is also a haunt. *Salacia* is a critique of that very double bind, wherein the version of freedom is bound to slavery. *Salacia* dramatizes intramural tensions that cut across and through the Black community, a community rendered always already under duress by so-called slave catchers in the North (which kidnapped both fugitives from slavery and purportedly free Blacks), as well as by white civil society. A Black abolitionist, Peter Dermot, runs a Black free press and a boarding house and watches with disdain out the window as Mary Jones engages in illicit sex work/trade with white men outside. The intramural is not without its fractures and fission and factions, however. "Man monster" posters circulate, and the lithographs are pasted to walls and trees, signifying that Jones is wanted, and in one scene she tears them down.

Yet, so too are many others, as the community is always subject to capture. Jones's situation is a collective and intramural and, at the same time, particular and singular predicament. Dermot disapproves of Jones's supposed immorality and vice but still provides her refuge. While he judges her for carnality and sins of the flesh, he nevertheless is not protected by the aura of respectability. The police storm his home looking for Jones, showing that Black life is never autonomous but always under duress, violated, "available in the flesh—immediate, hands on . . . for the slave masters," as Hortense Spillers asserts in Arthur Jafa's film *Dreams Are Colder than Death,* and we can add the police and white civil society as instruments and deputized avatars of the enslaver or, better yet, as instantiations of a general field of racial capitalist mastery, an enterprise that is as affective (an anti-black structure of feeling) as it is materialist.[24] The police threaten to close Dermot's entire establishment. Jones is on the run. Fugitive, she is cornered, trapped, and resists and fights but is overpowered and arrested. Jones, however, knows magic and the occult: a spiritual cosmo-technics. Magic and time travel present in both the Black speculative imaginary of nineteenth-century fiction and in slave narratives, one of the most famous being Frederick Douglass's encounter with Master Covey wherein he attributes his ability to overpower Covey to the gift of a magical root amulet by Sandy. Jones uses water as transport and moves through and between time, allowing her to escape the confines of her jail cell. The title of the film references water, Salacia being the Roman goddess of the sea. The opening lines recount the story of flight that traces through slave narratives, of enslaved people who could fly and left the plantation/world. Jones escapes one version of capture—the pre-emancipation past—to end up in another—the present-day Central Park. The cop and Jones land in a Central Park that sits on the demolished grounds of Seneca Village, which was destroyed in 1855 and had been the largest community of so-called free Blacks in the pre–Civil War period. There is no teleological progress narrative to claim, only an anti-black and antitrans temporal torsion. From Reconstruction's recoil into historical opacity and temporal knot: the historical aporia of antiblackness. Tourmaline's abolitionist intervention might be seen as an iteration of refusal and nonperformance that Sora Han argues situates blackness as "a performative against all performances of freedom and unfreedom dependent on the historical dilemma of a lack of meaningful distinction between freedom and slavery."[25]

Jones escapes one version and legal, social, and political grammar of capture—the pre- emancipation past—to end up in the midst of another: contemporary Central Park as a site of antiblackness and racial capitalist modernity. With *Salacia,* director Tourmaline discloses how the temporality of blackness exceeds teleology, is ecstatic: "We can be anything we want to be," says Jones in the film, and this necessarily includes anytime and place. Tourmaline's critical fabulation of Jones in the film reveals space-time as a fold. Jones's space and time travel reveals the entanglement of freedom and slavery—not only the coupled temporality of past and present but also the insufficiency of linear imaginary of time as past and present itself. Antiblackness structures the conception of time and is a spatial project—geographic and topographic in the sense that racial capitalism is literally etched and written and inscribed into the landscape—be it climate apartheid or gentrification as the ongoing legacy of anti-black atmospherics and displacement in the historical present. Fugitive from the past, Jones jumps to the future—leaving Sing Sing prison and transporting herself, along with the police officer who is chasing her, to Central Park. The Sing Sing scenes were filmed on Governors Island at Castle Williams, which was originally a Civil War penitentiary, and the entire island was one of longest-running military installations—a base for the U.S. Army and Coast Guard. Governors Island links to Henry Hudson, of the Dutch East India Company and plantations that lined the Hudson River valley. In *Black Skin, White Masks*, Frantz Fanon theorizes a leap of invention that is a rupture and an event that alters the coordinates of existence:

> I should constantly remind myself that the real leap consists in introducing invention into existence. In the world in which I travel, I am endlessly creating myself. And it is by going beyond the historical, instrumental hypothesis that I will initiate my cycle of freedom.[26]

Jones makes the inventive leap (in a Fanonian sense) past the anti-Black epoch of the 1800s to the present day only to materialize through the portal at a modern Central Park under a new regime of carceral state racial capitalism. She is on the ground where Seneca Village used to stand, which has been destroyed and largely forgotten. Jones bends space-time and also plays with its governing protocols. Fugitive not only to the norms of aesthetic subjection, Jones is on the run from the aesthetic and spatiotemporal double bind of freedom and slavery. Jones doesn't see or experience time as linear; there is no progress—racial or otherwise—to be had. Rather, for Jones, space and time are entangled and mutable, not isomorphic. Jones declares that "we can be anything we want to be." Her voice strengthening along with her resolve as she emphatically shouts it again.

Jones is not bound by the aesthetic or even the spatiotemporal grammar of capture of this anti-Black and antitrans world, moving across and through space and time, on the run from the vicious durational field of antiblackness, as opposed to localized within any historically specific space/time. The film shows the ruse and insufficiency of any racial progress narrative. *Salacia* shows how modernity is both haunted by and forged by antitrans and anti-Black violence that is inescapable within the terms of the world. Mary Jones not only enacts Black trans "escapology" but also shows how the world requires abolition and how blackness and transness are in aesthetic and ontological excess of its confines.[27] The magic that she uses is an ancestral African Indigenous inheritance that would have traveled and been transmitted in the face of the Middle Passage that aimed to place under erasure all Indigenous African cosmology and cultural lifeworlds (an erasure that continues in the effacement of the Indigeneity of blackness). Jones's time travel is in defiance of colonial temporality, and she pursues temporality outside coloniality. Tourmaline's film moves in and through this generative dream of freedom that is incommensurable with and irreducible to emancipation. *Ecstasy* refers to being outside one's place, standing outside of oneself (from telepathy to bilocation to mysticism), which implies a refusal of grounding (to refuse the given term), and through Tourmaline's art work, Black transness moves ecstatically, out of this world: "anything we want to be."

Notes

1. See Nicole R. Fleetwood, *Marking Time: Art in the Age of Mass Incarceration* (Cambridge, Mass.: Harvard University Press, 2020); Kara Keeling, *The Witch's Flight: The Cinematic, the Black Femme, and the Image of Common Sense* (Durham, N.C.: Duke University Press, 2007); David Marriott, *Haunted Life: Visual Culture and Black Modernity* (New Brunswick, N.J.: Rutgers University Press, 2007); Kobena Mercer, *Travel & See: Black Diaspora Art Practices since the 1980s* (Durham, N.C.: Duke University Press, 2016); Tina M. Campt, *Listening to Images* (Durham, N.C.: Duke University Press, 2017).
2. See Frank B. Wilderson III, *Red, White & Black: Cinema and the Structure of U.S. Antagonisms* (Durham, N.C.: Duke University Press, 2010).
3. Fred Moten, *In the Break: The Aesthetics of the Black Radical Tradition* (Minneapolis: University of Minnesota Press, 2003).
4. Nicole R. Fleetwood, *Marking Time: Art in the Age of Mass Incarceration* (Cambridge, Mass.: Harvard University Press, 2020), 26.
5. Hortense J. Spillers, *Black, White, and in Color: Essays on American Literature and Culture* (Chicago: University of Chicago Press, 2003), 14.
6. Angela Y. Davis, *Freedom Is a Constant Struggle: Ferguson, Palestine, and the Foundations of a Movement* (Chicago: Haymarket Books, 2016).
7. Saidiya Hartman, "On Working with Archives: An Interview with Writer Saidiya Hartman," interview by Thora Siemsen, Creative Independent, April 18, 2018, https://thecreativeindependent.com/people/saidiya-hartman-on-working-with-archives/.
8. Anna Arabindan-Kesson, *Black Bodies, White Gold: Art, Cotton, and*

Commerce in the Atlantic World (Durham, N.C.: Duke University Press, 2021), 25.

9. Fred Moten, "The Case of Blackness," *Criticism* 50, no. 2 (2009): 180.

10. Nahum Dimitri Chandler, *X—The Problem of the Negro as a Problem for Thought* (New York: Fordham University Press, 2014), 11.

11. Saidiya Hartman, "Venus in Two Acts," *Small Axe: A Caribbean Journal of Criticism* 12, no. 2 (June 2008): 11.

12. *Salacia,* directed by Tourmaline (2019; New York: Museum of Modern Art), film; *Mary of Ill Fame,* directed by Tourmaline (2020–21; 59th Venice Biennale), film.

13. Tavia Nyong'o, *The Amalgamation Waltz: Race, Performance, and the Ruses of Memory* (Minneapolis: University of Minnesota Press, 2009).

14. Walter Benjamin, *The Work of Art in the Age of Its Technological Reproducibility, and Other Writings on Media* (Cambridge, Mass.: Harvard University Press, 2008), 19–55.

15. Ralph Lemon, *Come Home Charley Patton* (Middletown, Conn.: Wesleyan University Press, 2013), 187.

16. People v. Sewally, June 16, 1836, District Attorney Indictment Papers, Court of General Sessions, 89, NYDA Case Files, NYC Municipal Archives.

17. People v. Sewally, 89.

18. Elizabeth Freeman, *Time Binds: Queer Temporalities, Queer Histories* (Durham, N.C.: Duke University Press, 2011), 162.

19. Tourmaline and Xoài Phạm, "Two Artists on the Sacred Sisterhood of Trans Women," interview by Coco Romack, *New York Times,* April 20, 2023, https://www.nytimes.com/2023/04/20/t-magazine/tourmaline -xoai-pham.html.

20. *Salacia.*

21. J. Kameron Carter, "Paratheological Blackness," *South Atlantic Quarterly* 112, no. 4 (2013): 589–611.

22. Kyla Schuller, *The Biopolitics of Feeling: Race, Sex, and Science in the Nineteenth Century* (Durham, N.C.: Duke University Press, 2018), 17.

23. Ford Fessenden and Erin Agner, "Dens of Iniquity," *New York Times,* January 28, 2011, http://archive.nytimes.com/www.nytimes.com /interactive/2011/01/26/nyregion/gentleman.html.

24. Hortense Spillers in Arthur Jafa, *Dreams Are Colder than Death* (Pumpernickel Films, 2014), 52 min.

25. Sora Han, "Slavery as Contract: Betty's Case and the Question of Freedom," *Law & Literature* 27, no. 3 (2015): 401.

26. Frantz Fanon, *Black Skin, White Masks* (New York: Grove Press, 2008), 204.

27. See Daphne Brooks, *Bodies in Dissent: Spectacular Performances of Race and Freedom, 1850–1910* (Durham, N.C.: Duke University Press, 2006), 121–23.

PART III
Temporality, Technicity, and Bioethics of Becoming

Genealogies of Trans Technicity
Hil Malatino

To what extent is the theorization of trans engagements with tech-nomedical objects embedded in a colonial/modern, Eurocentric understanding of technicity?[1] Drawing upon the work of Jacques Derrida, Bernard Stiegler, and David Wills, I situate accounts of trans technicity that are near-canonical in trans studies (from Susan Stryker, Paul B. Preciado, Sandy Stone, and others) as rooted in a continental philosophical account of originary technicity that resonated with epistemological and technical revolutions in the biological constitution and transformation of sex in the lat-ter half of the twentieth century.[2] Tracing this resonance through accounts of technologies of transition in the late twentieth and early twenty-first centuries illuminates how an embrace of origi-nary technicity—the idea that human beings are fundamentally technical, that humans and tools are absolutely coconstitutive—transforms how bodies (both trans and cis) are understood and clari-fies why such an articulation has mattered deeply as a philosophico-political counter to trans-antagonistic claims that trans bodies are unnatural and inorganic.

I then trouble this account of trans technicity, drawing upon the intervention of C. Riley Snorton, who refers to this epistemo-logical and technical transformation as a part of a broader Eu-rocentric "narrative of somatechnical advancement and might," wherein the technical capacities of the white transsexual body operate as monument and living testimonial to the exceptional plasticity achieved by Western medicotechnical methods.[3] This narrative represents a privileged subset of a plurality of trans engagements with and theorizations of technicity, which are always shaped by class and racial positions that stratify access to technologies of transition. There are many forms of DIY transition that trans folks experiencing poverty (often nonwhite, sometimes sex workers) have availed themselves of as alternatives to a "regime of medical gatekeeping [that has] made transition through official means inaccessible to most and miserable for the few willing to attempt it."[4] If this attention to access, stratification, and differential orientation to technicity falls out of the analysis, I argue that we risk articulating a white trans futurism that exceptionalizes privileged trans relationships to technocorporeal making and remaking.

The Desire for Trans History and/as the Logic of Rebuttal

I'm curious about the desire for trans history. Which is to say that I'm curious about several things: what motivates the desire for history, the ideas about what history is that circulate in conversations about trans pasts, what evidentiary proof of history legitimates or defends against, the origin stories about the emergence of transness that circulate and the specificities—geopolitical, biopolitical, racial, technical—they're rooted in. I'm also skeptical about the desire for trans history, or at least claims about the long-standing existence of trans subjects—the idea that trans subjects aren't necessarily new, historically speaking, that there are trans (or proto-trans) figures extant cross-culturally, in earlier historical epochs. The skepticism isn't grounded in disagreement. I'm open to the idea that something like transness, or at least adjacent to transness, well predates mid- to late twentieth-century Eurocentric sexological protocols of surgical and hormonal transition, that what was "invented" wasn't transness but a very specific protocol for the medical, legal, and political management of transness. What I am skeptical of is a reactive position to the idea that trans existence is legitimate only if authenticated through proof of duration, at the scale of the individual and at the scale of the species. In other words, that transness is legible and legitimate only if demonstrably long term, only if trans subjects have "known" for as long as they can remember, or since a very young age, and only if scholars can furnish evidence that speaks to a long historical lineage of trans or trans-adjacent subjectivity and experience. I worry that this is an argumentative tactic that emerges in response to a particular form of trans antagonism: the claim, so often repeated, that transness is unnatural. The claim that posits transness as a late modern technomonstrosity that serves as an indicator of postlapsarian dystopia where the coordinates of reason, logic, and common sense are scrambled, lost, perhaps willfully abandoned. Trans existence as harbinger of end-times, proof of collective irrationality. This motivates counterclaims about duration and longevity: trans subjectivity is not a new thing—it's an old thing. Look how many of us have always known, have always felt this way. Look at how many of us pepper the historical record. This counterclaim works in more than one way, of course. It can be, and has been, used by folks of color as a response to understandings of transness as not only a recent thing, or a violation of the natural order of things, but a particularly culturally white thing. Efforts to establish trans and two-spirit ancestors work to reposition noncis folks as part of multiple cultures and lineages, ranging beyond white, Eurocentered conceptions of trans identity.

If and when this historical-cum-personal narrative of duration and longevity is offered as a response—tacit or explicit—to such trans-antagonistic accusations, it falls squarely within the parameters of what Sara Ahmed terms a "rebuttal system," a system that consistently places trans people in a defensive/reactive posture that is not just incidental or situational but existential. Ahmed writes of the logic of rebuttal, positioning it as "a form of evidence that is presented to contradict or nullify other evidence that has been presented by an adverse party . . . a form of evidence that is directed against evidence that has already been presented." For trans subjects facing recurrent claims of inauthenticity, irreality, and unnaturalness, the contradictory evidence isn't an artifact, isn't an object other to the self; it *is* the self. The (hopefully) countervailing evidence is trans life itself. Ahmed goes on to ask:

> What if you are required to provide evidence of your own existence? When an existence is understood as needing evidence, then a rebuttal is directed not only against evidence but against

an existence. An existence can be nullified by the requirement that an existence be evidenced. The very requirement to testify to your existence can end up being the very point of your existence.[5]

When Ahmed writes that "an existence can be nullified by the requirement that an existence be evidenced," I hear her as saying that placing subjects in a consistently defensive existential posture produces a kind of labor—testimonial, but not only—that exhausts, or threatens to exhaust, subjective possibilities for living beyond the reach of the demand to furnish proof of life. This labor aims to have the simple fact of one's existence taken for granted, to have the fact of one's existence understood as factic, and being forced or coerced into such labor significantly compromises one's ability to live well, or perhaps to persist in living altogether.

The refrain of existential duration—we've always felt this way, we've always been here—is, however partially, embedded in the logic of such a rebuttal system. It is a response to the demand that trans subjects prove the legitimacy and legibility of mere being, rendering trans existence subject to proof rather than merely extant, factic, obvious. Insofar as it is a reactive response to trans-antagonistic accusations of irreality, delusion, and fakery, a response to the "requirement that an existence be evidenced," it acquiesces to the primary assumption that shapes such accusations: that trans being is of a fundamentally different order than that of cis folks and, thus, that trans subjects better explain themselves, better prove our beingness.

The terms of a rebuttal system presume a gulf between cis and trans existence, insofar as being cis is naturalized, taken for granted, ceded reality status. The terms of a rebuttal system also override the right to (and desire for) opacity. They demand, instead, that trans subjects furnish proof of deep investigation into the lastingness of a motivating drive toward transition, as well as—and in addition to—historical evidence. The phenomenon of privacy, the refusal of disclosure, the ability to choose the terms according to which information about one's existence is shared, and the simple fact of remaining a mystery to oneself (not knowing fully, or even at all, why we are how we are) are all foreclosed by the terms of such a system. It would be hard to underestimate the extent to which this constitutes an invasion of one's inner (we might say psychic) life, but it constitutes much more than that. It serves as a justification for violence in the name of, and for the supposed sake of, revelation (finding out what we "really" are). It serves a gaslighting logic that too often becomes viciously internalized, prompting a trans variant of deep existential doubt ("Am I really that? How could I be that, that thing I'm being told is impossible to really be?"). And insofar as it elicits reactive testimony while constraining the terms of response, it produces too-simplistic accounts of trans existence and the (varied, mutable, multivalent) specificities of trans experience.

Trans studies has formed, in part, as a rebuttal to the trans-antagonistic rebuttal system itself. A number of the texts that have become canonical for the field take up the refutation of the structuring logic of such a system, and they do so in two ways that are linked. One strategy is articulating a universalizing, rather than minoritizing, approach to trans experience—that is, arguing that aspects that have been thought to distinguish and be unique to trans experience are much more generalizable or widespread, as true of cis folks as they are of trans folks (or in ways that productively muddy the ostensible divide between being cis and being trans). Another is developing an account of embodiment that refutes both essentialism and constructivism by insisting on the fundamental technicity of the body.

Universalizing Technicity: Alternative Ontologies of Embodiment and the Emergence of Trans Studies

By *technicity,* I refer to the idea that technology is inseparable from the human—that is, that one can't rend apart the tool and the human, that the two are coconstitutive. Philosophically, this idea has traveled under a couple of different names: Jacques Derrida theorizes what he calls "originary technicity," and Bernard Stiegler writes extensively about what he terms "originary prostheticity."[6] The fundamental insight is that technology and the human are coevolved and, thus, that there has never been a rift or divide between the technical and the human. As Derrida writes, "There is no natural originary body: technology has not simply added itself, from the outside or after the fact, as a foreign body. Or at least this foreign or dangerous supplement is 'originarily' at work and in place of the supposedly ideal interiority of the 'body and soul.' It is indeed at the heart of the heart."[7] Originary technicity works against the idea of technological alienation that emerged as a critique of industrialization: the idea that, through the development of technology, humans become more and more estranged from (call it what you want) their essence, core self, ground of being. This commonly circulating notion, undergirding everything from keto diets to homesteading movements to social media fasts, has also played a significant role in transphobic imaginaries of trans people as fundamentally "unnatural."

There's the infamous framing of trans women as the devious inventions of medical patriarchs on an antifeminist mission to produce the ideal patriarchal form of femininity, first articulated by Janice Raymond and echoing in the works of trans-exclusionary feminists like Sheila Jeffreys and Julie Bindel. Getting to the crux of this in her 1994 introduction to a reprinting of *The Transsexual Empire* (and writing back directly to Sandy Stone's imperative critique of the work, which I'll address shortly), Raymond writes, "Unlike impersonators, transsexuals are not participating in a performance in which the audience suspends disbelief for the duration of the show. They purport to be the real thing. And our suspension of disbelief in their synthetic nature is required as a moral imperative."[8] The real and the synthetic circulate here as alibis for the true and the false, the factic and the make-believe. To understand trans people as anything other than delusional mimes is to commit the same grave logical error as mistaking a film for real life. In other words, to be made—synthetic—is to be fake, insofar as the synthetic is that which is made by human agency and is understood as counterposed to "the natural." This division between the natural/synthetic (as real/fake) is repeated in TERF and TERF-adjacent literature ad nauseam: Sheila Jeffreys insists on referring to trans women as "male-to-constructed females," with *constructed* doing the work that *synthetic* does in Raymond's text.[9] WoLF—the Women's Liberation Front, who notoriously opposed the Obama administration's trans-inclusive interpretation of Title IX—uses *women* as a term meaning "human females," synonymous with "a class of people called women"; the language of "gender" is understood to elide the ostensibly fundamentally "human" distinction between "females" and "males."[10] All of these thinkers, by extension, understand trans men as fundamentally and irrevocably female. The territory of the human is again ceded to this biologically dimorphic-cum-sex-class distinction, over and against the made/constructed supposed irreality of gender.

But it's not just within forthrightly transphobic discursive and political formations that this distinction is repeated; it's the crux of what Talia Mae Bettcher refers to as the "natural attitude" about sex; it circulates as common sense.[11] The "natural attitude" refers to the consistent inference of genitalia from what Bettcher calls "sex-presentation" and the corresponding "subjection of bodies to sex-differential boundaries of privacy and decency."[12] In the workaday understandings of many, there isn't an operative distinction between gender—a socioculturally constructed thing—and the biological body; there is rather a practice of genital inference on the basis of "sex-presentation" and a moral system of sex-differentiated concealment in the name of privacy and decency scaffolded upon that naturalized inferential practice. Bettcher rightly points out that the insistence on sex and gender as constructions—though no less real for being constructed—misses the way that "trans people are constructed as *constructions*."[13]

In a way, trans-exclusionary feminists are just saying the quiet part out loud. In their insistence on a system of sex-differentiation that positions trans people as deceptive, fraudulent, constructed-as-constructions, they are only doubling down on the logic that structures the thinking of anyone who has ever wondered what a trans person "really" is (that which is revealed, of course, by genital configuration or the supposed sex assigned at birth). The workaday feminist distinction between gender (sociocultural) and sex (biological) does nothing to disrupt the logic of this system and is cold comfort to many trans folks, as asserting that "everyone does gender"—all the world's a stage, and all of us actors—flattens, indeed overrides, the specificities of trans experiences of accusations of fakery, unnaturalness, and inauthenticity, which work to consign trans folks to the status of irreal, illegibly human, inexistent.

Bearing this in mind, it's not necessarily surprising that field-forming accounts of sex/gender that emerge in the nascent days of this thing now called trans studies don't merely repeat the assertion that gender is a cultural construct; they offer a much more complex account of the fundamental technicity of embodiment that entirely disrupts the account of the natural and the synthetic, the real and the fake outlined above. I want to briefly canvass a small but relatively representative handful of them to bear out their implications, focusing on the argument that what emerges is not a more capacious, trans-inclusive account of the supposed "sex/gender distinction" but instead an ontology that is thoroughly informed by continental philosophy of technology that has been significantly overlooked in the move to theorize the relationship of trans accounts of embodiment to feminist accounts of embodiment, the positioning of transfeminism in relation to other currents of feminist theory, and, relatedly, the framing of trans studies as a distinct subfield of women's, gender, and sexuality studies.

A quick tour through two foundational works in trans studies clarifies this traffic between philosophical accounts of originary technicity and the theorization of trans embodiment. Rather than a long, exegetical take on these works, my aim here is only to highlight their shared emphasis on the imbrication of the human and the technical, the fundamental madeness of the body (all bodies, not just trans bodies). This is a through line of Susan Stryker's work, extending from her imperative early 1990s essay "My Words to Victor Frankenstein above the Village of Chamounix" through her 2008 meditation on the poetics of transsexual sadomasochism, "Dungeon Intimacies," to her recent work on trans inhabitations of built space. In "My Words to Victor Frankenstein," she begins with a monologue that forthrightly declares transsexuality as made: "The transsexual body is an unnatural body. It is the product of medical science. It is a technological construction. It is flesh torn apart and sewn together again in a shape other than that in which it was born."[14] In a ground-clearing move, Stryker begins by confirming what, in transphobic imaginaries, is supposed to be that which consigns trans people to pathology, deviance, non-humanity, or subhumanity: technological constructedness. But the arc of the essay makes plain that the pejorative work of this conjecture is a product of psychic disavowal—that is, cis refusal to come to terms with their own technological constructedness, projecting onto trans folks what they can't bear to fully admit: the "revelation of the constructedness of the natural order" itself.[15] Stryker writes that "confronting the implications of this constructedness can summon up all the violation, loss, and separation inflicted by the gendering process that sustains the illusion of naturalness."[16] Accusations of trans unnaturalness are a way of shooting the messenger: an outraged displacement and disavowal. Instead, Stryker implores cis audiences to discover the "seams and sutures" within and upon themselves, to grapple with the implications of their own madeness.[17]

Sandy Stone's "The *Empire* Strikes Back: A Posttranssexual Manifesto," widely understood as integral to the formation of trans studies, is similarly concerned with technicity, with questions of madeness and the seams and sutures that are part and parcel of the gendering process. She begins with a geographical-cum-historical tour-montage of sites central to the medical-technical history of transsexuality, locating her readers first in the "verdant hills of Casablanca" with its "narrow, twisted streets filled with the odor of spices and dung," where the clinic of Dr. Georges Burou sits in a "more modern quarter."[18] Burou, an ob-gyn by training, developed and refined vaginoplasty techniques in this Moroccan clinic; he made no secret of vetting patients according to their femininity, operating only upon those surgical candidates he believed were, or would be, cis-passing. Among his patients were Coccinelle, the French celebrity showgirl, and the writer Jan Morris, who would detail her time in the Casablanca clinic in her transition memoir *Conundrum*. This memoir, with its deeply heteronormative tropes of conventional, patriarchal femininity, would become a centerpiece of Stone's analysis of the replication of "the stereotypical male account of the constitution of woman" in the mid- to late twentieth-century memoirs of trans women.[19] In Stone's telling, these narratives parrot back the caricature of femininity at work in the midcentury male medical imaginary. She writes:

> In the time period of most of these books the most critical of
> these moments was the intake interview at the gender dys-
> phoria clinic, when the doctors, who were all males, decided

whether the person was eligible for gender reassignment surgery. The origin of the gender dysphoria clinics is a microcosmic look at the construction of criteria for gender. The foundational idea for the gender dysphoria clinics was first, to study an interesting and potentially fundable human aberration; second, to provide help, as they understood the term, for a "correctable problem."[20]

There is a narrative mimesis occurring here wherein trans women are confirming, for the sake of legibility and access, the accounts of femininity that medical professionals expect—one might also say "extort" or "demand"—from them.

To develop this account of the relation between trans narratives of embodiment and medical practice, she cinematically transports the reader from Morocco to California: "Imagine now a swift segue from the moiling alleyways of Casablanca to the rolling green hills of Palo Alto. The Stanford Gender Dysphoria Program occupies a small room near the campus in a quiet residential section of this affluent community."[21] We've time-traveled, too, but just a few years: it's now the late 1960s and '70s, the peak years of the Stanford program, a time of working out the etiology, diagnosis, and treatment protocol for "gender dysphoria" that would concretize in its 1980 listing in the American Psychiatric Association's *Diagnostic and Statistical Manual of Mental Disorders*. Here, she is again concerned with the medical vetting process, with the narratives offered up by trans people—almost entirely trans women—in order to be greenlit for surgical and hormonal transition (a similar vetting process was happening for trans men at this historical moment, though it's not the focus of Stone's analysis in this essay). In other words, Stone homes her focus on the function of narrative in the medicopsychological assemblage of transition. It's tempting, though facile, to interpret her fixation on language as Stone theorizing the relation between narrative and technology and the ways in which both are subjected to heteropatriarchal regulation and gatekeeping. But Stone is doing something a bit different, here: she is positioning narrative *as* technology. Not only that: she is suggesting that, as far as transition is concerned, narrative is at least as important as surgery or hormones in the production of gender, the making of selfhood, the legibility of embodiment. "The clinic," Stone argues, "is a technology of inscription."[22] The story that is being written upon trans bodies in the early years of the Stanford program is one that confirms cisness, that props up idealized, normative, bourgeois, and binary gender difference. It is also one that erases actually existing trans people (and all nonideal cis people, for that matter). If "the highest purpose of the transsexual is to erase h/erself, to fade into the 'normal' population as soon as possible," then it is exceedingly difficult to "generate a counterdiscourse" with the "ability to authentically represent the complexities and ambiguities of lived experience."[23] The problem: the trans body-as-text/text-as-body is trapped within the confines of a heteropatriarchal medical imaginary that extorts a narrative of binary bodily entrapment ("man trapped in a woman's body," "woman trapped in a man's body"); the dominance of this narrative disappears the complexity and nuance of trans experiences. This matters because the stories we tell, need to tell, about how and what we are aren't mere fictions—they construct our embodied lives. Different stories are different technologies; they produce different beings, allow making and remaking on other terms.

A deep engagement with Jacques Derrida's concept of originary technicity undergirds Stone's argument, and it's important to parse that influence, as it matters deeply for the field of trans studies that is, in part, built upon (but not particularly attentive to) that influence. Moreover, it matters because it troubles the terms according to which a certain prevalent counterdiscourse of trans experience has developed.

Stone cites Derrida only once in "The *Empire* Strikes Back," quoting a well-worn set of commands he issues at the opening of his 1980 essay "The Law of Genre": "Genres are not to be mixed. I will not mix genres. I repeat: genres are not to be mixed. I will not mix them."[24] Stone calls this the "Derridean imperative" and asserts that "a transsexual who passes is obeying" them.[25] The schoolmaster vibe of Derrida's repetition, and Stone's repetition of this repetition, conjures a sense of a punished student who, rather than writing these words on a blackboard, is instead writing them through the entire gestural, corporeal, and aesthetic repertoire

that enables a reading of the body as cis. Stone is not merely recon-
ceptualizing embodied gender in line with Derrida's comments on
genre; Derrida himself brings the sexed body into it, on the second
page of "The Law of Genre":

> As soon as the word "genre" is sounded, as soon as it is heard,
> as soon as one attempts to conceive it, a limit is drawn. And
> when a limit is established, norms and interdictions are not
> far behind: "Do," "do not" says "genre," the word "genre," the
> figure, the voice, or the law of genre. And this can be said of
> genre in all genres, be it a question of a generic or a general de-
> termination of what one calls "nature" or *physis* (for example, a
> biological *genre* in the sense of *gender,* or the human genre of all
> that is in general), or be it a question of a typology designated
> as nonnatural and depending on laws or orders which were
> once held to be opposed to *physis* according to those values as-
> sociated with *techné, thesis, nomos* (for example, an artistic, po-
> etic, or literary genre).[26]

Both genre and gender serve a taxonomizing function, establishing criteria and sorting according to type. Derrida's articulation
of gender as a "biological genre" is meant to demonstrate that the
linguistic sorting of kinds thought to be specific to literature applies to the "natural" as well, disrupting the opposition between
physis and *techné,* the natural and the made. Just as there are literary and linguistic hybrids, so too are there "biological" hybrids; or
rather, the firmly delimited law of genre that prohibits intermixing
actively invents excess and misfitting, relegating those "texts"—
bodies included—that do so to a position of monstrosity and exclusion upon which whole systems of legibility rely. Constitutive
exclusion. There is no "natural" that we might have recourse to
beyond or untouched by these systems of definition and classification; it's the law of genre all the way down.

This is why Stone is so concerned with questions of narrative,
with the conditions of foreclosure that have historically limited
the speech of trans subjects, constraining trans narrative to the
overdetermined typological accounts of masculinity and femininity that circulated among midcentury medical men. She ends the
essay directly exhorting trans subjects to speak in the service of

troubling such typologies, making space for more complex and nuanced articulations of selfhood:

> I ask all of us to use the strength which brought us through the effort of restructuring identity, and which has also helped us to live in silence and denial, for a revisioning of our lives. I know you feel that most of the work is behind you and that the price of invisibility is not great. But, although *individual* change is the foundation of all things, it is not the end of all things. Perhaps it's time to begin laying the groundwork for the next transformation.[27]

The next transformation, for Stone, is an era of "posttranssexuality," inaugurated by the necessarily collective act of trans folks writing themselves "into the discourses by which one has been written."[28] One way to think of the field of trans studies is as an explicit, concerted effort to do that.

The discursive shift conjectured by Stone, and realized over the thirty-plus years that separate the drafting of this essay from the appearance of "The *Empire* Strikes Back," was not merely discursive; importantly, Stone's call for such a shift wasn't, either. Because Stone understands language *as* a technology, discursive shifts engender different realities. They effectively mutate and transform the conditions under and through which making occurs. Stone's embrace of the concept of language as technology is not unique, either to trans thought or the broader Left intellectual and cultural mise-en-scène of the United States in the 1980s and '90s, deeply influenced by poststructuralist thought and its dovetailing with the technological developments enabling the emergence of the internet. The articulation of the body as embedded in and part-object of an extended assemblage, a nonsovereign complex combinatory of the technical and organic, was at work across a wide range of cultural-technical production: in dystopian cyberpunk imaginaries that fueled the work of authors like William Gibson and Bruce Sterling, in the widespread popularity of synth music, the speculative Afrofuturist literature of Samuel R. Delany and Octavia E. Butler, in the collective fascination with emergent technologies that enabled file-sharing, email, and Usenet, and in Donna J. Haraway's articulation of cyborg feminism (which owed as much to continental philosophy as it did to Chicana feminist theo-rists of hybridity and resistance like Chela Sandoval and Cherríe Moraga).[29] David Wills, a Derrida scholar perhaps best known for his work on the question of prosthesis, describes the turn away from the sovereign, liberal human subject and toward a reconsid-eration of originary technicity as the articulation of "a theory of the human animal in its relations to technology and a hypothesis according to which the animate in general will have always, from the get-go, been negotiating with the inanimate."[30]

Derrida's "The Law of Genre" itself had a proliferative after-life in early trans studies scholarship, well beyond Stone's essay: Jay Prosser cites it in *Second Skins* in support of his general the-sis that positions narrative as an integral technology of trans bodily inscription.[31] Jack Halberstam takes it up (alongside Jean Baudrillard's essay "We Are all Transsexuals Now," which was shaped by a similar commitment to originary technicity) in his 1994 essay "F2M: The Making of Female Masculinity" to argue for gender as necessarily fictive.[32] His argument produced significant dissensus in FTM spaces, with many folks protesting relegation to the status of fiction. A paradigmatic example is a review of the essay in *FTM Newsletter*. The author, Isabella, identifies at the out-set of the review as "the 7-year partner of FTM [trans photographer, author, and activist] Loren Cameron" and indicts Halberstam for refusing to pay notice to actually existing trans men, writing that "nowhere in the entire essay is the successfully integrated post-op FTM, living his ordinary day-to-day life."[33]

Claims about originary technicity are ontological claims and thus transhistorical claims. Even as the technological transfor-mations of the 1980s seemed to herald the emergence of a certain posthumanism, they coincided with a series of philosophical ex-hortations to remember that the human has never not been tech-nical, that we are not "natural" bodies alienated (or liberated) by technology but rather always thoroughgoingly technical ourselves.

Because I'm deeply persuaded by accounts of originary technic-ity, I'm simultaneously agnostic about the historicity of transness and outright hostile to accusations of trans embodiment as uniquely inorganic, especially unnatural. It seems clear enough that a se-ries of technological, political, and cultural transformations—ably mapped by Paul B. Preciado (a student of Derrida) in *Testo-Junkie,* another now-canonical work for trans studies, and given the label of "the pharmacopornographic era"—precipitated the emergence of a particular form of trans legibility in the mid- to late twentieth century. Preciado even offers a hand-drawn chart of these developments unique to the pharmacopornographic era; it includes "transformation of pornography into popular culture," the "invention of gender as a clinical tool," the "endocrinological management of sexual identities," and the "technical separation of heterosexuality and reproduction."[34] I would add to this list the ongoing refinement of surgical techniques such as vaginoplasty, phalloplasty, breast augmentation, mastectomy, chest reconstruction, and tracheal shaves; the widespread availability of electrolysis; and the dissemination of information about transition techniques via sensationalistic news media narratives, popular sexological texts, and burgeoning social and activist organizing in the 1950s and '60s. Even so, this historico-technical conjuncture should not be taken as the beginning (or end) of a thoroughly (post)modern trans identity. Rather, as C. Riley Snorton rightly points out in *Black on Both Sides,* this narrative of mid-twentieth-century trans identity takes "shape in relation to a national narrative of somatechnical advancement and might."[35] This narrative is inseparable from whiteness and continues to circulate "in subsequent iterations of trans historiography" wherein (white) trans identity has a special status in relation to ideas of self-realization, self-surpassing, and becoming: "a peculiar emblem of national freedom," he pointedly writes, "not beloved but somehow incorporable."[36] Its hallmark is a fascination with the special madeness, flexibility, plasticity, and transformative capacity of trans subjects.

Let's call this *white trans futurism.* Conceptually, it hinges on positioning trans subjects as a posthumanist avant-garde, some of the first people to really grasp the idea that we have always already been technical-organic assemblages or, to put it differently, that we have never really been "human" (in the post-Enlightenment, liberal, self-contained, sovereign sense of the word). On this view, we're emissaries of future gender, here to enlighten others to the stifling and stultifying imaginary of embodiment that undergirds normative, binary, sexually dimorphic understandings of gender.

White trans futurism hinges on a superficial understanding of originary technicity—a misunderstanding that enables those who embrace it to position themselves as heroic avatars of a world to come. The desire for this ennobling narrative, in the face of ongoing, rampant trans antagonism, is understandable, but it is ultimately too steeped in violent modern/colonial logics to be either applicable to a multiplicity of trans subjects or useful for a coalitional trans politics that centers multiply marginalized and deeply materially disenfranchised trans subjects. When technicity comes up in the early trans studies scholarship discussed above, it is deployed with reference to the madeness of gender, which comes to stand in for the madeness of the human body; there is minimal mention of narrative and genre as also, crucially, technologies that make race and species. This limits the scope and argumentative force of the concept and overlooks the fact that many of the other thinkers taken with the concept in this long historical moment (Afrofuturists, Third World and cyborg feminists, and Derrida himself—self-described as "a little black and very Arab Jew") were centrally concerned with the entwinement of technicity and race, as well as technicity and gender.[37]

We might follow the guidance of Sylvia Wynter, whose scholarship is also grounded in the concept of originary technicity and is in deep dialogue with Derrida's work. She understands narrative as a tool, storytelling as technology, and genre as about more than gender differentiation. Moving from this ground, she forces us to ask hard questions about the social and political embeddedness of the technology of storytelling and the impacts it has on our understanding of the category of the human itself. She proposes that, rather than an organic, natural fact of evolutionary speciation, "being human is a praxis."[38] She explains that a particular Western "secular liberal monohumanist conception of our being human" has been overrepresented as "the being of being human itself" and implores us to "speak instead of our *genres of being human*."[39] This draws our attention away from Eurocentric, post-Enlightenment accounts of the human and toward the "relativity and original multiplicity of our *genres* of being human."[40] This shift in attention enables a recognition of the central role that "our discursive formations, aesthetic fields, and systems of knowledge must play in the performative enactment of all such genres of being hybridly human."[41] Instead of repeating a story of late modern Western technological transformation that effectively births the modern/ colonial transsexual, or a story of trans existential duration across all of time and space, we might take the idea of originary technicity more seriously and assert that we have always already been technical, trans or otherwise. Trans people aren't special in that regard, nor is there anything radical about it, regardless of what the transphobes might say. Let's not shit ourselves: that is not where the locus of trans resistance or social transformation in the service of justice lies. But the stories we tell about where we've been, where we're at, where we might go: those have real, material possibility for making self and world otherwise.

Notes

1. Using *colonial/modern,* I reference the work of decolonial thinkers like Aníbal Quijano and María Lugones who understand processes of colonization and the emergence of a Eurocentric conception of modernity as inextricably interwoven with one another and entailing the imposition of a naturalized hierarchical conception of race as well as a gender system that was used to sort beings into what Lugones refers to as "light" and "dark" sides in order to justify "very different forms of violent abuse." María Lugones, "Heterosexualism and the Colonial/ Modern Gender System," *Hypatia* 22, no. 1 (2007): 186–209.
2. Susan Stryker, "My Words to Victor Frankenstein above the Village of Chamonix," *GLQ: A Journal of Lesbian and Gay Studies* 1, no. 3 (1994): 237–54; Paul B. Preciado, *Testo-Junkie: Sex, Drugs, and Biopolitics in the Pharmacopornographic Era* (New York: Feminist Press, 2013); Sandy Stone, "The *Empire* Strikes Back: A Posttranssexual Manifesto" (1987), Sandy Stone (website), https://sandystone.com/empire-strikes-back .pdf.
3. C. Riley Snorton, *Black on Both Sides: A Racial History of Trans Identity* (Minneapolis: University of Minnesota Press, 2017), 142.
4. Jules Gill-Peterson, "Doctors Who? Radical Lessons from the History of DIY Transition," *Baffler* 65 (2022), https://thebaffler.com/salvos /doctors-who-gill-peterson.
5. Sara Ahmed, "An Affinity of Hammers," *TSQ: Transgender Studies Quarterly* 3, nos. 1–2 (2016): 29.
6. Jacques Derrida, "The Rhetoric of Drugs," in *Points . . . Interviews, 1974–1994,* ed. Elizabeth Weber, trans. Peggy Kamuf (Stanford, Calif.: Stanford University Press, 1995), 244–45; Bernard Stiegler, *Technics*

and Time, 1: The Fault of Epimetheus (Stanford, Calif.: Stanford University Press, 1998).

7. Derrida, "Rhetoric of Drugs," 244–45.
8. Janice Raymond, The Transsexual Empire: The Making of the She-Male (New York: Teacher's College Press, 1994), xxiii.
9. Sheila Jeffreys, "Transgender Activism: A Lesbian Feminist Perspective," Journal of Lesbian Studies 1, nos. 3–4 (1997): 55.
10. Women's Liberation Front, "Our Work," https://womensliberationfront.org/our-work.
11. Talia Mae Bettcher, "Trapped in the Wrong Theory: Rethinking Trans Oppression and Resistance," Signs 39, no. 3 (2014): 392.
12. Bettcher, "Trapped in the Wrong Theory," 394.
13. Bettcher, 398.
14. Stryker, "My Words to Victor Frankenstein," 238.
15. Stryker, 250.
16. Stryker, 250.
17. Stryker, 241.
18. Stone, "Empire Strikes Back."
19. Stone.
20. Stone.
21. Stone.
22. Stone.
23. Stone.
24. Jacques Derrida, "The Law of Genre," Critical Inquiry 7, no. 1 (1980): 55.
25. Stone, "Empire Strikes Back."
26. Derrida, "Law of Genre," 56.
27. Stone, "Empire Strikes Back."
28. Stone.
29. Donna Haraway, "A Manifesto for Cyborgs: Science, Technology, and Socialist Feminism in the 1980s," in Simians, Cyborgs, and Women (New York: Routledge, 1991), 149–81.
30. David Wills, Prosthesis (Minneapolis: University of Minnesota Press, 1995), xiii.
31. Jay Prosser, Second Skins: The Body Narratives of Transsexuality (New York: Columbia University Press, 1995).
32. Jean Baudrillard, "We Are All Transsexuals Now," in Screened Out (London: Verso, 2022), 9–14; Jack Halberstam, "F2M: The Making of Female Masculinity," in The Lesbian Postmodern, ed. Laura Doan (New York: Columbia University Press, 1994), 210–28.
33. Isabella, "Review of 'F2M: The Making of Female Masculinity,'" FTM Newsletter 29 (1995): 13, 14.
34. Preciado, Testo-Junkie, 81.
35. Snorton, Black on Both Sides, 142.
36. Snorton, 142.
37. Jacques Derrida, Circumfession, in Jacques Derrida, ed. Geoff Bennington (Chicago: University of Chicago Press, 1993), 58.

38. Sylvia Wynter and Katherine McKittrick, "Unparalleled Catastrophe for Our Species?," in *Sylvia Wynter: On Being Human as Praxis,* ed. Katherine McKittrick (Durham, N.C.: Duke University Press, 2015), 23.

39. Wynter and McKittrick, "Unparalleled Catastrophe for Our Species?," 31.

40. Wynter and McKittrick, 31.

41. Wynter and McKittrick, 31.

Misgendering as Temporal Capture

Megan Burke

The point of this chapter is to consider the phenomenon of misgendering as a condition of trans (im)possibilities. Philosophical scholarship on misgendering has largely centered around the phenomenon as an epistemic injustice—in interpersonal encounters as testimonial injustice and at the structural level as hermeneutical marginalization, drawing attention to how misgendering harms one's status as a knower to perpetuate asymmetrical relations of social power.[1] Stephanie Julia Kapusta pushes the philosophical account of misgendering, arguing that it functions as a political harm to marginalize and exclude transgender women from the category "woman."[2] These accounts help us make sense of misgendering as an ethical and political matter, not just a psychological one. My goal is to think through how the historicity of gender shows up in and inflects the trans experience of being misgendered. I argue that misgendering is a kind of temporal capture that shores up normative gender—understood as a racialized, sexualized, classed, and ableist project. This critical phenomenological consideration provides a framework to help describe how misgendering operates to secure a world where forced gender assignments in the present are bound to historical legacies of power and violence.

Misgendering

Misgendering generally refers to the intentional or unintentional use of improper or inadequate modes of address that mischaracterize, misrecognize, or misname someone in relation to their gender. Although most often described as such, misgendering is not an event that only happens to trans subjects. For instance, a nontrans woman whose appearance is unintelligible as a woman in dominant contexts may be regularly taken to be a man. She may experience "the bathroom problem" in ways similar to trans people—that is, she could be surveilled while in and policed out of the women's bathroom because her gender presentation exceeds the expected condition of femininity. So even though she is not trans, her experience of the bathroom problem accords with transphobic logics since, as Talia Mae Bettcher argues, a basic form of transphobia is predicated on the expectation that gender presentation communicates genital status.[3] Moreover, given that the perceptual frames of normative gender are authorized through whiteness, misgendering may also be understood to occur when a Black man is addressed as a "boy" or when a Black boy is denied his boyhood because he is taken to be a dangerous predator.

As a result of the social, historical, and political contours of gender categories, misgendering is a complex and messy phenomenon. In the aforementioned instances, existing in excess of normative gender could result in an experience of misgendering that, while not necessarily explicitly transphobic, is nevertheless bound up with transphobic logics. I want to be very careful, then, not to suggest that misgendering is a simple phenomenon; it is not. Misgendering is a gendering apparatus that works in different ways as an instantiation of normative logics and, at times, for some subjects, as justification for violence.

For the purposes of this essay, though, I conceptualize misgendering as a trans experience. I do so following Bettcher's account of transphobia as a basic denial of authenticity, which makes it all too common that "transpeople are identified in ways that are contrary to or even hostile to their own self-identifications."[4] I take misgendering to be a common articulation of such misidentification, and so I take the experience of misgendering to be a common feature of trans subjectivity in a world fraught with trans antagonisms. For this reason, here I understand misgendering as an ontologically violent crafting and maintenance of cis gender.[5] Even if it is unintentional, it is affectively powerful. In focusing on misgendering in this way, I am thinking about misgendering as a "trans genre of misrecognition."[6]

To be sure, trans experiences of misgendering are diverse and complex. Usually, my experience is as a nonbinary person who, when addressed by others, is hurled back into their gender assigned at birth. But, it could also be the case that a genderqueer person is not hurled back into their initial assignment but still interpreted in ways incongruent with their self-defined gender. It could also be the case that a trans femme is (mis)read as a woman. Since a descriptive account of every event of misgendering is impossible to undertake here, it is important to note that my account offers tools to think through what is happening in these instances, even if I do not and cannot speak to a variety of cases. My concern, then, is to understand what misgendering is doing in addition to making us feel bad, in addition to making us confront time and time again that the world overwrites our self-definitions. Given that I live in a transphobic world, I cannot say what it would be like to be misgendered if the world were otherwise.

It is my view that misgendering works to consolidate the logics of normative gender by interrupting a subject's personal time. That interruption is instituted, in part, by the arrival of historical time in a subject's lived present. By focusing on the arrival of lived historical time in one's present, I draw attention to the typically unthematized historical dimensions of misgendering, highlighting how misgendering operates as what Sara Ahmed names an "orientation device."[7] In the discrete experiences of misgendering I consider, I highlight how the commingling of personal and historical time shores up various legacies of power and normative gender in the life of a subject. I acknowledge that the experiences I tend to are limited in generative ways, as well as ways that foreclose insight into other experiences. Yet, through this analysis I hope to encourage further thinking on the constitutive encounter and tension between historical time and personal time as a key feature of misgendering. Regardless of how we are addressed, when others declare our gender for us, we are being oriented by a historically grounded sense-making apparatus.

Critical Phenomenology, Trans Phenomenology

Phenomenology is an investigation into the way things appear in first-person experience; it is the philosophical study of "lived experience." In its classical or transcendental form, phenomenology aims to describe the essential or a priori structures of experience. The intention is to radically and critically encounter the meanings and conditions of our conscious lives in order to describe phenomena untarnished by habitual perceptions. For the classical phenomenologist, we have to bracket the contingent dimensions of existence in order to grasp the true meaning of being, of existing, of things themselves. Critical phenomenology challenges and refuses this transcendental gesture. Critical phenomenology does not seek to get below the historical, social, and political phenomena that shape our lives; it takes it to be constitutive of experience itself.

The point of critical phenomenology is to transform how and who we are in the world by paying acute attention to how relations of power, histories of oppression, and conditions of domination show up in a subject's embodied experience. What critical phenomenology contributes to politicized inquiry, then, is the way it tends to subjective experience. It demands attention to the meanings disclosed in experience, to the ways the social world and political relations are made through our embodied experience, and it requires considering what is overlooked by our usual understandings in order to perceive how the textures of social and individual embodiment emerge in the webs of history and power. This sustained attention to how first-person experience is structured by and animates socially constituted realities of privilege and oppression can help us understand how injustice and resistance structure and are negotiated in the everyday lived experiences of trans people.

Thinking at the intersection of trans studies and critical phenomenology is still a relatively new endeavor.[8] Jay Prosser and Henry Rubin offer foundational texts in trans phenomenology— their analyses focus on the felt experience of trans embodiment and subjectivity.[9] Gayle Salamon expands on these considerations of trans embodiment, highlighting how the lived or felt body is constituted by and laden with cultural meaning.[10] In her later work, *The Life and Death of Latisha King,* Salamon considers how transphobic meanings are ascribed to gendered embodiment and comportment such that they come to motivate, justify, and conceal transphobic violence.[11] Finally, Tamsin Kimoto considers the experiences of hormonal transition and transphobia, underscoring how they undo and reconstitute embodiment and intersubjectivity.[12] My contribution to this body of scholarship is less about the experience of trans people's discontent with gender and more closely aligned to Salamon's and Kimoto's concerns with the lived experience of transphobia and its consequences. Yet, instead of focusing on what it is to be the target of transphobia, I turn to the trans experience of misgendering to highlight how it animates historical legacies and logics of gender. While there are various modes of inquiry that can help shed light on misgendering, I turn to critical phenomenology specifically because of the way it helps us get at how history shows up in our lived experiences.

In phenomenological terms, *temporality* refers to a subject's experience of time. Lived time, or temporality, is a structure of our experience; it is a matter of how the present that I live is enveloped in retentional moments of my past and an anticipation of the future. This triadic structure is the temporal flow of subjectivity; my experience is generated by and generative of a past, present, and future that I live. A critical phenomenology of temporality must address not only how experiences of time emerge from and in relation to this interplay but also how lived time is altered, modified, and differently structured as a result. The notion of lived historical time is one way to develop such a critical phenomenological account of time.

Lived historical time refers to the way a subject's lived time is modified by historical meanings and events.[13] It highlights how the historical past shapes the course of experience and subjectivity itself. It is a way to understand how "history is renewed and animated in the moment of" an experience without us having to consciously draw on it.[14] For individuals of historically privileged social positions, living historical time often guarantees that time is lived as dynamic and open, unencumbered by the world and others. Historical time is often weaponized against those of historically marginalized and devalued social positions, such that historical realities of oppression and domination become living legacies, persisting not only in the collective present but also undoing and often upending a subject's personal experience of time.

The possibility for and the consequences of such weaponization is temporal harm, a particular kind of suffering that is not physical, psychological, or epistemological but temporal in character.[15] Temporal harm occurs when the historical past is weaponized against an individual such that their lived time is altered to that extent that forecloses an open, malleable experience of time. Temporal harm is central to how a subject comes to live historical injustice.

Misgendering as a Temporal Orientation Device

In *Time Binds,* Elizabeth Freeman offers an analysis of chrononormativity, which she understands as "the use of time to organize individual human bodies towards maximum productivity" as a way to work against queer existence.[16] For Freeman, chrononormativity constitutes social relations in a particular way, along linear and "teleological schemes of events or strategies of living such as marriage, accumulation of health and wealth for the future, reproduction, childrearing, and death" through the use of time to organize our lives.[17] Bound up with capitalism, chrononormativity arranges our lives along lines of gender, sexuality, race, and class in ways that propel the national, economic interests of Western industrialized nations like the United States. This use of time is one that structures how an individual experiences gender and time.

The experience of being assigned a gender at birth, although not one consciously remembered, is one that is, under current sociopolitical conditions, likely to persist over the course of many years, if not a lifetime. That initial assignment aims to organize one's life chrononormatively. So, when I was assigned "girl" at birth, there followed an entire developmental trajectory that was structured by a specific gendered temporality.[18] At the moment of the initial assignment, an event that enveloped my existence in narratives and histories of gender, race, class, and sexuality, my lived time was structured to follow a chronological narrative. My gendered past, present, and future, my time as a girl/woman, was established for me. Certainly, that need not fix the kind of girl/woman I could become, but that I would become one was and is expected. When I am misgendered, I am not only reminded that others do not perceive me the way I perceive myself. I am not just reminded of my gender assignment. I am hurled back into a gendered timeline that enforces and produces normative subjectivities and social relations. It's not that I am without agency and cannot resist this enforcement. Rather, in the collision of how I constitute my time and how my time is constituted for me by others, my present and future are interrupted by how the past arrives.

A more concrete story of misgendering from my own experience may help elucidate this point. In the fall of 2020, I was in a Zoom meeting with two colleagues on my campus from different departments, both white nontrans women, whom I had met with at least three times before as part of a campus initiative we were tasked with. My Zoom tile read "Megan/they, them, theirs/PHIL." The meeting seemed to be going like most other meetings—intellectually dull and administratively tedious. In two ways, though, this meeting was also different. We finally had the initiative ready to send out to other colleagues, which meant it was our last meeting, and it was also the first meeting in which I didn't have to correct my colleagues' use of she/her pronouns when they referred to me. While being misgendered by my colleagues is so routine I feel particularly adept at brushing it off, I was nonetheless relieved to not have to brush it off. But then, just when we were saying our goodbyes, one of my colleagues said, "Thanks, *ladies*." I doubt *ladies* was even said with emphasis, but it sure felt that way. It hit me as if the wind had been knocked out of me.

Before I had the chance to recover my breath and make a correction, the host ended the meeting. I sat at my desk trying to figure out how to unhinge myself from that moment of being misnamed. Should I write an email? Should I let it go? How was I to deal with the immediate past in order to secure a future for myself in which I was not misnamed again? The questions turned into frustration for not reacting quicker. I remember wanting to rewind time. This one brief experience of being misgendered pushed and pressed on my time. My future felt stunted. All I could think about was how to dislocate myself from that specific gendered address. My present felt disoriented. My past came bearing down; I was still "that girl"—the one who would become a lady. When *ladies* compromised my present, I was left to stitch together a break in my time.

This breaking and restitching of time is a kind of time travel, one that indexes crip time. As Ellen Samuels writes, crip time is a kind of *"broken time,"* an experience of being "cast . . . into a wormhole of backward and forward acceleration, jerky stops and starts, tedious intervals and abrupt endings," an enforcement of breaks, even when one doesn't want to endure them.[19] This temporal experience is a site of both alienation and liberation—a temporal disposition to be embraced because of the way it bends normate existence. And yet, it is also an excruciating time warp imposed onto one's existence in a world structured by linear, progressive time. The latter dimension of crip time emerges because of the dominant temporal frame that, as Alison Kafer puts it, "casts disabled people as (out) of time, or as obstacles to the arc of progress."[20] The temporal logic of the dominant frame is a fictive seamless developmental linearity; those who can approximate it do not experience time as broken. In contrast, those who do not meet the expected patterns of progress are out of sync, their temporal orientations deemed dysfunctional, in need of a cure.

My own stitching and restitching of broken time certainly can be a relief from—that is, a liberatory departure from—the gendered linearity demanded by white, Western, bourgeois, colonial, hetero norms of gender. Yet, first and foremost, when *ladies* interrupted my present, I experienced a temporal malfunction, one rooted in and that reminded me of my gender "dysfunction." *Ladies* folded me (back) into the norm, a likely unintentional but nonetheless curative response to my refusal of the logic of the normative gender system. *Ladies* exploded my present, instituting dominant temporal logics and curing the reality of my gendered irrationality. It indexed the nonsensicality of my self-defined gender. It was the wormhole of jerky stops and starts.

My own gender/temporal malfunction can only be understood in relation to the historical baggage of *ladies.* In the instantiation of the category "lady," there are historical meanings at work, which makes the social conferral mean more than just a mistaken mode of address. Historically, the term designates social nobility and civility. It is to be a polite woman, the complement to a gentleman, a woman who knows and follows the gendered and sexual rules of her social class, which, historically, is that of the white, property-owning class. To be a lady is also therefore to be perceived as cultured and esteemed, and therefore not of diminished capacities. In this sense, it is possible to understand *lady* as a legacy of what

María Lugones refers to as the "light side" of the colonial, modern gender system, the ordering of life for white, bourgeois subjects.[21] That ordering speaks to the ways meaning is constituted by and imposed onto the life of white, bourgeois men and white, bourgeois women for the sake of reproducing the project of colonial power and violence. As Lugones accounts for it, in the colonial gendered arrangement, only bourgeois, white Anglo-European subjects are marked as "men" or "women," a mark that secures their status as both civilized and fully human. This mark is achieved through the genocide of Indigenous peoples of the Americas and the enslavement of Africans, who are classified as not human, uncivil, and wild. As a result, "only white bourgeois women have consistently counted as women so described in the West."[22] Bearing the mark of civility, in the colonial order white, bourgeois women—*ladies*— are positioned as temporally advanced, ahead of those deemed nonhuman. The categorical institution of "ladies" comes at the expense of the colonized; it is an institution central to the project of colonial violence.

Far from being a phenomenon of the past, these historical meanings do not lie dormant. To be given a gender as a white, bourgeois subject is not, then, an innocent act. For me, to be named a "lady" is to be drawn into this history. It is to be positioned in the timeline of the coloniality of gender. So when my personal present is interrupted by *ladies,* that interruption animates a particular history of gender, one predicated on various legacies of violence. Because of how I am situated downstream from the history of colonial violence, *ladies* is a reminder of who I am supposed to be in the context of history. My personal time is therefore laden with lived historical time and thus bound to historical meanings.

Accordingly, it is possible to understand misgendering as what Sara Ahmed refers to as an "orientation device."[23] Ahmed accounts for orientation as a "powerful technology" that directs bodies to inhabit the world in specific ways.[24] As a temporal orientation device, misgendering interrupts and reshapes one's personal time. It does so by the arrival of historical meanings in one's lived present. That is, misgendering throws one (back) into an assignment, one that not only attempts to reorient one's personal history but also reinforces the collective history of that assignment. Ultimately, it does its work on a subject by interrupting their personal experience of time.

It is certainly not the case that a white subject like me escapes perpetuating historical violence just because I do not exclusively inhabit the gender I was assigned at birth. Because of how I am situated, my subjectivity is still bound up with historical legacies in complex ways that likely elude my direct perception and shield me from certain harms even as I do not conform to my gender assignment. My point here, however, is that misgendering functions to explicitly hold me to that assignment, regardless of whether the person, people, or institution mean to do so, and that this reorientation, even if temporary, reanimates the social power of the living history of gender (violence). It is not merely that my present gender, the gendered future I envision for myself, and my gendered past that I negotiate are undermined when I am misgendered, although they are. Lived historical time cuts into my present and pins me to a certain schema, a timeline, a host of historical meanings. Even in experiences of misgendering that look markedly different from mine, historical schemas show up and cut into personal time.

I take this cutting to be a mode of temporal capture, which institutes an interruption and potential closure of how personal, lived time can unfold by holding a subject to a particular historical structuring of time. For me, and those similarly situated along lines of race and class, this closure of lived time undermines possibilities for living in ways that can challenge the historical legacies of violent norms. The concern here is not that someone like me cannot still resist those habits. The concern is with their further collective sedimentation. To be held captive to historical legacies of gender by others is a way to maintain cruel attachments and social relations.

Temporal Capture

In *The Life and Death of Latisha King,* Gayle Salamon offers a phenomenological reckoning with the conditions of the transphobic murder of Latisha King, a trans girl of color who was shot in the back of her head by her classmate Brandon McInerney on February 12, 2008.[25] Salamon considers how homophobic and transphobic norms, especially the ones structuring life at Latisha's high school and those lived out by her peers and the adults around her, subjected her to scrutiny, left her unshielded from hate and violence, and inspired her murder.[26] Salamon exposes, through intricate consideration of the testimonies from Brandon's trial, the way normative gender embodiment is reinstituted and reimagined by the expectations and demands of others, by the way others foreclose possibilities for who Latisha could be. In this sense, Salamon reckons with how Latisha was perceived and killed, socially and physically, by those around her precisely because her life was held to their expectations, precisely because of how others oriented her in the world. I turn to Latisha's life and her death here with an awareness that another recitation of her murder is not in itself a condition of doing justice to who she was. In recounting a dimension of her life and death, my aim is to show how misgendering vis-à-vis lived historical time becomes fatal with the hopes that such a consideration can help interrupt the dominant movement of time.

Although not explicitly discussed by Salamon, misgendering plays a significant role in how Latisha's life was and is recognized. A little more than a week before her death, Latisha had asked some of her teachers and peers to recognize her as Latisha. This was not necessarily the first time she called on others to recognize her in this way, but it was the most explicit. It's unclear to what extent, if any, her request was fulfilled in the days prior to her death.[27] Even if people around her "were not working with the idea" that she was transgender, even as she would still respond to her name assigned at birth, it is certainly the case that Latisha had already asked to be recognized as Latisha.[28] Her peers knew this to be true. Her teachers knew this to be true. And even Brandon knew this to be true when he saw her name on a computer screen, as she had typed it. Nevertheless, in almost all of the narratives about her, in the testimonies at the trial, and in the majority of the reports about the murder, Latisha is misgendered. Salamon's read of the trial testimonies, for instance, draws our attention to how the conflation of gender and sexuality are central to this misrecognition and to the misrepresentation of Latisha's murder "in the press as a gay story . . . as many trans stories historically have been."[29]

Importantly, Latisha's ask to be named on her terms encouraged Brandon to pull the trigger. As Diane Michaels, a white, nontrans woman who was a juror in the trial explains, Brandon's "having second thoughts about doing it. But then, the green light when he says, 'Hey, Larry, I hear you're changing your name to Letitia,' to him that's a green light. He pulls out the gun and shoots him [Latisha]."[30] According to Michaels, "He [Brandon] was solving a problem." Brandon's denial of Latisha's existence is not, on the surface, an event of misgendering. It seems clear that Brandon recognized "something" about her—that she was acting out of bounds, that she was transgressing who she was supposed to be. To understand how Brandon's intentional and lethal refusal to recognize Latisha is a form of misrecognition, it is important to consider the commingling of personal time and historical time.

Andrea J. Pitts argues that the "the sociohistorical fabric" of Oxnard, California, as a white place, designed on white settler ideals of exploitation and extraction, is central to Latisha's murder.[31] This is not only because Brandon doodled swastikas, read *Mein Kampf,* or had been staying with a local neo-Nazi leader before he murdered Latisha. It is also because, as Pitts makes clear, "Oxnard was designed to keep Mexican American and Black residents from living in the predominantly white east side of the city."[32] Even further back in its historical formation, Oxnard was formed through colonial conquest in the eighteenth century and, in particular, "the displacement and forced labor of the Chumash peoples by Franciscan missionaries and Spanish soldiers."[33] Carving out Oxnard as a white space is not a one-time event but a legacy of the place itself. Phenomenologically speaking, Oxnard's white settler values are not in the past, they are of the present—not just the historical present, but the present as it is lived by those who live in Oxnard. This historical past arrives not just in a place but in the lives of teenagers like Brandon and Latisha, as a structure of their experience.

Alia Al-Saji's work on the *durée* of racism and colonialism points out how the historical past is an enveloping atmosphere of the present, pushing and pressing on it. For Al-Saji, it's not merely that histories endure. Rather, it's that they can press on a subject's lived present, weighing down, generating pain, even.[34] In contrast, white subjects like Brandon (and myself) do not inherit these histories as a weight. They are temporally light. White supremacy ensures a certain kind of temporal ease and seamlessness for white subjects in the commingling of personal time and historical time. So although our personal time is also structured and inflected by this historical past, whiteness cushions and comforts its arrival in the lived present. In this sense, the arrival or explosion of historical legacies of racism do not bear down on the present in such a way that would require us to escape them, even if we come to resist them. Following Al-Saji's account, such temporal lightness is not the case for subjects like Latisha.

The historical legacies of racism arrive in Latisha's life in ways that frame her not only as an abject, racialized other but also as a maladjusted subject. Cameron Awkward-Rich's account of trans maladjustment in *The Terrible We* underscores how "personhood is premised on the capacity to cultivate certain forms of feeling, habits of thought, and styles of relating—on meeting certain requirements."[35] Latisha, in her attempts to define herself, to assume an existence on her terms, was always already positioned as a failed subject. The way she thought about herself, the way she moved, dressed, and the activities she undertook were taken to be a sign that she was maladjusted. Thinking about her supposed maladjustment highlights how Latisha's death is also rooted in the eradication of all "problem bodies" from public life.[36] This is to say that Brandon's commitment to expunge Latisha from the present was not just a white supremacist gendered project but also an ableist one.

Working against the durée of normativity, of proper gender, Latisha walked into the computer lab, sat down, and typed her name. In doing so, she opened up time for herself. Brandon, however, fired his gun, to end her time. This refusal is an explosion and crystallization of historical legacies not only because neither Brandon nor Latisha are outside of historical time but also because when Brandon walked into the computer lab carrying a gun with a premeditated plan to murder Latisha, he carried with him lived historical time as a loaded weapon. When he fired the gun, he called on and restored the institution of normative gender central to the fabric of Oxnard, which includes its various rituals of racialized violence. These rituals exploded in her present in the form of two bullets, ending her future.[37]

An extreme form of misnaming is instituted when Latisha is shot. She is refused her name, deadnamed by two bullets. Those gunshots assure that she dies by a different name and that, in doing so, her personal time is anchored to the normative ordering of gender and time, and that legacy is sedimented in her life. In this sense, it's not just that the gun was fired to deny her existence, though it was. Rather, it's also that the gunfire assures that Latisha will not be named on her terms. Importantly, Brandon's demand that Latisha not be named continues to echo, haunting her after death, in the lives of those without guns but loaded with the authority to name her. That authority comes loaded with historical meanings that refuse futures to trans girls of color, even in their afterlife. Ultimately, by focusing on how misgendering shapes Latisha's existence, we can better understand what Latisha was up against and how historical time was weaponized against her, how she was captured by time. Historical legacies are mobilized against her, and they fired into her present, such that the past explodes to eliminate her time.

This critical phenomenological analysis of misgendering draws attention to the temporal dimensions of being misgendered in order to show how the experience itself is one where lived personal time and lived historical time collude to further sediment normative gendered logics. I've argued that temporal capture is a central structure of the experience of being misgendered and that it functions as an orientation device. A key dimension of the distress of misgendering is thus structured by a tension between historical time and personal time. When one is misgendered, they are confronting a constellation of hostile forces and meanings that reanimate and work to sediment dominant logics into the lived present. As a trans genre of misrecognition, misgendering is therefore an apparatus that doesn't simply deny self-defined gender but also consolidates histories of power and violence.

Notes

1. Rachel McKinnon, "Allies Behaving Badly: Gaslighting as Epistemic Injustice," in *Routledge Handbook on Epistemic Injustice,* ed. Ian Kidd, José Medina, and Gaile Pohlhaus (New York: Routledge, 2017), 161–75; Konstantinos Argyriou, "Misgendering as Epistemic Injustice: A Queer STS Approach," *Las Torres de Lucca* 10, no. 19 (2021): 71–82.
2. Stephanie Julia Kaputsa, "Misgendering and Its Moral Contestability," *Hypatia* 31, no. 3 (2016): 502–19.
3. Talia Mae Bettcher, "Appearance, Reality, and Gender Deception: Reflections on Transphobic Violence and the Politics of Pretense," in *Violence, Victims, Justifications: Philosophical Approaches,* ed. Felix Ó Murchadha (New York: Peter Lang, 2006), 175–200.
4. Bettcher, "Appearance, Reality, and Gender Deception," 181.
5. Here I'm thinking with Marquis Bey's account of the cistem and the making of cis gender. Marquis Bey, *Cistem Failure: Essays on Blackness and Cisgender* (Durham, N.C.: Duke University Press, 2022).
6. Hil Malatino, *Side Affects: On Being Trans and Feeling Bad* (Minneapolis: University of Minnesota Press, 2022), 53.
7. Sara Ahmed, *Queer Phenomenology: Orientations, Objects, Others* (Durham, N.C.: Duke University Press, 2006), 4.
8. As Tamsin Kimoto puts it, "Relatively few scholars working in trans studies deploy the language and tools provided by phenomenology or use trans experience to challenge and rework text in the history of phenomenology." Tamsin Kimoto, "Merleau-Ponty, Fanon, and Phenomenological Forays in Trans Life," *APA Newsletter on LGBTQ Issues in Philosophy* 18, no. 1 (2018): 16.
9. Jay Prosser, *Second Skins: The Body Narratives of Transsexuality* (New York: Columbia University Press, 1998); Henry Rubin, "Phenomenology as Method in Trans Studies," *GLQ: A Journal of Lesbian and Gay Studies* 4, no. 2 (1998): 263–81.
10. Gayle Salamon, *Assuming a Body: Transgender and Rhetorics of Materiality* (New York: Columbia University Press, 2010). In *50 Concepts for a Critical Phenomenology,* Talia Mae Bettcher offers a good overview of the work on gender discontent and embodiment by Prosser, Rubin, and Salamon. Her entry also highlights how most work to date in phenomenology on trans experience has to do with matters of body image and bodily aesthetics. Talia Mae Bettcher, "Trans Phenomena," in *50 Concepts for a Critical Phenomenology,* ed. Gail Weiss, Ann Murphy, and Gayle Salamon (Evanston, Ill.: Northwestern University Press, 2020), 329–36.
11. Gayle Salamon, *The Life and Death of Latisha King: A Critical Phenomenology of Transphobia* (New York: New York University Press, 2018).
12. Kimoto, "Merleau-Ponty, Fanon, and Phenomenological Forays."
13. Megan Burke, Martina Ferrari, and Bonnie Mann, "Toward a Femi-

nist Phenomenology of Temporal Harm," *Signs: Journal of Women in Culture and Society* 48, no. 2 (2023): 269–90.

14. Burke, Ferrari, and Mann, "Toward a Feminist Phenomenology," 270.
15. Burke, Ferrari, and Mann, 270.
16. Elizabeth Freeman, *Time Binds: Queer Temporalities, Queer Histories* (Durham, N.C.: Duke University Press, 2010), 3.
17. Freeman, *Time Binds,* 4.
18. Megan Burke, *When Time Warps: The Lived Experience of Gender, Race, and Sexual Violence* (Minneapolis: University of Minnesota Press, 2019).
19. Ellen Samuels, "Six Ways of Looking at Crip Time," *Disability Studies Quarterly* 37, no. 3 (2017): https://dsq-sds.org/article/view/5824/4684.
20. Alison Kafer, *Feminist, Queer, Crip* (Bloomington: Indiana University Press, 2013), 28.
21. María Lugones, "Heterosexualism and the Colonial/Modern Gender System," *Hypatia* 22, no. 1 (2007): 186–209.
22. Lugones, "Heterosexualism and the Colonial/Modern Gender System," 202.
23. Ahmed, *Queer Phenomenology.*
24. Ahmed, 85.
25. Salamon, *Life and Death of Latisha King.*
26. I have made a conscious choice to use the first names of Latisha and Brandon here insofar as both were children at the time of the event.
27. As the documentary *Valentine Road* shows, Latisha's gender is misrecognized even by those who were more empathetic toward her gender nonconformity. *Valentine Road,* directed by Marta Cunningham (Bunim-Murray Productions, 2013).
28. Ken Corbett, *A Murder over a Girl: Justice, Gender, Junior High* (London: Picador Books, 2016), 86.
29. Salamon, *Life and Death of Latisha King,* 23.
30. *Valentine Road.*
31. Andrea J. Pitts, "Commentary on *The Life and Death of Latisha King: A Critical Phenomenology of Transphobia* by Gayle Salamon," *Philosophy Today* 65, no. 4 (2021): 1–7.
32. Pitts, "Commentary," 2.
33. Pitts, 2.
34. Alia Al-Saji, *"Durée,"* in *50 Concepts for a Critical Phenomenology,* 103.
35. Cameron Awkward-Rich, *The Terrible We: Thinking with Trans Maladjustment* (Durham, N.C.: Duke University Press, 2022), 8.
36. As Awkward-Rich importantly notes, "The withholding of rights and personhood from any groups has long been justified through imputations of impairment, incapacity, irrationality, and idiocy" such that disability is a "master trope" that regulates the contours of the category of "human" and thus of the humanizing categories of gender. Awkward-Rich, *Terrible We,* 32.

37. Salamon points out that although racism played some role in Brandon's life and his disposition toward Latisha, a biracial, Black-identified trans girl, it was not discussed during the trial. Salamon herself doesn't offer a critical reckoning of the way the gendered violence Latisha experienced is explicitly racialized violence. Tamsin Kimoto, "What Does (Not) Appear," *GLQ: A Journal of Lesbian and Gay Studies* 26, no. 3 (2020): 614–16; Pitts, "Commentary."

Sylvia Rivera and the Fight against Carceral Medicine

Andrea J. Pitts

In a 2018 interview with *Vice* magazine, Black trans activist Miss Major Griffin-Gracy states: "We used to accept this crap of: *We're not worthy,* and *We shouldn't exist,* like this government is trying to push down our throats. We've got to revolt, and we've got to reclaim who the fuck we are and let these people realize, before they came along, we were honored and worshipped and appreciated and adored."[1] Harkening here to dense histories of gender variance, Miss Major's own biography and political organizing is itself a testimony to the forms of reclamation that she describes in this interview. Miss Major also notes in this interview that she wants trans people to understand that "we have a culture, we have a history, we have a reason to be here."[2]

Following Miss Major's insights, this chapter seeks to continue to locate the contours of such cultures and histories of trans life and futurity. Specifically, within trans of color genealogies we find intergenerational commitments to the flourishing of communities of color within and beyond the constraints of carceral institutions. The philosophical praxis of trans of color activists, including Miss Major, Sylvia Rivera, Marsha P. Johnson, Jennicet Gutiérrez, and others, foregrounds projects to analyze histories of refusal within systems of confinement, as well as stories of resistance to the neoliberal marketing of trans rights as a tactic for the expansion of the carceral state. This chapter focuses on such a project of historiographical reframing, to read the activism of Sylvia Rivera as one such trans of color activist who extended her critique of the carceral state to health-care systems and medicalized forms of confinement. That is, following disability justice critiques, I read Rivera as part of a trans of color genealogy that critiques the ableism of forced systems of confinement across psychiatric, medical, and punishment industries. First, I turn to some framings of prisons and forced confinement that expand the critical scope of prison abolitionist praxis. Then, I turn to Rivera's role in critiquing psychiatric confinement, and last, I examine the role of neoliberal austerity measures in perpetuating carceral logics that harm racialized and disabled communities, and Rivera's responses to such austerity measures.

Trans of Color Genealogies of Abolition and Disability Justice

Turning to Miss Major as a central critic of the prison industrial complex, it may be helpful to understand how abolition projects frame the relationship between prisons, as brick-and-mortar institutions, and the expansiveness of carceral logics as they exist beyond prison walls. Notably, Miss Major describes her relationship with mentor and prison activist Frank "Big Black" Smith, a pivotal organizer and head of insurrectionist security during the 1971 Attica prison uprising, as profoundly shaping her political life. Smith, as one interview with Miss Major states, encouraged her to read Black history and politics while she served time in Clinton Correctional Facility in upstate New York during the early 1970s.[3] Turning briefly to the words of Miss Major's mentor, we find genealogical connections among prison activists to questions that exceed common neoliberal framings of identity-based politics or isolated single-issue demands for rights that obscure the mutual dependencies between forms of state and interpersonal violence. That is, in a 1991 interview, Smith discusses a slogan from the Attica uprising. He states:

> We had a slogan, and it's not rhetoric, that "Attica is all of us." We wasn't talking about escaping, we were talking about conditions. And the conditions that we were speaking about at Attica State Prison is on a national, international and inter-community level. We're talking about the same conditions in

our community as well as what's in prison. Because we came from communities. They're talking about rehabilitation. For what? For the facility? For the institution? You got to be rehabilitated for some other location. And where's that location? Back in our communities. . . . It wasn't just isolated in the prison perspective. That's why we say Attica is all of us, Attica is everything. In order for Attica to change, out here's got to change.[4]

Smith's remarks here offer a core insight regarding the ways in which the conditions inside prisons reflect broader societal conditions outside prisons. That is, his remarks direct our attention to how forms of medical neglect, interpersonal harm, bureaucratic control, forms of surveillance, and toxic living conditions shape the lives of many who are considered "unproductive" or "undeserving" members of society, regardless of their confinement status.

This framing of prisons as shaping forms of social existence both inside and outside prison walls harkens to what Liat Ben-Moshe calls differing "carceral locales." Carceral locales are both forms of enclosure, such as "prisons, jails, psychiatric hospitals, and residential institutions for those with intellectual or developmental disabilities," and the associated rationales, public discourses, and legislative justifications that rely on those systems of enclosure.[5] In this sense, as Michel Foucault asked decades earlier, "Is it surprising that prisons resemble factories, schools, barracks, hospitals, which all resemble prisons?"[6] Ben-Moshe and other abolitionists link the reasons and public discourses of prisons beyond their brick-and-mortar existences. That is, carceral locales attempt to remove people from society and thereby seek to further eliminate unwanted values, behaviors, and beliefs within a given social setting. In this vein, Perry Zurn, similarly detailing discourses of enclosure, argues that gender-segregated spaces like prisons and public restrooms rely on an "eliminative logic" that involves "(1) iterative segregation, which (2) purifies the social center and (3) presumes the reduced or thin relationality of marginal persons."[7] By "thin relationality," Zurn refers to "the eliminative belief that trans people . . . are unrelatable, solitary folks who, while belonging to a highly stereotyped and stylized category of 'the transsexual,' nevertheless have little to no needs to belong either to their own community or to the world at large."[8] Criminality functions in this way, creating beliefs and sensibilities regarding presumably pathological "others," whose confinement and isolation from the world supposedly protects or ameliorates the society from which they've been removed. Yet, Smith's claim that "Attica is all of us" clearly rejects this purification narrative, and his work, alongside that of Miss Major's call to know our histories, attests to the interrelations between trans politics and anticarceral politics.

More specifically, we can find a number of interrelations between prisons and medical industries that themselves remain worthy of critique and refusal. For example, Smith's interviews following the Attica uprising directly document the medical neglect and abuse suffered by prisoners before, during, and after the uprising, including the humiliation and daily forms of violence suffered by people in prisons. Additionally, Miss Major's efforts to address the needs of people with HIV/AIDS in the 1980s and 1990s, including her work as a home health-care worker and with the Tenderloin AIDS Resource Project, demonstrate a keen attention to the lack of health resources affecting trans and queer communities and the patterned stigmas and fears associated with HIV/AIDS.[9] Miss Major also describes her early anticarceral organizing work beginning in San Francisco in the 1990s, after working with legal advocates with the San Francisco Community Health Improvement Plan who were trying to lessen the sentences that trans women who were being targeted as potential sex workers were receiving at the time. Miss Major states in a 2017 interview: "They were giving a girl a sentence of five years if she had more than four bags of condoms in her purse. Really? How stupid is that? Know what I mean, especially in San Francisco! The hell? So justice and fair play, that shit doesn't exist."[10] What these histories of activism from Miss Major and Smith demonstrate are patterned and interconnecting relationships between medical conditions inside and outside prisons. The conditions that Smith decries are pointing to the need to work across prison walls to address systemic shared patterns of violence affecting Black communities, and the Black trans people targeted outside of prisons who Miss Major discusses are being locked up for seeking to address those very same health crises and forms of deathly economic and societal neglect within their communities.

We can thus begin to consider, in response to these important connections, specific dimensions of carceral medicine—which we can distinguish from terms like *correctional health care* or *correctional medicine*. *Carceral medicine* refers, in this chapter, to the co-constituting relations between carceral and medical discourses, such as the overlap between punishment and health discourses, systemic patterns of confinement affecting disabled people, the intertwining assumptions regarding criminality and pathology, conceptions of civic order and social hygiene, eugenics and reproduction practices, and the institutionalization of correctional health care. This last term, *correctional health care,* includes the development, since the mid-1970s, of institutionalized medical care within prisons, jails, and detention facilities in the United States and Canada. However, the carceral dimensions of medicine and the medical dimensions of carceral systems extend much further back historically, including the control of Indigenous peoples and their bodies through residential schools, missions, and other colonial mechanisms of confinement and violence.[11] Such dimensions of carcerality and medicalization also include the reliance of the biomedical and psychiatric sciences on the violated flesh of enslaved Black peoples, which has been examined by authors such as Therí Alyce Pickens, C. Riley Snorton, and Zakiyyah Iman Jackson.[12]

This critique of carceral medicine also exists in conversation with approaches to the medical industrial complex, including disability justice and mad activism, both of which have long implicated the carceral dimensions of psychiatric institutionalization. Such discourses continue to call attention to and condemn the confinement, abuse, sexual violence, forced sterilization, and experimentation conducted on disabled people. Likewise, authors within crip-of-color critique such as Ben-Moshe and Jina B. Kim express the long-extant threads of resistance to the mutually reinforcing relations between systemic racism, ableism, and cisheteronormativity. For example, Kim suggests:

> Rather than reading for evidence of self-ownership or resistance, then, [crip-of-color critique] reads for relations of social, material, and prosthetic support—that is, the various means

through which lives are enriched, enabled, and made possible. In so doing, it honors vulnerability, disability, and inter/dependency, instead of viewing such conditions as evidence of political failure or weakness. A crip-of-color critique thus recognizes and centers the vast networks of support that enable contemporary life. . . . It highlights modes of affirming, organizing, and supporting racialized life in which self-sufficiency no longer registers as an ideal.[13]

In this framing, Kim gestures to the critiques of individual autonomy and self-determination discourses within rights-based liberal discourses and suggests instead that crip-of-color critique strives to honor and sustain the deep vulnerabilities, shared relations, and forms of mutual dependency among racialized and disabled communities.

Trans prison abolitionists likewise pose forms of embodied, aesthetic, and technological interdependencies to reject the atomistic and individualistic beliefs that undergird criminal law and systems of punishment. For example, Morgan Bassichis, Alexander Lee, and Dean Spade, three trans prison abolitionists, collectively reject "pull yourself up by your bootstraps" narratives of agency and social mobilization. Akin to what Kim notes above regarding the need for "the vast networks of support," these author-activists critique government efforts to dismantle "laws and social programs meant to protect people from poverty, violence, sickness, and other harms of capitalism."[14] As they note, policies like the North American Free Trade Agreement and the Personal Responsibility and Work Opportunity Reconciliation Act perpetuate the myth that poverty and unemployment are due to individual failings, and they reject forms of conservative skepticism that consider people who utilize welfare programming as worthy of suspicion and surveillance. In these senses, they likewise suggest that we must "reclaim a radical legacy" of political movements that "have nurtured and guided transformative branches of queer and trans organizings working at the intersections of identities and struggles for collective liberation."[15]

Within such reclamation practices, Leah Lakshmi Piepzna-Samarasinha describes the importance of the framework of disability justice for recognizing the lives of disabled queer and trans people of color. They note that disability justice "gifts me with a sweeping glance at the queer and trans histories I have been taught and that were hidden from me, that have kept me alive, asking me to look at them again and see and know them in a different way that does not erase or 'forget' the disability stories in them."[16] Echoing Miss Major's call "to reclaim who the fuck we are," Piepzna-Samarasinha engages in memory work, calling in disabled, queer, and trans of color organizing and life that has resisted erasure and political suppression. Specifically, they describe a 1992 interview with Sylvia Rivera in which Rivera recounts how her beloved friend and fellow organizer, Marsha P. Johnson, struggled with suicidality, systemic ableism, and the police killing of her partner, Cantrell. Rivera also describes how she and Johnson had both been locked up several times in psychiatric hospitals in New York.

Forced to become familiar with medical and state violence, Johnson and Rivera dedicated theirs lives to affirming queer and trans communities, including as Piepzna-Samarasinha writes, offering a kind of crip kindness. They note:

> When I look . . . at Marsha and Sylvia's refusal of respectability politics, their radical kindness and openness to anyone coming through STAR House—including multiply marginalized street queens and trans women and other trans people, poor and of color, who no doubt were seen as "crazy," "too much," and shunned from other queer communities—I see a kind of "crip kindness" . . . where we are firm in our refusal to throw people away because of our own experiences of madness and being shunned.[17]

Accordingly, as a form of memory work and reclamation, I want to place this legacy of trans crip kindness within the long history of resistance to carceral medicine. In the next section, I turn to Rivera's interviews and public speeches to outline how her work contributes to a politicized response against the mutual entanglement of carcerality and medicalization within crip-of-color genealogies. Notably, her work resonates with Smith's wisdom that "Attica is all of us" and, as Kim describes, that we must attend to the "relations of social, material, and prosthetic support" that make life possible for some and impossible for others. To carry out this analysis, I first turn to her role in a 1970 protest against psychiatric confinement at Bellevue Hospital in New York. Then, in the final section, I turn to Rivera's critiques of neoliberal austerity measures and patterns of criminalization affecting trans of color communities. These analyses thereby seek to place Rivera's activism and its legacy within a critical genealogical strand of trans of color disability and abolitionist organizing.

Against Psychiatric Prisons

Rivera is most often known for her work with STAR, Street Transvestite Action Revolutionaries, and the efforts she and Johnson provided through securing housing, clothing, and food to queer and trans people in New York in the 1970s. However, we can also consider Rivera's legacy as working against the mutual imbrication of medicalization and carcerality. The 1960s to 1990s marks a pivotal period in the history of carceral medicine. This period includes massive upward trends in rates of incarceration, including shifts in sentencing, criminal and immigration law, and policing practices that heightened forms of harassment, abuse, and surveillance affecting Black, brown, and Indigenous communities. During this same period, police squads often raided bars and other businesses frequented by queer and trans patrons and would commonly arrest persons suspected of sex work, a policing tactic that disproportionately targets people of color. Rivera herself notes in a 2001 interview that such raids were common during this era and that she was thrown in jail during this period as well. She states, "If you did not have three pieces of male attire on you, you were going to jail. Just like a butch dyke would have to have three pieces of female clothing, or *he* was going to jail."[18] Rivera's remarks note that she is quite familiar with the hypervisibility and surveillance of trans and queer communities and that carceral forms of control and constraint were attempting to criminalize gender nonconformity in New York at the time.

Also during these decades, however, coalitional struggles formed among a number of antiracist and queer/trans liberation

groups to respond to the conditions of police harassment and societal divestment that communities of color and queer and trans
communities were both experiencing. Rivera notes that one of the
first times STAR marched as a group was in an October 1970 demonstration against police repression organized by the Puerto Rican
activist collective the Young Lords.[19] That protest marched from
East Harlem to the United Nations, demanding an end to the colonization of Puerto Rico. While some of the primary efforts of STAR
were to provide housing, food, and clothing to homeless youth,
the group found solidarity and respect among the Young Lords,
who were also fighting against health-care injustices and police
violence in New York. In this, Rivera and a number of other Puerto
Rican, African American, and Latinx activists were advocating
both for an end to the forms of systemic harm that communities
of color face in the mainland United States and an end to the continued colonial occupation that the United States enforces within
and outside its own territorial borders. Rivera's solidarity with the
Young Lords and with the Black Panther Party, for example, demonstrates a form of radical solidarity taking place at that time, and
on this point, Rivera notes that when she met Huey P. Newton in
Philadelphia in 1971, "he decided we [members of STAR] were part
of the revolution—that we were revolutionary people."[20] Among
such radical groups, the health politics, survival programs, and
critiques of police brutality and surveillance were considered interrelated revolutionary struggles.

Turning to Rivera's early critique of carceral medicine, we can
consider Rivera's participation in an October 1970 demonstration wherein, Rivera—nineteen years old at the time—picketed in
front of Bellevue Hospital. In one photograph, Rivera's sign reads
"Community Control of Bellevue," referring to the public psychiatric hospital affiliated with the New York University School of
Medicine. Rivera is seated next to Bob Kohler, an organizer from
the Gay Liberation Front (GLF), and several other demonstra-
tors who are also holding signs. One demonstrator's sign reads
". . . Prisoners from Bellevue's Auschwitz of Sexist Brainwashing,"
and Kohler's sign states "NYU Robs the World. The People Will
Take NYU." Other photographs from this demonstration include
Marsha P. Johnson, who is also photographed holding a sign that

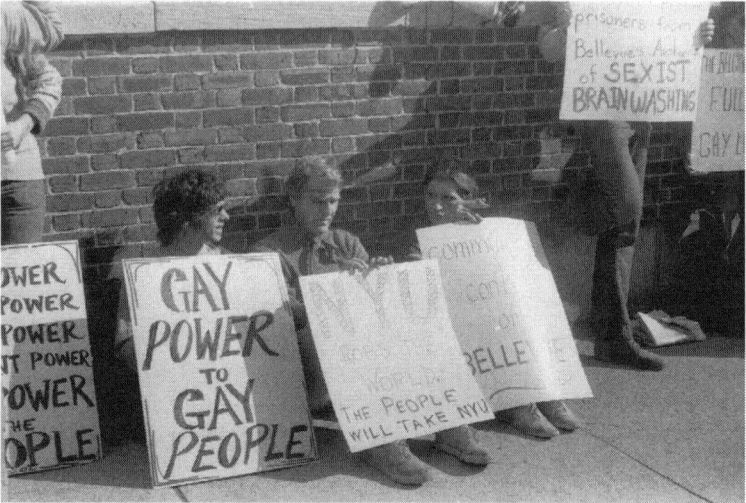

"Sylvia Rivera at Gay Liberation Front's Demonstration at Bellevue Hospital, 1970," Richard C. Wandel Photographs, 217B, LGBT Community Center National History Archive.

reads "Power to the People" in front of the hospital. Here, we find early demonstrations among core members of STAR protesting the confinement of disabled people in Bellevue's psychiatric hospital, a medical institution in which both Rivera and Johnson had been involuntarily committed during their time in New York.

Regarding the demands of that demonstration, a newspaper clipping from the *Village Voice* on October 1, 1970, lists the aims of the protest. The text mentions the Gay Liberation Front and "Street Transvestites for Gay Power," an early name of STAR, as organizers for the event.[21] The clipping announces the following demands held by both the Gay Liberation Front and Street Transvestites for Gay Power:

(1) An end to the oppression of homosexuals and all people in Bellevue Psychiatric Prison—the end of shock treatment, drugs, imprisonment, and mental poisoning.

(2) Free medical care, dental care, and preventive medicine under community control, including free abortions controlled by community women, with no forced abor-

tions and no forced sterilization, without regard to age or obtaining permission from anybody.[22]

Note that the demands listed are certainly considering the confinement of queer and trans people within the psychiatric hospital. However, these demands also extend beyond this specific carceral configuration affecting this specific group of pathologized people. Moving beyond siloed identarian logics, they insist on an end to oppression for "all people" in the "Bellevue Psychiatric Prison." Naming here the unjust confinement of all people forcibly housed in the hospital, Rivera and Johnson's early work with STAR and the Gay Liberation Front appears to directly address involuntary medical confinement.

Ben-Moshe's arguments to abolish psychiatric incarceration build on demands like these articulated in the demonstration organized at the Bellevue protest. Ben-Moshe, informed by political mobilizations of the 1950s, '60s, and '70s, describes abolition of psychiatric incarceration as occurring along three fronts: "abolition as the act and process of closing down psychiatric hospitals; abolition of the rationale for long hospitalization; and last, abolition of psychiatry."[23] These three strategies, taken together, Ben-Moshe provides as a method to link the shared logics of prison abolition and psychiatric deinstitutionalization.[24] That is, the first of these abolitionist goals is to build alternative worlds that do not rely on carceral institutional settings such as "prisons, nursing homes, psychiatric hospitals, residential facilities for those with intellectual and other disabilities" and even the carceral locales that can circulate within our own homes.[25] The second and third strategies focus on the forms of rationalization and justification offered for long-term, involuntary hospitalizations and the field of psychiatry itself. Ben-Moshe specifically turns to the work of influential white academics like Wolf Wolfensberger and Thomas Szasz who "moved the pendulum" regarding psychiatric institutionalization from reform to abolition within public discourses, legal contexts, and political imaginaries.[26] Ben-Moshe notes, for example, that Szasz called on gay liberation activists in the 1970s to denounce psychiatry as a whole.[27] Rather than simply critiquing the psychiatrization of homosexuality alone, as some gay and lesbian reformists proposed, Szasz urged activists to reject models of social change that relied on the view that an approach to "abolition by attrition" (a phrase from Ben-Moshe) would be effective in destabilizing the institutional force and guiding rationales for psychiatry.[28] Ben-Moshe thus considers Szasz's approach as a direct challenge to the idea that abolition can occur via the naming and advocating for the depathologization and removal of one social group from the surveillance and institutional power of psychiatry while not advocating for a critique of psychiatry as a whole. She writes on this point:

> Decarcerating or removing from psychiatry's control by attrition would mean that some populations would be closer to freedom, as in the case of demedicalizing certain conditions such as homosexuality or hysteria, but the system and its power imbalance remains; we are still left with a punitive and vengeance-driven system of capture, only now it does not apply to one population or another.[29]

In this sense, Ben-Moshe points to Szasz's critique as a core concern within both antipsychiatry and antiprison projects. "The problem of chipping at the margins of the system," she states, "is that the center, the logic of incarceration itself as neutral and essentially benign (as long as those incarcerated are healthy and not mistreated), remains intact."[30]

In the demands outlined by the Gay Liberation Front (GLF) and STAR during that October protest of the Bellevue psychiatric hospital, we thus see a variety of responses from the protestors. Some clearly seem to be holding signs that are directly advocating for an end to the pathologization and forced treatment and confinement of queer and trans people directly. The first part of their stated demands listed in the *Village Voice* ("An end to the oppression of homosexuals . . . in Bellevue Psychiatric Prison") names this explicitly. However, the broader scope of their demands ("An end to the oppression of . . . *all people* in Bellevue Psychiatric Prison—the end of shock treatment, drugs, imprisonment, and mental poisoning") appears to reject the "abolition by attrition" model that Ben-Moshe and Szasz critique.[31]

The approach appears to be one much more akin to the forms

of solidarity between disability justice and queer and trans justice projects. For example, Alison Kafer notes that "the inability to value queer lives is related to the inability to imagine disabled lives. Both are failures of the imagination supporting and supported by the drive toward normalcy and normalization."[32] Accordingly, to thread out coalitional spaces among queer, trans, and disability justice projects, Kafer examines differing sites for such political solidarity work, including issues of bathroom access, environmental justice, and reproductive justice. As such, the demand to release all people from the Bellevue psychiatric hospital is an early example of Rivera's long-term collaborations with projects that interweave the lives and futures of disabled, queer, and trans communities.

Likewise, the second demand outlined in the Bellevue demonstration—"Free medical care, dental care, and preventive medicine under community control, including free abortions controlled by community women, with no forced abortions and no forced sterilization, without regard to age or obtaining permission from anybody"—also appears as an important precursor to those expressed by reproductive justice activists today. For example, Loretta J. Ross, a founding activist within the women-of-color–led reproductive justice movement of the 1990s, writes in a coauthored piece with historian Rickie Solinger that the approach "goes beyond the pro-choice/pro-life debate and has three primary principles: (1) the right not to have a child; (2) the right to have a child; and (3) the right to parent children in safe and healthy environments."[33] In this, the demands outlined in the Bellevue protests trace the first two principles, and we can note resonances of the third principle in their call for "free medical care, dental care, and preventive medicine under community control." Living in "safe and healthy environments" was a core demand among organizations such as the Young Lords and the Black Panther Party during the 1960s and 1970s, and both organizations had concerted platforms to address the health care and safety of Black and brown communities in New York at the time.

Writing on Rivera's remarks about the Bellevue protests, Stephen Dillon notes that "to STAR, gay power was antagonistic to police power. . . . STAR warned of the dawn of a new political horizon when queer activists would work with the police, applaud the police, join the police, argue for more police, and demand harsher forms of state power to be enforced by the police. STAR argued that queer desire didn't have to lead back to the racial state."[34] Accordingly, following groups like the Young Lords and others, "community control" for members of STAR such as Rivera and Johnson likely referred more directly to reconfiguring the institutional apparatuses that were coalescing at the time and that were strengthening relationships between carceral control and medical institutions. It is thereby important to note that Rivera's involvement in the NYU protest did not frame the project of gay liberation, as articulated at the time, as one merely of depathologizing homosexuality. The effort to reject depathologization alone was part of a broader set of negotiations in the 1960s and 1970s among LGBT activists. There were, for example, a number of reformist efforts among gay and lesbian activists of this same period, including activists who were working closely with the American Psychiatric Association (APA) to declassify homosexuality as a mental illness.[35] Rejecting the more confrontational and militant aspects of the Gay Liberation Front and other militant antiracist and anti-imperial groups at the time, New York–based groups like Gay Activists Alliance formed to focus on single-issue gay reform goals. Among these goals were reforming the APA's diagnostic categorization of homosexuality via tactics that demanded gay professionalization and an affirmation of the authority of the psychiatric sciences, imploring them to do better science by adhering to the empirical evidence that gays and lesbians were hardworking consumers, just like everyone else.[36] This approach contrasted sharply with groups like the GLF and the Flaming Faggots in New York, who rejected the psychiatric sciences as a tool for LGBT oppression.[37] The GLF, for example, embraced madness as part of their political project and rejected reformist efforts to mainstream and rationalize their demands to a professional medical audience.

Within this milieu, Rivera aligns with the GLF and other militant groups like the Young Lords who are protesting the exploitation and abuse of racialized communities within the medical sciences. Rivera's participation is thus part of a broader call echoing at the time for an end to psychiatric confinement and a demand for community control of and free access to health, dental, and reproductive services, all alongside a critique of police violence. As such, Rivera's remarks and political participation in the NYU protests more closely align antipsychiatry and antipolicing abolitionist projects and thereby serve as critiques of the ongoing carceral and medical intertwinements at the time.

Carceral Medicine and Neoliberal Austerity

Extending beyond Rivera's participation in the NYU protests, we also find commentary in her interviews in which she critiques measures to limit access to health-care resources. Rivera remarks that, by the late 1990s, her work included "[fighting] back against the government" and that "they're cutting back Medicaid, cutting back on medicine for people with AIDS. They want to take away from women on welfare and put them into that little work program. They're going to cut SSI. Now they're taking away food stamps. These people who want the cuts—these people are making millions and millions and millions of dollars as CEOs."[38] In this quote, Rivera offers a prescient critique of neoliberal austerity reforms in which welfare programming began to shift to workfare programming in the 1990s across the United States, the United Kingdom, and elsewhere. Loïc Wacquant describes such a shift as "the downsizing of the social-welfare sector of the state and the concurrent upsizing of its penal arm [as] functionally linked, forming, as it were, the two sides of the same coin of state restructuring in the nether regions of social and urban space in the age of ascending neoliberalism."[39]

In this vein, the increased cutbacks that Rivera points to functioned alongside patterns of carceral expansion in these very decades. Prison populations steadily grew every year from the 1970s onward, while rates of crime fluctuated or even decreased by the mid-1990s. There are a number of reasons that scholars use to explain the prison boom in the United States. Some scholars, such as Ruth Wilson Gilmore, argue that the boom in prison industries resulted from a crisis in the state's capacity to maintain "the formal inequality of capitalism," including the laws, bureaucracies, budgets, taxation, and educational sectors that produce

"primary definitions of social reality."[40] Gilmore states: "The peculiar welfare-warfare, or military Keynesian, state form began to
lose its legitimate ability to manage crisis, and thus to reproduce
itself and endure, at about the time the profit rate started to flatten
and then fall in the mid to late 1960s."[41] The seeming "safety nets"
put into place through welfare programming since the New Deal,
while always stratified across racial lines, began to decline further, and Gilmore notes the rise of workfare programming, which
attempted to solve multiple crises, including labor surpluses, limitations and restrictions regarding access to welfare programming,
and the reinvestment of surplus land and circulation of finance
capital into prison industries. Such programming ties wage labor,
prison labor, and other labor pools with the distribution of social
goods. Such standards, including employment requirements, drug
testing, etc., then justify the denial of housing, health care, and
nutritional resources to populations who are considered irrespon-
sible and thus undeserving of public aid.

Considered through this lens, Rivera's comments likely refer to
the 1996 Personal Responsibility and Work Opportunity Reconciliation Act, which was signed into law by Bill Clinton that year. This
legislation mandated that people had to be employed in order to receive financial, housing, and food assistance and placed limits on
the amount and the timeline of receipt of cash assistance. This program, as many critics agree, has exacerbated conditions of poverty
in the United States. For example, Ben-Moshe notes that the "deci-
mation of the social safety net" and increased austerity measures
are manifestations of neoliberal economic and social reforms that,
in part, explain the emergence of mass incarceration and continue
to offer dividing forms of state inclusion and exclusion that harm
disabled queer and trans people of color.[42]

Additionally, we could likewise consider Rivera's work later in
life coordinating a food pantry at the Metropolitan Community
Church of New York, as well as her lifelong commitment to housing
politics through STAR, the Transy House Collective in Brooklyn,
and her work at the queer homeless encampments near the Hudson
River, as directly responsive to the forms of governmental limita-
tion and denials of social support for queer and trans communities. For example, Transy House Collective operated from 1995

to 2008 and provided housing as well as financial assistance and counseling services to transgender youth.[43]

However, recalling only these service-oriented aspects of Rivera's life also risks, as Lawrence La Fountain-Stokes notes, "sanitiz[ing] her legacy."[44] Importantly, to interpret Rivera's activism against carceral medicine, we must also emphasize her efforts to legitimize and analyze the politics of sex work. In this sense, La Fountain-Stokes and trans activist, filmmaker, and writer Tourmaline offer important documentary, scholarly, and artistic works that frame Rivera's legacy within the context of discussions of sex work and trans politics. Such a call underscores that Rivera's experiences with sex work began when she was very young, and she describes her own experiences of "turning tricks with my uncle for money" before age ten. At ten years old in the early 1960s, she left home to "live and hustle" in Times Square, where she was "adopted" by several older Puerto Rican drag queens.[45] She also engaged in sex work at various points throughout her life, including as a means to pay rent at STAR House. Notably, Rivera criticizes a romanticized view of sex work wherein one might highlight agential possibilities within this form of labor for trans people while obscuring the risks of criminalization and violence that often accompany sex work as survival work.

In this regard, La Fountain-Stokes points to Rivera's critiques of sex work as being the only employment option for trans women of color. Rivera states:

> Everybody thinks that we want to be out on them street corners. No we do not. We don't want to be out there sucking dick and getting fucked up the ass. But that's the only alternative that we have to survive because the laws do not give us the right to go and get a job the way we feel comfortable. I do not want to go to work looking like a man when I know I am not a man. I have been this way since before I left home and I have been on my own since the age of ten.[46]

La Fountain-Stokes thus reminds scholars and activists invested in Rivera's legacy to remember the importance of her activism and support for sex workers. Adding to such points, Michelle O'Brien notes that sex work serves as one of the "major sites of class struggle for trans women of colour. . . . Sex work and nightlife entertainment financially sustained strata of otherwise socially marginal trans women of colour. Though they were almost entirely excluded from wage labour and were largely unable to access urban social welfare programmes, Black and Latinx queer and trans communities were able to build out extensive networks of mutual aid practices."[47] O'Brien then lists the work of Rivera and Johnson as participating in such radical forms of community organizing among sex workers.

Additionally, Nat Raha describes the organization of STAR House as reconfiguring forms of kinship and community that address the systemic forms of vulnerability and harm that queer and trans youth of color confront. Raha writes:

> STAR House functioned with a division of labour: the older group members selling sex to shield the younger queens from the dangers of working on the street, while the younger queens "liberated food." . . . STAR asserted that the lives of street queens of colour who were sex workers were valuable, in need of support, and worth protecting and nourishing, serving as a lasting testament to the value of acting for one another in solidarity.[48]

When read through these interpretations, Rivera's organizing strategies point to the need for basic material resources, such as housing and food, but also to the need for forms of kinship, joy, and spiritual uplift among queer and trans of color communities. For example, on this latter point regarding spiritual aspects of Rivera's politics, Martin Duberman writes of STAR House:

> Before everyone went out in the evening, [Rivera] "worked with the saints." Devoted from childhood to Santería, and convinced that St. Barbara was the patron saint of gay Hispanics, Sylvia set up an altar, complete with incense and candles, around which everyone would gather and "pay tribute" before they left the house.[49]

In these ways, Rivera's legacy and activism operate outside of notions of respectability politics and assimilationist strategies and actively work against a necessarily secular approach to political organizing.

Recalling the aforementioned remarks of Kim and Piepzna-Samarasinha, Rivera's framing of crip kindness builds mutual networks of solidarity, support, and kinship among disabled communities of color. Accordingly, as Kim likewise reminds us regarding the threats of individualism, we can view Rivera's work as functioning against the medicalization of trans health and mainstream rights-based approaches that seek to fold trans life and futurity into existing institutional structures. Such liberal and neoliberal inclusionist tactics often remain antithetical to the many possible trans futures that Rivera's work has opened and that, as La Fountain-Stokes notes, many scholars and activists continue to address today.[50] For example, trans health programs that do not address the criminalization of sex work or the forms of systemic labor injustices that affect trans of color communities run the risk of perpetuating the very harms against which Rivera fought.

Through these interpretive resources, Rivera's legacy remains attuned to issues of societal divestment, institutionalization, structural poverty, and incarceration, interlocking conditions that shape the mutual entwinement of penal and medical institutions today. As Miss Major, Smith, Johnson, and Rivera all insisted, carcerality shapes the institutions and communities we live in, both inside and out. My hope is, then, that by turning to this history and understanding how queer and trans of color people have resisted patterned carceral and medical entwinements, we can begin the reclamation work to honor their legacies and thereby allow them to continue to shape our collective work ahead.

Notes

1. Miss Major Griffin-Gracy, "Trans Icon Miss Major: 'We've Got to Reclaim Who the Fuck We Are,'" interview by Zackary Drucker, *Vice*, November 21, 2018.
2. Griffin-Gracy, "Trans Icon Miss Major."
3. Miss Major Griffin-Gracy, "'Nothing Is Set in Stone': Miss Major Reflects on the Significance of the Stonewall Riots," interview by Andy Wright, Medium, September 22, 2015, https://medium.com/gender-2-0/nothing-is-set-in-stone-68093f328e93.
4. Frank Smith, "Attica Is All of Us," *Agenda* 6, no. 7 (1991): 5.
5. Liat Ben-Moshe, *Decarcerating Disability: Deinstitutionalization and Prison Abolition* (Minneapolis: University of Minnesota Press, 2020), 1–2.

6. Michel Foucault, *Discipline and Punish: The Birth of the Prison,* trans. Alan Sheridan (New York: Vintage Books, 1995), 228.

7. Perry Zurn, "Waste Culture and Isolation: Prisons, Toilets, and Gender Segregation," *Hypatia* 34, no. 4 (2019): 677.

8. Zurn, "Waste Culture and Isolation," 681.

9. Miss Major Griffin-Gracy, "Interview Transcript #054: Miss Major Griffin-Gracy," interview A. J. Lewis, December 16, 2017, *NYC Trans Oral History Project,* 32, available at https://nyctransoralhistory.org /content/uploads/2021/11/NYC-TOHP-Transcript-054-Miss-Major -Griffin-Gracy_UPDATED.pdf.

10. Griffin-Gracy, "Interview Transcript #054," 33.

11. See, for example, Maureen Lux, *Separate Beds: A History of Indian Hospitals in Canada, 1920s-1980s* (Toronto: University of Toronto Press, 2016); Charles Sepulveda, "To Decolonize Indigenous Lands, We Must Also Abolish Police and Prisons," *Truthout,* October 13, 2020, https://truthout .org/articles/to-decolonize-indigenous-lands-we-must-also-abolish -police-and-prisons/.

12. See Terrí Alyce Pickens, *Black Madness :: Mad Blackness* (Durham, N.C.: Duke University Press, 2019); C. Riley Snorton, *Black on Both Sides: A Racial History of Trans Identity* (Minneapolis: University of Minnesota Press, 2017); Zakiyyah Iman Jackson, *Becoming Human: Matter and Meaning in an Antiblack World* (New York: New York University Press, 2020).

13. Jina B. Kim, "Toward a Crip-of-Color Critique: Thinking with Minich's 'Enabling Whom?,'" *Lateral: Journal of the Cultural Studies Association* 6, no. 1 (2017): 2.

14. Morgan Bassichis, Alexander Lee, and Dean Spade, "Building an Abolitionist Trans and Queer Movement with Everything We've Got," in *Captive Genders: Trans Embodiment and the Prison Industrial Complex,* ed. Eric A. Stanley and Nat Smith (Oakland, Calif.: AK Press, 2011), 20.

15. Bassichis, Lee, and Spade, "Building an Abolitionist Trans and Queer Movement," 29.

16. Leah Lakshmi Piepzna-Samarasinha, "Disability Justice/Stonewall's Legacy, or Love Mad Trans Black Women When They Are Alive and Dead, Let Their Revolutions Teach Your Resistance All the Time," *QED: A Journal in GLBTQ Worldmaking* 6, no. 2 (2019): 57.

17. Piepzna-Samarasinha, "Disability Justice/Stonewall's Legacy," 59.

18. Sylvia Rivera, *Street Transvestite Action Revolutionaries: Survival, Revolt, and Queer Antagonist Struggle* (n.p.: Untorelli Press, 2013), 32.

19. Sylvia Rivera, "I'm Glad I Was in the Stonewall Riot," in *Trans Liberation: Beyond Pink or Blue,* ed. Leslie Feinberg (Boston: Beacon Press, 1998), 108.

20. Rivera, "I'm Glad I Was in the Stonewall Riot," 108.

21. "Scenes," *Village Voice,* October 1, 1970.

22. "Scenes."

23. Ben-Moshe, *Decarcerating Disability,* 20.

24. Ben-Moshe, 21.
25. Ben-Moshe, 23.
26. Ben-Moshe, 32. See also Thomas Szasz, *Liberation by Oppression: A Comparative Study of Slavery and Psychiatry* (Piscataway, N.J.: Transaction, 2003); Thomas Szasz, *The Myth of Mental Illness: Foundations of a Theory of Personal Conduct* (New York: Harper Perennial, 1974).
27. Ben-Moshe, 97.
28. Ben-Moshe, 97–98.
29. Ben-Moshe, 98.
30. Ben-Moshe, 264.
31. "Scenes," emphasis added.
32. Alison Kafer, *Feminist, Queer, Crip* (Bloomington: Indiana University Press, 2013), 45.
33. Loretta J. Ross and Rickie Solinger, *Reproductive Justice: An Introduction* (Oakland: University of California Press, 2017), 9.
34. Stephen Dillon, *Fugitive Life: The Queer Politics of the Prison State* (Durham, N.C.: Duke University Press, 2018), 120.
35. See Abram Lewis, "'We Are Certain of Our Own Insanity': Antipsychiatry and the Gay Liberation Movement, 1968–1980," *Journal of the History of Sexuality* 25, no. 1 (2016): 83–113.
36. Lewis, "'We Are Certain of Our Own Insanity,'" 94.
37. Lewis, 101.
38. Rivera, "I'm Glad I Was in the Stonewall Riot," 108–9.
39. Loïc Wacquant, *Punishing the Poor: The Neoliberal Government of Social Insecurity* (Durham, N.C.: Duke University Press, 2009), 43.
40. Ruth Wilson Gilmore, *Golden Gulag: Prisons, Surplus, Crisis, and Opposition in Globalizing California* (Oakland: University of California Press, 2007), 78.
41. Gilmore, *Golden Gulag,* 79.
42. Ben-Moshe, *Decarcerating Disability,* 11.
43. See Michael Bronski, "Sylvia Rivera: 1951–2002," *Z Magazine,* April 1, 2002.
44. Lawrence La Fountain-Stokes, "The Life and Times of Trans Activist Sylvia Rivera," in *Critical Dialogues in Latinx Studies: A Reader,* ed. Ana Y. Ramos-Zayas and Mérida M. Rúa (New York: New York University Press, 2021), 249.
45. Lawrence La Fountain-Stokes, *Translocas: The Politics of Puerto Rican Drag and Trans Performance* (Ann Arbor: University of Michigan Press, 2021), 99.
46. Sylvia Rivera, "Sylvia Rivera's Talk at LGMNY, June 2001, Lesbian and Gay Community Services Center, New York City," *Centro: Journal of the Center for Puerto Rican Studies* 19, no. 1 (2007): 121.
47. Michelle O'Brien, "Trans Work: Employment Trajectories, Labour Discipline and Gender Freedom," in *Transgender Marxism,* ed. Jules Joanne Gleeson and Elle O'Rourke (London: Pluto Press, 2021), 56.

48. Nat Raha, "A Queer Marxist [Trans]feminism: Queer and Trans Social Reproduction," in *Transgender Marxism,* 104.

49. Martin Duberman, *Stonewall* (New York: Plume, 1994), 253.

50. La Fountain-Stokes, "Life and Times of Trans Activist Sylvia Rivera," 249.

tRacing Face
A Racial Genealogy of Beauty
Tamsin Kimoto

Fuckably Me

The primary claim animating this essay is that a medicalized aesthetics of gender, in this case femininity, is also necessarily a racial aesthetics. I claim that this is so because of how the underlying norms surrounding femininity and beauty, which are implicitly white norms under white supremacy, are understood as achievable through the altering of facial bone structure. Given the role skulls in particular played in the development of our racial categories, these procedures inevitably end up reproducing ideals of beauty as whiteness. First, I consider the various literatures on facial feminization surgery (FFS) very briefly in order to highlight certain key features of them and to contrast them with a political aesthetics informed by trans feminisms of color. Next, I look back at the history of racial science through the work of Johann Friedrich Blumenbach to highlight the role of aesthetics in constructing a concept of race and the ongoing work that beauty does in constructing categories of identity. Finally, I consider how we might think expansively about what Talia Mae Bettcher calls "reality enforcement" as a racializing and gendering phenomenon in light of a somatechnics of beauty.

Before I begin my argument, however, I wanted to take a moment to reflect on what brought me to this topic. There are two reasons beauty was on my mind. Like so many things, it started with Tinder. I am the kind of trans person who makes sure it's crystal clear that we both understand I am trans before we ever meet in person; I am, after all, not trying to die. Despite including that information in my profile, it nevertheless catches a number of people off guard. One such person, we'll call him Z, responded, "I legit didn't realize that . . . well I gotta say they did a damn good job!" This, along with a number of other such interactions, really began my interest in thinking about fuckability but also about what it means to be read as gendered in certain ways under prevailing conditions of white cisheteropatriarchy. These kinds of responses demonstrate certain underlying assumptions about the aesthetics of gender that I want to explore more here. Importantly, Z points to his belief that the only way I could have become fuckable enough to swipe right on is through medical intervention.

At the same time, I happened to have been doing some digging through my family's genealogy and came across my great-great-grandmother, Shige, who immigrated to Hawai'i in the early twentieth century. She was more than a decade younger than my great-great-grandfather and very likely immigrated as one of the early picture brides.[1] While our experiences with it are undoubtedly quite different, photography is a central site in which both Shige and I encounter assessing gazes that determine value and desirability on the basis of determinations of physical beauty (along with perhaps a few other details). Indeed, while the racial norms we encounter in this assessment are somewhat different, they are not entirely discontinuous with one another, and this is partly what primed me for a consideration of how our faces have played significant roles in the courses our lives have taken.

The Literatures on Facial Feminization Surgery

There are three relevant sets of literature we can point to when thinking about what it might mean to "review the literature" on FFS. The first includes the literature created by transfeminine people seeking FFS or those who've already had FFS reporting on their experiences. This archive exists across discussion forums, qualitative research on FFS, and anecdotal accounts from trans people. There's so much material—too much to cover here—but what I want to highlight is the way in which FFS is framed as a necessary but not sufficient procedure for achieving an ideal of beauty by some transfeminine people. Forums are filled with examples of people referring to procedures as "necessary" for feminization. Susan's Place user EmilyMK03 writes in response to another person's complaint about complications with their recovery, "There are some surgical procedures that are truly necessary to feminize a face (brow bossing removal and trachea shave, for example). . . . But you have to think really hard before the surgery about what you want done to feminize your face, versus what you want done to look more beautiful."[2] What I want to draw our attention to here is how femininity and beauty are both linked to and delinked from one another; what is necessary to achieve an ideal of femininity is framed as potentially part of a process of becoming beautiful and simultaneously as a distinct concern. The mere fact of being read as feminine is not yet sufficient to be beautiful.[3]

The second set of literature we might consider is the practical literature—the work done by plastic surgeons that largely focuses on discussions of technique and outcome. Surgeons working in this vein report the structure of male and female faces as given; for example, a "state of the art" overview of FFS notes that "male chins are often long, square and angulated as opposed to female chins, which are shorter, narrower and more pointed."[4] Other surgeons note the increasing importance placed on FFS: "Facial feminization is a key element in the treatment of gender dysphoria and . . . it can be more important from the patient's psychological point of view, in terms of their psychosocial adaptation, than the sexual reassignment itself, which is related more to the patient's personal life."[5] Beauty is rarely directly mentioned in these kinds of entries—though it's not entirely absent and is often framed in much the way EmilyMK03 does. Instead, the emphasis tends to be on identifying what are the objective parameters of feminine versus masculine faces.[6] This set of texts is replete with discussions of surgical alterations, both minor and major, that allow a physician to alter one's "facial gender." Key here, then, is the assumption of not just the objectivity of masculine and feminine facial features but also an investment in the plasticity of the face as radically informed by these inflexible standards.

We can find this question of beauty throughout the archive of plastic surgery, and this in turn points us to the influence of physical anthropology on the development of modern plastic surgery. For example, many of the terms that more recent plastic surgeons use were developed in the early twentieth century by surgeons explicitly drawing from the work of physical anthropologists detailing the bone structure of human skulls.[7] In even this early literature, race is often featured as part of the discussion, given how the variation among skulls has been used to track and develop categories of race thanks to the legacy of Johann Friedrich Blumenbach (whom I'll discuss later).[8] This variation comes with a recognition that certain features are aesthetically pleasing relative to race with, however, the tacit or even explicit understanding that features coded as European are the most pleasing.

The final body of literature is what I'll refer to here as the critical literature on FFS. This includes people working in both trans studies and science and technology studies who put the topic of FFS into conversation with broader sociopolitical dynamics. While there are a number of people writing in this area, I'll focus here on the work of Eric Plemons. In *The Look of a Woman,* Plemons argues that FFS is a "project of ontological invention" in which what is at stake is "changing the patient from an unrecognizable woman into a recognizable woman."[9] Central to the claim is the idea that gender exists in the act of being recognized as gendered in a particular way. Part of what interests me in all three of these bodies of literature is how race does or does not figure into the overall conversation. Race often appears much more in terms of how it is absented from the conversation. In the case of Plemons's work, race appears briefly but is not really thematized. He notes that norms of femininity and masculinity are clearly entangled with race in the opening pages of the book, but then the topic largely vanishes from view. Indeed, he later wrote an article that attempts to address this problem, but here the focus is on "ethnicity" rather than race, and two of the three examples are of European faces.[10] If the aim is to demonstrate how whiteness is an implicit principle guiding the practice of FFS, then I think we need a clearer account of how it is that race, science, and aesthetics are bound up with one another. The danger otherwise is that an account of "ethnic" features seems to more or less level the racialized field in which transfeminine people live our lives. Furthermore, it elides the specific precarities that transfeminine people of color face by decentering the threat of violence.

Lurking throughout these literatures is the notion of facial gender. Facial gender, of course, tracks beliefs about the legibility of gender through facial morphology. It is therefore yet another way of thinking through how concepts of sex and gender are thoroughly intertwined. In addition to plastic surgery journals, one might find the notion explicitly referenced in literature on algorithmic facial recognition technologies. In a critical review of the field, Os Keyes notes how both the technologies themselves and the academic and industry discussions of the technologies often fail to incorporate any kind of trans analysis that might complicate how gender is being written into algorithmic recognition.[11] The irony that a similar failure occurs in academic and industry conversation of surgical interventions aimed at trans audiences is palpable.

In a wide-ranging interview with *Vice*, Miss Major Griffin-Gracy is asked about the first trans person she ever saw and responds, "I don't remember her name, but I remember her look. I was 12, and I ran into her in Chicago on the elevator train."[12] The young Miss Major goes on to befriend this woman, who eventually asks her if she's a "little sissy" too. Miss Major also points to tensions within trans communities and spaces between those who seek medical interventions and those who don't, which she attributes to an erosion of solidarity among trans people as some are able to gain provisional acceptance through, among other things, inhabiting the terms of beauty as a racialized cis norm. Striving to fit into these norms of beauty might be another way of bolstering wrong-body models. The wrong-body model of trans identity—the idea that trans people are essentially people who are trapped in bodies that do not align with their genders—has a particular and enduring hold on the public imaginary around trans people.[13] Such a model centralizes the phenomena of medical transition through both hormonal and surgical intervention in ways that delegitimize and obscure the lives of the many trans people who do not or cannot seek out such changes. The right body, as my thwarted Tinder connection indicates, is the desirable body that must only be achievable through these interventions.

I can't help but wonder how many of us have similar experiences of seeing another trans person and feeling the kind of pull Miss Major describes. A pull that is animated in part by the clockability of the person in front of us—that is, our ability to perceive them as trans. Clockability runs counter to the prevailing norms of trans assimilation through embracing racial norms of beauty. Being clockable certainly isn't without risk; getting clocked is often a prelude to violence if it happens in the wrong time and place. At the same time, given the right set of conditions, clocking is an occasion for communal recognition and reciprocity and the generation of the pull Miss Major describes. I am not advocating for a position that demands that we stop seeking out plastic surgery like FFS; however, it does seem necessary for us to interrogate what we lose when we become unclockable. Given the racial logics underlying procedures like FFS as it is commonly practiced, we may lose the variety of possible trans beauties afforded by trans of color faces. That kind of narrowing of our aesthetic sensibility might also hasten the erosion of lines of solidarity between trans people and limit our capacities for the kinds of world-making that have enabled trans of color lives to endure and flourish. A genuinely trans of color aesthetics, then, might be one that is rooted in the political histories and wills of the sissies Miss Major describes.[14]

Skulls, Race, and the Coloniality of Beauty

Philosophers and historians who work on the notion of racial science tend to emphasize the constitutive role of Immanuel Kant in developing our modern racial categories as biological categories.[15] At least among philosophers, however, this is often treated as the end of a discussion about the origins of racial science such that other figures recede into the background or do not appear at all as part of the conversation. I want to turn our attention to one such figure who is more widely discussed outside of the philosophical literature on race. I'm not interested here in the fight over who actually invented the modern concept of race or whose views are the most influential. Instead, I want to focus on how Blumenbach went about developing the five race categories. Unlike Kant, who relied largely on travel narratives, Blumenbach used measurements and analyses of human skulls in order to develop his own account.[16] The five categories Blumenbach developed are largely intact today. His account includes measures of bone structure and the prominence of varying facial features in order to differentiate the categories from one another; for example, he notes that the skulls of some North American Indigenous people present "some similarity to the skull of a dog." While scholars are quick to note that Blumenbach did not link race to mental or moral capacity in the way Kant did, lines like this recur throughout his writings, and his work is still explicitly invested in a colonial project.

This is perhaps nowhere more apparent than in his assessment of Caucasian skulls. He notes that he calls them "Caucasian" because that region "produces the most beautiful race of men. . . . That stock displays, as we have seen, the most beautiful form of the skull," and therefore functions for him as the mean from which the two extremes (the Mongolian, or yellow, and the Ethiopian, or black, types) diverge. Here, beauty is an explicit part of how Blumenbach is developing the very categories of race as he measures the skulls in his collection. The most beautiful skull belongs to whiteness, and the other four categories are measured by their distance from that beautiful skull. In the very same moment that racial science is being developed, then, a racial aesthetics also emerges. Though moral and cognitive ability may not mark the differences between the races for Blumenbach, beauty certainly does. Insofar as the ordering principle is beauty, and beauty across the sexes in the case of the Georgian skull that is the most beautiful, beauty and race are ossified together as both are able to be read from an examination of a skull.

Beauty, then, is part of what María Lugones calls the "colonial/modern gender system." In her essay "Heterosexualism and the Colonial/Modern Gender System," Lugones takes to task what she sees as thinkers of colonialism's uncritical naturalization of gender. She looks particularly at the work of Aníbal Quijano, whose discussion of gender, she notes, looks entirely to the political economy of a supposedly biological sex.[17] Lugones points to the fact that Quijano assumes that gender relations prior to colonization were virtually identical to gender relations under the coloniality of power; we can see this when he says that race has replaced gender as the most effective and enduring form of social domination.[18] This depends not only on the belief that men have always subordinated women across cultural differences but also, Lugones argues, on strict assumptions about heterosexuality and a rigid conception of the gender binary as demanded by early modern sciences. These beliefs, however, are as much the effects of the coloniality of power as the ideology of race that Quijano himself addresses. The sexual otherness, real or imagined, of the non-European others encountered and dominated in the process of colonialism was also a condition on which coloniality/modernity developed. Part of the very structure, then, of colonialism is the imposition of Eurocentric conceptions of gender that subordinate women to men and work to eliminate entirely those who do not fall neatly into either category. Using Quijano's own understanding of the structural axis, Lugones demonstrates that gender and sexuality, as well as class and race, are structural axes of coloniality/modernity in such a way that they cannot be neatly separated from one another in the way that Quijano's project, or the work of white feminists, might tacitly suggest.[19]

What I want to suggest here in conversation with Lugones is that the development of physical beauty as whiteness is part of this process and becomes a measure by which non-European others are evaluated. One way we can see this in the present is by considering the popularity of eyelid modification surgeries among East Asians such that there is a surgical procedure referred to as "Asian blepharoplasty" or "double eyelid surgery." This procedure aims to transform the eyelid of a patient from what's referred to as a "monolid" to an eyelid shape that appears more like the eyelids of Europeans.[20] While people who seek out the surgery report a number of reasons for doing so, a desire to improve oneself or a response to external pressure are both frequently cited.[21] In either case, the desire is to shift one's face toward a more Eurocentric standard of beauty that aligns with how global beauty industries have reinforced Blumenbach's formulation of whiteness as the center of beauty. Beauty, then, is a rich site for thinking through the structural axes of the colonial/modern gender system.

One way to think through this is to attend to one of the poles of Blumenbach's racial categories. The yellow, or Mongolian, race constitutes one-half of the ugliest races. In an analysis of the history of Down syndrome, Mel Y. Chen turns our attention to this pole by noting that the original diagnosis for the condition labeled it "mongoloid idiocy."[22] The racialized term would persist in the popular imaginary such that one can find it being used as a slur against disabled people well after its nineteenth-century repurposing. Race and disability are articulated together in the history of Down syndrome and remain tethered together through both the popular usage of the term *mongoloid* and its continued use in physical anthropology and medicine. They also notably remain tied through how blepharoplasty and epicanthoplasty are figured as a kind of treatment-cum-management for both. As supposed treatment, such surgeries aim to bring a face into a resemblance of the presumptively normal (white, nondisabled). The interplays of race, disability, and aesthetics embedded in the developments of these techniques also signal to us the role of profitability in beautification as a response to racism and ableism. Meeta Rani Jha describes these sorts of processes as "beauty capitalism" in order to highlight how global flows of capital intersect with race, gender, and sexuality in the proliferation of industries devoted to beautification.[23] While Jha's focus is not on disability, Chen's history of Down syndrome brings this into sharp relief. The potential influence of Blumenbach's typology in the naming of Down syndrome and the ongoing entanglements of them in modern plastic surgery matters precisely because of how enmeshed the histories of transness and disability have been. As Cameron Awkward-Rich argues, disability and madness haunt transness.[24]

Reality Enforcement and the Somatechnics of Beauty

It's worth noting that much of what opens women of color, as well as white trans women, to the kinds of violent assessment embedded in reality enforcement is the occasionally implicit but often explicit claim that we are ugly. Ugliness has an ugly history, of course. In her work on staring, for example, Rosemarie Garland-Thomson notes how ugliness often serves as a structure governing access to the realm of public life both literally in the case of the so-called ugly laws and implicitly through the kind of force that repeated stares bear on us.[25] Being an "ugly" woman, then, is a risk because of how it can expose us to the possibility of violence.

Hewing closer to normative standards of beauty potentially offers a kind of refuge, then, for transfeminine people. Features marked as deeply racialized, such as hair texture or eye shape, have been the sites of a great deal of discourse both decrying and defending their relative beauty. Laverne Cox notes in her discussions of FFS that, for transfeminine people of color, we risk distorting precisely those features that mark us as raced in particular ways. And, of course, for trans femmes of color, beauty brings with it the possibilities of what Asian American feminists refer to as "racial abstraction" or "ornamentalization," processes by which (in)human objects of desire are drained of any semblance of subjectivity or even life in order to appease the aesthetic appetites of the presumptively white audience consuming them.[26] Beauty as possible guarantor of survival works ironically by severely restricting the boundaries of that life.

Talia Mae Bettcher describes reality enforcement as "the basic type of transphobia grounding the deceiver representation."[27] The "deceiver representation" refers to the notion that trans people, under conditions of cisnormativity, are always figured as engaging in a kind of deceptive practice due to the ways in which our gendered presentation is construed as misaligning with a sexed reality. Bettcher frames reality enforcement as an explicitly transphobic phenomenon due to the role of the deceiver representation and especially because it often manifests through what she calls "genital verification," a kind of violence that takes a number of forms up to and including the murder of the trans person whose genitals are verified. Bettcher also notes, however, that this does not mean that trans people who have had gender-affirming surgical procedures are exempt from genital verification; indeed, the form it takes instead is to articulate one's genitals as unnatural in contrast to the supposedly natural genitals of cis people.

Bettcher rightfully notes that the most violent forms of reality enforcement tend to affect those who are multiply oppressed: "Since reality enforcement can be understood as a form of violence that cuts across racial, class, and gender differences differently, we can talk of a form of violence that cannot be reduced to sexism, racism, or classism while at the same time being fundamentally interwoven with all three."[28] While I don't necessarily disagree with Bettcher, I do wonder if we should understand reality enforcement as a strictly transphobic phenomenon. In his discussion of Carlett Brown and Ava Betty Brown, C. Riley Snorton points to the ways in which both Browns were, irrespective of their own particular histories, cast as mimetic repetitions of Christine Jorgensen.[29] This mimetic recasting reflects broader discourses of femininity and womanhood, though, in which nonwhite, and especially Black, cis women are also figured as mimetic reproductions of an idealized white cis woman. We can think here of the histories of gender and genital verification embedded within the developments of racial science, like Sarah Baartman, as well as a variety of contemporary phenomena like the case of Caster Semenya or TERFs attacking Asian cis women runners online.[30] Reality enforcement, understood more broadly, might help us link how Eurocentric discourses of gender necessarily figure all nonwhite and noncis people as mimicries of European prototypes—that is, to think about how theories of racial degeneration, like those put forth by Blumenbach, might also inform how it is that we think and do gender—and such an expanded notion might allow us to do so without collapsing gender or race into one another.

For trans women living under the threat of trans panic, this presents the following situation: one must present in ways that read as woman in all situations in order to avoid a particular sort of scrutiny that might reveal a sexed body that supposedly misaligns with one's gender presentation. This is a kind of experience of the figure/ground relationship. What makes an object figure as opposed to ground is the extent to which it is attended to by the perceiver. For many trans women, then, one's ability to present successfully as a woman can be read as an attempt to remain ground in the perceptual experiences of heterosexual men or to present as figure in a certain way; both of these are strategies to avoid being subject to the transphobic violence that trans panic makes possible. This kind of hypervigilance, both of one's own bodily habit and of the possibility of being exposed to a particular sort of violence, directly affects the ways in which trans women experience the world and their possibilities in it. At the same time, even the most well-disciplined bodily habits do not guarantee that one will still be safe from transphobic violence. Because heteropatriarchy means, at least in part, that men attracted to women experience all women as available to them, presenting as a woman means opening oneself up to the possibility of sexual violence. However, for a trans woman, this presents the added danger that one will be outed as a trans woman and be subject to a different sort of violence, and it will be one that is supposedly legitimated by trans panic. For trans women, then, the world presents itself as always potentially violent regardless of whether one successfully presents as a woman according to cisnormative standards.

Throughout these experiences, we have the very real politics surrounding beauty and ugliness and how they shape our life possibilities. If we read reality enforcement through the lens of aesthetic judgments of desirability, then we start to see how the demand to move toward more normative standards of beauty can be coercively taken up as a project. In her *New York Times* opinion piece, Andrea Long Chu calls our attention to what is an often-familiar feeling for many trans women. In response to her girlfriend calling her beautiful, Chu notes that she, of course, doesn't believe her partner because she "has eyes."[31] This particular performance of a kind of expected trans misery calls our attention to how we might come to see ourselves this way. Of course we don't all see ourselves this way, but it does provide an interesting lens for how to think through the problem of dysphoria.

What I'm suggesting here is that we might think through dysphoria in at least some instances as a question of perceiving oneself as ugly and therefore as a kind of misfitting, to pull again on the entanglements of trans and disability histories, into a given gender category.[32] In order to begin thinking through the function of self-perception in beauty and its relation to gender, we might revisit Simone de Beauvoir's famous "One is not born, but rather becomes, a woman."[33] Though the body has a preeminent place in Beauvoir's thought, precisely because "the world appears different to us dependent on how it [the body] is grasped," she importantly rejects any sort of determinism about how it is that the body structures our subjectivities.[34] "The female," Beauvoir writes, "is a woman, insofar as she feels herself as such. Some essential biological givens are not part of her lived situation. . . . Nature does not define woman: it is she who defines herself by reclaiming nature for herself in her affectivity."[35] Regardless of the conceptual sleight of hand here in claiming that "biological givens" do not play a role in woman's lived situation while also relying upon the "female," I think we can begin to appreciate the reasons why Beauvoir's arguments resonate with Laverne Cox and other trans persons. In her criticisms of biological determinism, Beauvoir has perhaps unintentionally opened the door for thinking through the peculiarities of trans embodiments in light of prevailing conditions of cisnormativity.

While emphasizing the role of self-perception, Beauvoir also points to the ways in which such an understanding is radically shaped by the background conditions of patriarchy.[36] Background conditions of patriarchy, and the supposed biological truths they construct and the myths and histories they build, make it impossible for women to see themselves in ways that are not conditioned by these, but, for Beauvoir, the existential task is to work through and against these conditioning structures in ways that open up the possibilities of subjectivity. Importantly, such work seems to require a concerted and intersubjective effort, which might be, and often is, foiled or circumvented in a variety of ways. Beauvoir's emphasis on self-perception is especially important for thinking through trans subjectivities, particularly in light of Toril Moi's crucial reorientation of our understanding of the body in Beauvoir's thought. Moi places her study of Beauvoir in the context of thinking through the ways in which Beauvoir both rejects biological determinism and avoids the problems of falling into the sex/gender distinction, which falls into the trap of either "uphold[ing] the 'objective' or 'scientific' view of the body as the ground on which gender is developed" or rejecting the notion of "woman" as an inherently oppressive tool of heteropatriarchy.[37] In contrast, Moi emphasizes that Beauvoir sees the body as itself a situation.[38]

At its most redemptive, the fact of being a body, for Beauvoir, is an occasion to work through and on the body rather than simply treating it as a mere given; that is, though one's body is inevitably part of one's facticity, it can also be a site of transcendence precisely because it is not absolutely determinant. A more cynical reading of the body might turn us back to Chu's eyes and the eyes of the real and imagined others we catch staring. The desire to avoid those stares and the violences they entail and the concomitant desire to fit a gender category feeds well into the project of beauty capitalism. In his discussion of the norm, Lennard J. Davis contrasts it with the ideal; whereas the ideal was the unattainable divine of prior aesthetic imaginaries, the norm is an achievable and therefore necessary goal.[39] Sabrina Strings makes remarkably similar observations in her analysis of fatphobia and its deep indebtedness to white supremacist norms of embodiment.[40] The body as perfectible through individual effort and through increasing forms of intervention, and the failure to do so as a failure that then warrants possibly violent response, is key to how beauty capitalism operates as a background condition governing gendered self-perception.

We can begin to think through here what I'm provisionally calling a "somatechnics of beauty." By this, I mean to capture the notion that beauty is conceived of as both an embodied and a technological category in ways that are mutually informative and reinforcing. If we think here of the various archives on FFS I pointed to earlier, we can see how beauty is framed as an additional concern beyond the mere goal of achieving a "feminized" face. In so doing, the implicit claim is that beauty, relative to gender, requires different kinds of surgical intervention to achieve—that is, beauty is measured by a somewhat distinct set of embodied and technical standards than bare gender. While we might be able to articulate an understanding of facial gender as at least theoretically sensitive to a consideration of race, as Blumenbach's declaration of the white race as the closest to the ideal of beauty indicates, it's not clear that we can bring such similar sensitivities to a consideration of achieving a standard of beauty. Beauty, then, as it has been taken up under this somatechnics, remains an implicitly white category in ways that occlude or even preclude the consideration of nonwhite beauty within the practice of medicalized trans discourses. Thus, trans people are beautiful, fuckable, and provisionally worth saving to the extent that we can approximate a norm that is white as well as cis.

Notes

1. For a discussion of picture brides, see Alice Yun Chai, "Women's History in Public: 'Picture Brides' in Hawaii," *Women's Studies Quarterly* 16, no. 1/2 (1988): 51–62.

2. EmilyMK03, reply to Maybebaby56, "My FFS Experience with Dr. Zukowski," Susan's Place, October 15, 2016, https://www.susans .org/?topic=215448.0.

3. It is worth noting here that there is a great deal to be said as well of facial masculinization surgeries (FMS) and their potential imbrications in the racial politics of beauty that I will be analyzing here. Masculinity obviously has its attendant forms of beauty and desire. Given, for example, the extensive discussions of race and masculinity that have occurred within the bodies of literature composing ethnic and gender studies, it would be shocking if these surgical procedures are not bound up with much of the same concerns we find in the literatures on FFS I take up here. I leave off, for now, a more thoroughgoing engagement with FMS because it does warrant a closer look than I can take up here.

4. Keith Altman, "Facial Feminization Surgery: Current State of the Art," *International Journal of Oral and Maxillofacial Surgery* 41, no. 8 (2012): 886.

5. Luis Capitán et al., "Facial Feminization Surgery: The Forehead—Surgical Techniques and Analysis of Results," *Plastic and Reconstructive Surgery* 134, no. 4 (2014): 613.

6. Jeffrey H. Spiegel, "Rhinoplasty as a Significant Component of Facial Feminization and Beautification," *JAMA Facial Plastic Surgery* 19, no. 3 (2017): 181–82. Spiegel frames rhinoplasty for trans patients as entirely concerned with beautification and addresses, in particular, the role of evolutionary biology in justifying the pursuit of beauty.

7. B. E. Lischer, "Variations and Modifications of the Facial Features: An Introductory Study," *International Journal of Orthodontia and Oral Surgery* 5, no. 9 (1919): 495–507.

8. John Bingham Roberts, *War Surgery of the Face: A Treatise on Plastic Restoration after Facial Injury* (New York: William Wood and Company, 1919).

9. Eric Plemons, *The Look of a Woman: Facial Feminization Surgery and the Aims of Trans-Medicine* (Durham, N.C.: Duke University Press, 2017).

10. Eric Plemons, "Gender, Ethnicity, and Transgender Embodiment: Interrogating Classification in Facial Feminization Surgery," *Body & Society* 25, no. 1 (2019): 3–28.

11. Os Keyes, "The Misgendering Machines: Trans/HCI Implications of Automatic Gender Recognition," *Proceedings of the ACM on Human-Computer Interaction* 2, no. CSCW 88 (2018): 1–22.

12. Zackary Drucker, "Trans Icon Miss Major: 'We've Got to Reclaim Who the Fuck We Are,'" *Vice*, November 21, 2018, https://www.vice.com/en /article/j5z58d/miss-major-griffin-gracy-transgender-survival-guide.

13. Talia Mae Bettcher, "Trapped in the Wrong Theory: Rethinking Trans Oppression and Resistance," *Signs* 39, no. 2 (2014): 383–406.

14. Here's where a note of hermeneutic caution might be due. This is not an argument against passing, but it would be easy to read what follows that way. Sandy Stone famously presents an argument for not passing in her "Posttransexual Manifesto." Because of the underlying racial logics of how facial gender tends to operate, we might pass or not pass without the kind of intention that is embedded within how Stone conceptualizes passing. And, as the literatures I surveyed suggest, passing and beauty are overlapping but not identical concepts. I am interested in opening a space for us to think through how we might rethink beauty, but that requires getting the messiness of it on the table. Passing is inevitably part of that picture, but we risk falling into the racial logic of beauty if we think that clocking registers aesthetic value. Sandy Stone, "The *Empire* Strikes Back: A Posttransexual Manifesto," *Camera Obscura: Feminism, Culture, and Media Studies* 10, no. 2 (1992): 150–76.

15. Emmanuel Chukwudi Eze, "The Color of Reason: The Idea of 'Race' in Kant's Anthropology," *Postcolonial African Philosophy: A Critical Reader* (Cambridge: Blackwell, 1997), 103–40; Robert Bernasconi, "Will the Real Kant Please Stand Up: The Challenge of Enlightenment Racism to the Study of the History of Philosophy," *Radical Philosophy* 117 (2003): 13–22.

16. Johann Friedrich Blumenbach, *On the Natural Varieties of Mankind* (New York: Bergman Publishers, 1969).

17. María Lugones, "Heterosexualism and the Colonial/Modern Gender System," *Hypatia* 22, no. 1 (2007): 194.

18. Aníbal Quijano, "Coloniality of Power, Eurocentrism, and Latin America," *Nepantla* 1, no. 3 (2000): 535.

19. Lugones, "Colonial/Modern Gender System," 192–93.

20. Notably, blepharoplasty may also be accompanied by epicanthoplasty. This will be important momentarily.

21. Soo-Ha Kwon et al., "Experiences and Attitudes toward Aesthetic Procedures in East Asia: A Cross-Sectional Survey of Five Geographical Regions," *Archives of Plastic Surgery* 48, no. 6 (2021): 660–69.

22. Mel Y. Chen, "'The Stuff of Slow Constitution': Reading Down Syndrome for Race, Disability, and the Timing That Makes Them So," *Somatechnics* 6, no. 2 (2016): 235–48.

23. Meeta Rani Jha, *The Global Beauty Industry: Colorism, Racism, and the National Body* (New York: Routledge, 2015).

24. Cameron Awkward-Rich, *The Terrible We: Thinking with Trans Maladjustment* (Durham, N.C.: Duke University Press, 2022).

25. Rosemarie Garland-Thomson, *Staring: How We Look* (Oxford: Oxford University Press, 2009).

26. Leslie Bow, *Racist Love: Asian Abstraction and the Pleasures of Fantasy* (Durham, N.C.: Duke University Press, 2021); Anne Anlin Cheng, *Ornamentalism* (Oxford: Oxford University Press, 2019).

27. Bettcher, "Trapped in the Wrong Theory," 392.
28. Bettcher, 395–96.
29. C. Riley Snorton, *Black on Both Sides: A Racial History of Trans Identity* (Minneapolis: University of Minnesota Press, 2017), 157.
30. Siobhan Ball, "TERFs Accuse Chinese Women Runners of Being Men," Daily Dot, September 4, 2019, https://www.dailydot.com/irl/terfs -accuse-chinese-national-athletes-looking-like-men/.
31. Andrea Long Chu, "My New Vagina Won't Make Me Happy," *New York Times,* November 24, 2018, https://www.nytimes.com/2018/11/24 /opinion/sunday/vaginoplasty-transgender-medicine.html.
32. Rosemarie Garland-Thomson, "Misfits: A Feminist Material Disability Concept," *Hypatia* 26, no. 3 (2011): 591–609.
33. Simone de Beauvoir, *The Second Sex,* trans. Constance Borde and Sheila Malovany-Chevallier (New York: Vintage Books, 2011), 283.
34. Beauvoir, *Second Sex,* 44.
35. Beauvoir, 49.
36. Beauvoir, 10.
37. Toril Moi, *What Is a Woman? And Other Essays* (Oxford: Oxford University Press, 1999), 73, 75–76.
38. Moi, *What Is a Woman,* 66.
39. Lennard J. Davis, "Constructing Normalcy: The Bell Curve, the Novel, and the Invention of the Disabled Body in the Nineteenth Century," in *The Disability Studies Reader,* 2nd ed. (New York: Routledge, 2006), 3–16.
40. Sabrina Strings, *Fearing the Black Body: The Racial Origins of Fat Phobia* (New York: New York University Press, 2019).

PART IV
Politics, Institutions, and World-Making

Scatter
A Trans/Crip Analytic
Perry Zurn

In the summer of 2015, I moved to Massachusetts to assume my first faculty gig. With all the gumption and anxiety of a newly minted PhD, I was eager to begin my academic sojourn as visiting assistant professor at Hampshire College. On the first day, I turned to my colleague Fae, who exuded genderfluid femme fabulousness, and asked where the nearest bathroom was located. They pointed me to an all-gender restroom down the hall and announced with evident glee that all the bathrooms on campus were gender-inclusive. As I turned to go, I could feel both shock and relief vying for my body. In that instant, I viscerally remembered my time as a graduate student: the relentless dehydration headaches; the rushing in and out of gendered restrooms, holding my breath; the waiting in line at the nearest gender-inclusive restroom several buildings away, only to run out of time and have to turn back (to attend class, to teach, to meet with my dissertation directors, to hold office hours) before relieving myself, with tears of frustration and shame pooling in the corners of my eyes, and searing heat in my throat. Using the nearby restroom in peace, I wondered, "How is this even possible?" How did Hampshire get this way and when? What stories of trans agitation and world-building lay behind the innocuous bathroom signs? Two years later, I returned to the valley to study not only the history of trans-inclusive policies at Hampshire and the surrounding colleges but also the history of trans life there and the poetics subtending it all.[1]

To track that story, I used a multimodal methodology. I consulted official and unofficial college archives, as well as the Sexual Minorities Archives' local holdings. I also interviewed, with the help of another colleague, dozens of Hampshire students, staff, faculty, and alum (and dozens more among the other schools).[2] Sifting through those archives and interviews, trying to piece together a story, I read widely in the trans theory and creative scholarship produced by trans folks who had intersected with Hampshire or the Five Colleges of which it forms a part (Amherst College, Mount Holyoke College, Smith College, and University of Massachusetts, Amherst). While maintaining a certain (uncertain) ground in theory and philosophy more generally, it was my hope that this ultimately be a local project guided by local theory. Perhaps unsurprisingly, the more I learned of trans life at Hampshire, the less I was interested in trans-inclusive policy writ large and the more I became interested in the poetics that precedes and exceeds any agitation for said policies. By *poetics,* I invoke Fred Moten's sense of how we "make things and make one another."[3] I also invoke trans poets' sense of messing with sense-making—breaking form, structure, and syntax in order to think the body/text otherwise.[4] What are the backward, backdoor, backyard ways in which trans folks make sense and break sense, make each other and unmake each other at the edge of the university?

When it comes to bathrooms, whether on college campuses or elsewhere, policy debates have been and remain germane to the terrain. But what are the trans poetics that subtend bathroom use and protest? What does one need to attend to, and how might one attune, to catch stories of an elsewhere here? I went looking for a frame—an analytic—that would permit this specific kind of noticing to set to work. And I could not shake the sound of scat and scatter. Bathrooms are heavily governed places of scat, for trans and nontrans people alike.[5] And while binary restrooms scatter us, as trans people, we scatter them in turn, making them more than and other than themselves. Indeed, we might even understand transness as a kind of gender scattering—smattering, slathering. More than this, however, the stories of bathroom activism suggest there is a scatter at the heart of transness itself, by which I mean the crip instability of the term *trans,* the unstable cripness of trans experience, and the coeval intimacies of crip life and trans life. In largely disavowing this scatter, trans studies and many trans people scatter transness from itself: what it is and what it could be.[6] But it is in this primordial "scatterscram" that we might more richly make things and make one another—in all the madness that trans makes possible.[7] I offer scatter, then, as a trans/crip analytic through which to catch sight of trans poetics.[8] Before turning to the main tale (i.e., Hampshire's bathroom saga), let me first situate scat and scatter in one of many possible theoretical contexts.

Scatterways

Scatter. Disperse, diffuse, dissipate. A word of obscure origin, the etymology of *scatter* is itself scattered across languages and millennia—Old and Middle English, Dutch, Low German, and Greek—and no one is quite sure when or where it all started.[9] To say its origin is obscure, then, is perhaps to say it has no single origin, no definitive anchor, no first place. Scatter has always already been scattered, never once unified or settled. Even the term *scat* (or *skat*) itself is split, meaning "treasure" in Old English but "dung" in Greek. Over the centuries, *scatter* has referred to the scattering of sheep and ships, of clouds and snow, and, perhaps quintessentially, of seeds—which are spread, sprinkled, and strewn about. It marks the pattern of fugitive flight. And the way laughter shatters the air, sending its peals bounding and bouncing along the ground. There is something onomatopoeic about it. Strangely, the transitive use—i.e., "to scatter oneself"—is now rare or obsolete, as if it were too hard to think. Nevertheless, one can imagine, without too much effort, oneself as scattershot, the very point of a scatteraway.

How scatters get made and what they make in scattering constitutes the poetics of scatter. Perhaps unsurprisingly, there are multiple levels and layers to that making. In nature, the scatter typically happens in tandem, an intimate dance between the scattered and scatterer. Birds and bees scatter pollens and seeds, squirrels strew the ground with acorns, while deer drop burly bristles across the forest floor, and a light breeze coaxes spores along. An ancient orchestration, companionate spreading allows for new life. But there is another kind of scattering. A noncompanionate, nongerminative one. Monocultures scatter plants from one another, while highways cut up wildlife habitats. In both cases, human projects undertaken without regard for other lives scatter those lives. Flora and fauna become isolated, and biodiversity declines. Thinking the vibrant and violent scatterings of concept and creature, Jacques Derrida and Édouard Glissant make a critical intervention: the violent scatter is never complete, never final; the vibrant scatter always exacts its revenge. Entropy wins over order every time. Frozen momentarily, the cycle of life and death inexorably returns.

For Derrida, a self-described Franco-Maghrebian Jew, a certain scatter subtends everything—every formation of matter into being, every substantiation of sense into meaning. Before and beneath concepts, institutions, and things, which are always determined via distinction and delineation, there is the indistinguishable and the irreducible. In a way, this is the point of Derrida's concept *différance*—the constant differing and deferring of sense that makes writing both possible and impossible.[10] Commentator Geoffrey Bennington calls this primordial scatter "a certain madness," which irrepressibly interrupts normative sense and sensemaking procedures; a "motley" multiplicity that cannot be reduced to identifiable, legible, respectable units.[11] Derrida's friend Glissant concretizes the scatter. As a Black Caribbean theorist, he thinks in and with that geography. When colonization swept through the region, it set out to replace the natural scatter of languages, histories, and customs with a culture of the continent. Solid, singular. Stationary and consistent. In doing so, it created peoples "scattered"—and isolated—from themselves.[12] Colonization, however, is never complete. In this case, the revenge of the Caribbean archipelago is creolization itself, a reassertion of nonreductive scattering, and, through it, a "poetics of Relation."[13] Ephemeral, multiple. Mobile and erratic. A scattering for, rather than against, life.

To think scatter, then, is to think a smattering of things. It is to think the vibrant force of multiplicity that drives things in various directions and without clear origin. It is also to think the violent force of dispersion that quells that multiplicity (although never absolutely). And it is to think creative processes—like creolization and writing—that, while they gather things into identifiable forms, nevertheless harbor a stash of dispersive power that frays them at their edges, making room for something else.

Consider trans is/as scatter. If transness is anything, it is an insistence that gender is—vitally and intimately—inherently more scattered, more diffused and dispersed, than a binary gender system can account for. The multiplicity that we are disrupts the binary gender system from within, always extending beyond and entangling between the clean lines, defined categories, and limited histories. But by instituting the swift and solid bifurcation of male from female, man from woman, that binary gender system scatters us and our scatter-selves, we gender disruptors and gender dissidents; it scatters us to the winds, throwing us from homes and havens, schools and restrooms, legibility and legality. We are scattered—isolated from each other, from our histories, and sometimes from our very own selves. But the story does not stop there. Trans always returns, gender disruption always erupts, even under conditions of erasure. And it is that return and eruption, we often think, that promise trans liberation.

These two scatterings, however, are tempered by a third sense: our trans selves as the site of a scatteraway. To the layers of vibrant and violent scatterings, we need to add the transitive sense, a self-scattering. We scatter ourselves from ourselves. We too are a source of our own scatteraway—especially, in this context, from the crip side of trans. There is a fraying force that fractures overly clean conceptualizations of what "trans" is, "trans" does, and the (non)sense "trans" makes. It is a mad force for which we are not always ready and which we do not always welcome. Likewise, there is an inherent instability by which transness misses the mark and breaks normative function (and misses its own mark, breaking its own normative function). There is something fundamentally dysfunctional about it. And of course, this is not to mention the embodied and enminded ways in which transness collides with and explodes into disability. The two misfitting and maladjusting together. This—all of this—is the crip content at the heart of trans. Too often, we institute divisions, denials, and disavowals about transness in order to scatter it precisely from its crip scatterself. It is this crip transitivity I hope to illuminate.

Scat!

While there were decades of bathroom skirmishes at Hampshire—
first through bathroom stall graffiti and then through bathroom
sign removal and tampering—it all came to a head on November 21, 2011, with what everyone ominously refers to as "the bathroom incident."

"Get out!" he screamed. "Scat!" he might as well have intoned.
Hampshire students in Jack Isaac Pryor's Performing Identities
class were tasked with developing site-specific final performances.[14] Three students chose to work in what was at the time labeled a "Bathroom with Urinals" in the Music and Dance Building
(immediately opposite which stood a "Bathroom without Urinals").
A professor was just leaving the restroom as they entered; he returned after ten to fifteen minutes to use the restroom again. With
some frustration, he asked the students to leave. They left momentarily to check with Pryor but then went back to work in the restroom. The professor returned a third time and, upon seeing them,
exclaimed in frustration, "Okay! This is it! You need to get out of
here! This is a men's room! You can't be in here. . . . It's a men's
room. It's my bathroom."[15] When they resisted, he called campus
police and reported "three girls in the men's bathroom."[16] By their
own description, one was a "Jewish cisgender woman," another a
"white transsexual man," and a third was a "genderqueer person of
color" of Middle Eastern descent.[17] On the heels of the queer studies awakening on campus, in which Pryor played a significant role,
and the heightened gender justice awareness that had produced
the inclusive bathroom signs in the first place, the incident was
shocking and struck like a flint.

Students read the scene in multiple ways. In the first, the professor is the Man, in more than one way. Patriarchy relies not only on
the superiority of one sex over the other but also on the presumed
rationality of one and an active infantilizing of the other.[18] His restroom, his assessment, his rights—and his material resources.
Historically, men's rooms—much like other public spaces such as
courtrooms and universities—were for centuries presumptively
masculine, only named (or signed) as such when women's restrooms were introduced in the late eighteenth century.[19] Against
the professor's claims to reason and property, then, Hampshire

students dubbed their resistance effort #OccupyBathroom. Occupy Wall Street was in the air and an Occupy Hampshire chapter had just started earlier that month. In continually occupying the restroom, students insisted that power and resources be redistributed in nonpatriarchal ways, especially around bathroom use and determination.

In a second reading of the scene, the professor's claims evince a certain coloniality. Developing in Europe in the late eighteenth century, binary-gendered restrooms were then introduced either as civilizing initiatives among the colonized or as distinguishing architectures of colonial culture.[20] Such initiatives and architectures were always already racialized and gendered, and they coincided with a larger effort to assert the colonial modern gender system and to police especially Indigenous, Latinx, and Black people.[21] The assertion that this is "my bathroom," this is a "men's bathroom," belies a conviction that whatever local gender flexibility might be signaled by the quaint "Bathroom with Urinals" sign, it is nonsense. Civilizing distinctions must be reasserted, even violently implemented. It is for this reason that the students' resistance effort came to be known as #DecolonizeBathroom.[22] To decolonize, in this context, meant to break down the gender and racial hierarchies that inform the production/possession of space.

The (admittedly tense) work of occupying and decolonizing involves a return or revenge of the scattered. Such work is a testament that the force of the scat(ter) is unable to be contained. Incidents like this are endemic; queer and trans people join a long line of gendered, racialized, and disabled bodies that have been scattered from bathrooms. We go looking for a gender-inclusive restroom in a different building, or a gendered bathroom in an out-of-the-way place, or we use the bathroom associated with (or not associated with) our sex assigned at birth because we will get yelled out of the other one. But queer and trans people—at Hampshire and elsewhere—also scatter. Our insistent presence in binary-gendered restrooms, using whichever we choose, is a dispersive force in the heart of these social institutions, demonstrating with insistent flesh that gender is more than dominant stories—and histories—would have us believe.

Hampshire's bathroom incident concluded with an insistent

critique of the event itself and of campus policy. The students final-
ized and staged their performance piece, which offered a "queer
magic ritual" through which they and others might heal from the
racist, homophobic, and transphobic "wounding" of the incident.[23]
This was a fundamentally poetic response. But the students also
demanded that the college clarify its policies (and, where appropriate, create new policies) about public space, bathrooms, signage,
enforcement, and accountability—demands the college went some
way toward fulfilling.[24]

The story could have easily stopped there, but it didn't. A student-
produced zine covering the incident reports, on its final page, that
the professor was said to require "medically necessary bathroom
access."[25] It is a cliff-hanger, left unaddressed. I interviewed an
administrator who confirmed the report.[26] It was the source point
for another scatter. What happens when disability hits the scene?
When queer and trans students practicing a performance piece
make a bathroom inaccessible for a professor with a medical need
for it—even if there is another, differently rendered restroom five
feet away? Neither the zine nor my interviews helped illuminate
this quandary.

Splits and Tangles

Before proceeding with the story, a quick step back. In *The Terrible
We,* neighboring University of Massachusetts, Amherst professor
Cameron Awkward-Rich refuses the split between transness and
disability—and especially the divisions, denials, and disavowals
that scatter transness from its (crip) self. He recalls two founding
moments for trans and disability studies. In 1990, as the Americans with Disabilities Act sat on the Senate floor, conservative
senators insisted on a rack of exclusions, including "transvestism,"
"transsexualism," and "gender identity disorders."[27] In the moment disability became protected, transness became unprotect-
able. Then, in 1995, Susan Stryker insisted, to a roomful of conference attendees, "I'm a transsexual, I'm not sick"—an anecdote she
deploys to introduce trans studies a decade later.[28] In the moment
transness became authoritative, then—enough to warrant its own
academic discipline—it also became nondisabled, nonsick. Against

these originary splits, Awkward-Rich insists on the scatterplot intimacies of transness and disability. His questions are haunting: "Might insanity, tragedy, and absurdity be integral . . . to trans life and thought? . . . And how might a trans studies, accountable to the world- and knowledge-making force of the maladjusted, the bad, the mad, the painful, . . . otherwise unfold?"[29] How, indeed, might trans studies and transness reject its founding disavowal of disability and instead embrace its existing crosshatch with disabled and mad knowledge-making and world-making practices?

In the annals of trans maladjustment, running apposite these split histories, Awkward-Rich finds a complex poetics. From the archive of transmasculine life, he culls moments of depression, reclusivity, trauma, and suicidality, as well as pathologizing run-ins with the courthouse, the prison, the asylum, the freak show, and the sensational newspaper. In doing so, he builds a poetics of "entanglement," which consistently marks and recreates the co-constitution and co-occurrence of trans/crip intimacies.[30] He thinks that poetics of entanglement (which refuses to scatter transness from disability) alongside a "dissociative poetics" (which places a crip scatter inside transness itself).[31] Rereading the work of Eli Clare and Elliott DeLine, he identifies a disaggregation constitutive of the transmasculine experience and of how that experience gets told—replete with a "fracturing epistemology," "narrative fragmentation," "halting repetition," split voices, and messy stories.[32] Paradoxically, then, one of the entanglements of transness and disability is dissociation. One of the ways they are gathered is through scattering. In locating a dispersion of crip elements in the very heart and histories of transness, he asks a simple question, over and over again: What would it mean not to quell this scatter?

Awkward-Rich takes his title, *The Terrible We,* from Carson McCullers's *The Member of the Wedding.* Twelve-year-old white tomboy Frankie Addams wants to belong to the girls' club, which meets in a clubhouse across the yard, but she is clearly not welcome. Frankie focuses on the pain of rejection and isolation, when in fact she belongs to "a much queerer collective" that meets around her own kitchen table. A cast of queer, crip, and of color characters, both real and fictive: this is "the terrible we."[33] A we more dispersed than the other but also more intimate. Reviewing the scene, Awkward-Rich calls for "sitting together" in the kitchen—with this "motley" we that is the mess of transness and disability, shot through with race, their histories and phenomenologies all wound up and scattershot with each other.[34] Sitting like an archipelago around the table. Stefano Harney and Fred Moten make a similar call to the kitchen, where fugitive communities—members of the undercommons—have repeatedly generated and nourished "the to come of the forms of life."[35] Amid anxious calls to rectify who is at the policy table—or the clubhouse table—Awkward-Rich invites us to think about the heterogeneity already integral to the offbeat spitballing and yarn-telling, shit-talking and big-dreaming tables at which we sit.

Back to stories, then. We—trans folks, trans studies folks—scatter ourselves. The obsolete transitive sense of the term is alive and necessary here. We are scattered in our accounts of ourselves. We tend to tell stories (and histories) of trans existence and resistance without reference to disability, whether in our own community or among those with (or against) whom we struggle. What would it mean to attune ourselves to the complicities and complexities that already exist, already form networks, between and among madness and transness, dysfunction and disruption, sickness and gender trouble? What does it look like to stand—or, perhaps better, sit—on this bridge of maladjustment?

The Scatteraway

Let us return to the scene in question: the bathroom with urinals in Hampshire's Music and Dance Building. The professor walks in. Is he simply the voice of patriarchy and colonialism? Is he merely the conduit of a violent scattering? If, and insofar as, he has a medical condition that structures his access needs down to the minute, he is a crip figure. A professor, yes; a man, yes; but also less and more than these norms signify. In a not uncommon twist, the story goes, he appeals to a discourse of colonial patriarchy in order to advocate for his needs. In this scene, what are the students doing? They possess, claim, and refuse to relinquish a space that they are not using to relieve themselves. Are they figures of ableist entitlement?

Are they enacting a differently violent scattering? What would it take to think of professor and students as one community and the histories and ideologies that keep us apart? What would it mean to imagine both parties joining at the point of access and sharing the ground of maladjustment?

Rereading the zine, it is impossible not to cup one's ear to its crip undercurrent. The Middle Eastern student, who assumes the name "Beast" in the performance, uses a wheelchair, identifies as neurodivergent, and describes their body as "twisted and taut," "fruity," and "brown."[36] All three students are described as "survivors of chronic and acute traumas."[37] They in turn describe the incident as a "trauma" and a "wound," causing one student to "shake" and another to have "an anxiety attack" in the stall.[38] The students also describe the incident as a "crazy-making experience."[39] The students felt "triggered" and "emotionally unstable."[40] Somehow, an ally's foot got caught in the professor's office door afterward and they came back "limping."[41] The student exchanges with the administration after the event are characterized repeatedly as "unhealthy" and as constructing a "toxic energy flow."[42] Against the professor's "rabid defense of male territory, cissexism/sexism, and a constant fear of abjection," then, is a less than sane and staid collective.[43] A motley we indeed. A motley we who, nevertheless, tried to craft a place of healing in a space of experiential violence: the bathroom. Indeed, there is one way to read the scene as a clash between access needs—the professor and students composing a circle of maladjustment and misfitting that produces further rifts and harms where there might have been, in another world and around another table, a bond of alliance.

Across the more than one hundred interviews with predominantly trans interviewees that inform my larger study of trans poetics at the Five Colleges, testaments to disabilities, disorders, and dysfunctions abound. They are named in tumble-fulls, with crip vectors cropping up in clusters across and within individual interviewees. A representative but nonexhaustive list is as follows: "always sick," angst, anorexia, anxiety, attention-deficit/hyperactivity disorder, autism spectrum disorder, autoimmune disorder, back injury, bad memory, bipolar disorder, burnout, cancer, childhood abuse, chronic fatigue, chronic illness, chronic pain, clinical depression, cluster migraines, diabetes, dyslexia, eczema, fatigue, flu, "fragile body," gender dysphoria, hard of hearing, heart defect, labyrinthitis, learning disability, long Covid, Lyme disease, mobility impairment, neurodivergence, obsessive-compulsive disorder, panic attacks, post-traumatic stress disorder, sexual assault, "six years of a bum right ankle," suicidality, trauma, and traumatic brain injury. Many interviewees list "disability" and "mental illness" without further description on the intake form, and some describe themselves as "mostly able-bodied" or as "appearing able-bodied."

What is perhaps most interesting about this list is not its length and diversity but how often these disabilities, disorders, and dysfunctions were disavowed in the very moment they were disclosed. Repeatedly, interviewees would find themselves mentioning something and then saying, "Sorry, that's not the trans story." They were apologizing because they assumed (perhaps in some way I communicated) that I wanted the trans story, not the disability story. Interviewees who easily spoke of their transness and experiences of racialization often avoided discussing their crip experiences. They assumed these stories were separate stories, not hyphenated stories, asterisked stories, elliptical stories. When explicitly invited to say more, for example, Joshua acknowledges his impulse to "play up" his transness but not his disability, to lean in to "passing as able-bodied" but to come out as trans.[44] Another interviewee, in telling their gender journey, told me they got sick, so sick, and still are sick, but "anyway, all this other stuff is not about trans identity." Yet another mentioned a virulent, chronic infection that required them to go off antidepressants and testosterone, which then sent them into years of depression and anorexia. They quickly righted course and confessed, "but that's not about trans things." But it *is* about trans things, it *is* trans stuff, it *is* the trans story.

Discussing trans-inclusive university policy, especially trans-inclusive sports, Mount Holyoke alum Blake poses what he considers the "crazy" idea of making transness count as a disability under the Americans with Disabilities Act (ADA).[45] What a wild thought. "That'll consume a whole six-pack and an afternoon if you let it," he says. But it would be effective and efficient, he adds. "Would it be pathologizing?" Sure. But would it be worth it? Probably. Blake's proposed tactical alliance is Awkward-Rich's constitutive intimacy—an intimacy disavowed by much of trans studies and trans people alike, but an intimacy that keeps returning to scatter transness at its core, shattering any illusion of a solely healthy, able, and sane trans bodymind and community.

Scattering Sense

As trans folks, we are always already scattered. Our bodies do not consolidate the way they are supposed to, whether pre- or post- or non-transition, and the way we think about ourselves and our worlds is, perhaps at its best, scatterbrained—jumping from here to there, breaking apart what appears together, taking a broom to the anthills of cisheteronormativity. We live and function in a world where we are scattered, despite ourselves, into two genders, two social roles, two bathrooms, and two boxes. And when we can't take the hint, we're scattered from two to nowhere. But the flesh is insistent and the spirit recalcitrant. We scatter people's categories; scategories. Much rides on this return, even revenge, of the dispersed. We pin our trans hopes and dreams to it, as if someday, finally, multiplicity will win out and the scatter of gender fluidity will reign. But what we spend too little time appreciating is that we often scatter ourselves from the depth of this potential. We tell our stories piecemeal, refusing, so very often, to look again, to look still more closely, and find there in our stories vectors and energies that tear trans from its own origins and send it scattershot in another—or several other—direction(s). Asterisked indeed.

To take scatter as an analytic of trans poetics is to look for these many scatterings in trans comings and goings. It is to follow the wind, the winged creatures, and the stockpiling, stashing squirrels of all gender-disrupting persuasions. It is also to track the split tracts and sealed silos. And the cracks—the fissures in every edifice through which the wind and the sun rush in. Something "trans" surfaces and squares off in each of these spaces. More than simply marking the scatterways, however, such an analytic must think the scattershot with scatterthot. With a hint or a haint of "transMadness," refusing the too-easy division between trans and everything else across and within which it sits. Cavar, a genderless and neurodivergent Mount Holyoke alum, defines *transMadness* as "a wandering and wondering praxis, anticipating and refusing neurotypical, sane, cis supervision in both the structure of our thought(s) and in the comportment of our bodies."[46] For them, transMadness "rewilds" the "wordstrokes" that condemn thought to reified disabilities, inflexible genders, and tyrannous common-sense concepts.[47] transMadness mobilizes ways of (un)knowing and knowing "-less," in spaces of "less" than cis sense and sanity.[48] Taking scatter as a trans analytic, then, might mean attending to these mixed and multiple scatterways in such a way as to set trans theory on edge. To make it unsteady on its own feet. Such an analysis would track what "trans" unsettles and also where "trans" settles—and upset the sediment there, where it happens.

Sonny Nordmarken, a University of Massachusetts, Amherst alum who helped organize a trans studies working group during his sojourn as a graduate student in the Department of Sociology, thinks deeply at the intersection of trans studies and disability.[49] He writes eloquently of the monstrosity of trans existence and, specifically, the way in which it disrupts "gender accomplishment practices"—the way we try to prove our genders (and our trans-ness).[50] He also published an autoethnography of living with Lyme disease, a tick-borne illness endemic to western Massachusetts.[51] In one especially memorable description of cognitive impairments precipitated by Lyme, he writes:

> Throughout my days, I forget what I'm doing in the midst of doing it, what I'm looking for in the midst of looking for it. . . . I strain to remember the first part of the sentence at the same time as retaining the last few words, but I'm not fast enough and many of the words evaporate. . . . It is a task to think of appropriate words in the moment I am forming sentences. Sometimes I say words that don't make sense. Sometimes I mis-speak. Sometimes my grammar is not right. Sometimes it is embarrassing.[52]

Nordmarken is lost in words, lost to words, at a loss for words. First and foremost, this is disorienting for him, as he loses an access to his body he previously had. It is also deeply frustrating because these symptoms are repeatedly disregarded and misdiagnosed by medical professionals. But Nordmarken's headspace might also signal possibility. What if his cognitive lapses were characteristic of trans(Mad) life itself and trans(Mad) studies, too? What if they, too, were full of absences, silences, muddles, and lost origins, as Cavar might insist?

What if this were all precisely as it should be? What if trans life and trans studies, shot through with crip intimacies, were full of illogics, silences, muddles, and dissonances? Lost in words, lost to words, at a loss for words? Indeed, what if it were only patriarchal, colonial, and ableist instincts that press for more consistency, more reliability, and less (crip) poetry? What would our stories— our histories and our archives—look like if we really reconciled with the scatter that is ourselves? And to the transMadness of that poetics? This is not simply a call to tell better (or more accurate) stories but also to break our storytelling praxis. Archipelagize it; mad-scatter it. And it is not simply to cite better (having more well-governed and well-disciplined reference lists) but rather to honor the scatter that is trans/queer/crip/of color community knowledge-building.[53] Such calls to destabilization put in question languages of centering. They insist that stories not simply be stabilized in another place but be held precariously in their inherent instability. This is a scatter that vibrates multilocally—twitching in the heart, shaking in the belly, skittering in the mind, and flapping across the page.

I have written before that a series of injuries and illnesses brought me to my knees just as I was graduating with a PhD and the several years thereafter.[54] And that in that moment, the vastness of what I had never wondered—about capacities and futurities—took my breath away. What I have not yet put to the printed page is this: I was so physically wrecked when I arrived at Hampshire that one of my sisters moved in with me for an entire semester to help care for me, get me around, and make life possible for me. I did not simply arrive at Hampshire trans. There were holes in my stomach and ribs scattered from my sternum. I remember grieving my (previous form of) trans masculinity, now that I was unable to carry things, push things, or hold myself up with my own two arms. I remember collapsing on a walk I thought I could make and thumbing a random car for the first time in my life. I stared down the barrel of a future that was nothing like what I had envisioned. It took me years to heal, but the vulnerability of my strength stays with me. More than that, I realize now, almost a decade later, I have been my own scatteraway. I am not claiming disability; but I am resisting the mirage of the sane and able trans body. Perhaps in writing this, and sending these many words splattering across the page, I will have gathered something together that can germinate otherwise, in another disordered and disordering ecology.

Notes

1. See Perry Zurn, *How We Make Each Other: Trans Life at the Edge of the University* (Durham, N.C.: Duke University Press, forthcoming).
2. Interviews conducted by author from 2017 to 2021 at Hampshire College. All names of interviewees have been redacted and replaced with pseudonyms.
3. Fred Moten, *A Poetics of the Undercommons* (Brooklyn: Sputnik & Fizzle, 2016), 24.
4. TC Tolbert and Trace Peterson, *Troubling the Line: Trans and Genderqueer Poetry and Poetics* (Callicoon, N.Y.: Nightboat Books, 2013); Andrea Abi-Karam and Kay Gabriel, eds., *We Want It All: An Anthology of Radical Trans Poetics* (Brooklyn: Nightboats Books, 2020).
5. Perry Zurn, "Waste Culture and Isolation: Prisons, Toilets, and Gender Segregation," *Hypatia* 34, no. 4 (2019): 668–89; Perry Zurn, "Bathroom," in *Keywords in Gender and Sexuality Studies,* eds. Aren Aizura, Aimee Bahng, Amber Jamilla Musser, Karma Chavez, Mishuana Goeman, and Kyla Wazana Tompkins (New York: New York University Press, 2021), 21–22.
6. By *crip,* I understand a critical positionality and politics that unmasks the ideological coconstruction of ability and white cisheteronormativity. See Robert McRuer, *Crip Theory: Cultural Signs of Queerness and Disability* (New York: New York University Press, 2006); Jina B. Kim, "Toward a Crip-of-Color Critique: Thinking with Minich's 'Enabling Whom?,'" *Lateral* 6, no. 1 (2017): https://csalateral.org/issue/6-1/forum-alt-humanities-critical-disability-studies-crip-of-color-critique-kim/.
7. I borrow the term *scatterscram* from Cavar, personal correspondence, May 7, 2023.
8. I offer this trans/crip analytic as supplement to the trans/crip temporalities and microtactics developed by Alexandre Baril and Max Thornton to highlight the shared misfitting of trans and crip life. See

Alexandre Baril, "An Intersectional Analysis of 'Trans-crip't Time' in Ableist, Cisnormative, Anglonormative Societies," *Journal of Literary and Cultural Disability Studies* 10, no. 2 (2016): 155–72; Max Thornton, "Trans/Criptions: Gender, Disability, and Liturgical Experience," *Transgender Studies Quarterly* 6, no. 3 (2019): 358–67.

9. *Oxford English Dictionary,* 2nd ed. (1989), s.v. "scatter."

10. Jacques Derrida, "Différance," in *Margins of Philosophy,* trans. Alan Bass (Chicago: University of Chicago Press, 1982), 3–27.

11. Geoffrey Bennington, *Scatter 1* (New York: Fordham University Press, 2016), 2; Geoffrey Bennington, *Scatter 2* (New York: Fordham University Press, 2021), 9.

12. Édouard Glissant, *Caribbean Discourse: Selected Essays,* trans. J. Michael Dash (1981; Charlottesville: University Press of Virginia, 1989), 19, 255n1.

13. Édouard Glissant, *Poetics of Relation,* trans. Betsy Wing (1990; Ann Arbor: University of Michigan Press, 1997), 33.

14. In my retelling, I rely on the student-produced zine covering the incident *Something Queer Happened Here* (2013), shared with me by interviewee Micah (personal correspondence, October 14, 2018), as well as corroborating accounts offered by multiple interviewees and by Jack Isaac Pryor in *Time Slips: Queer Temporalities, Contemporary Performance, and the Hole of History* (Evanston, Ill.: Northwestern University Press, 2017), 168–201.

15. *Something Queer Happened Here,* 3.

16. *Something Queer Happened Here,* 4.

17. *Something Queer Happened Here,* 6.

18. Kate Manne, *Down Girl: The Logic of Misogyny* (Oxford: Oxford University Press, 2017).

19. Sheila Cavanaugh, *Queering Bathrooms: Gender, Sexuality, and the Hygienic Imagination* (Toronto: University of Toronto Press, 2010).

20. Alison Moore, "Colonial Visions of 'Third World' Toilets: A Nineteenth-Century Discourse That Haunts Contemporary Tourism," in *Ladies and Gents: Public Toilets and Gender,* ed. Olga Gershenson and Barbara Penne (Philadelphia: Temple University Press, 2009), 105–25; Elizabeth Abel, "Bathroom Doors and Drinking Fountains: Jim Crow's Racial Symbolic," *Critical Inquiry* 25, no. 3 (2009): 435–81.

21. María Lugones, "Heterosexualism and the Colonial/Modern Gender System," *Hypatia* 22, no. 1 (2007): 186–209; Hortense J. Spillers, "Mama's Baby, Papa's Maybe: An American Grammar Book," *Diacritics* 17, no. 2 (1987): 64–81.

22. Hampshire College, "Disorientation Packet," 2017, https://www.hampshire.edu/disorientation-packet.

23. *Something Queer Happened Here,* 21.

24. *Something Queer Happened Here,* 5, 8, 12–13.

25. *Something Queer Happened Here,* 33.

26. Interview with Melissa by Perry Zurn and Aster (Erich) Pitcher, October 4–5, 2017.
27. Cameron Awkward-Rich, *The Terrible We: Thinking with Trans Maladjustment* (Durham, N.C.: Duke University Press, 2022), 55.
28. Awkward-Rich, *Terrible We*, 2; Susan Stryker, "(De)Subjugated Knowledges: An Introduction to Transgender Studies," in *The Transgender Studies Reader*, ed. Susan Stryker and Stephen Whittle (New York: Routledge, 2006), 1–2.
29. Awkward-Rich, *Terrible We*, 59.
30. Awkward-Rich, 32, 44, 58.
31. Awkward-Rich, 93.
32. Awkward-Rich, 94, 95, 108.
33. Awkward-Rich, 19, 20; Carson McCullers, *The Member of the Wedding* (1946; New York: Mariner Books, 2004), 42.
34. Awkward-Rich, 150, 165n16. See also Awkward-Rich's use of the "motley we" in "I Wish I Knew How It Would Feel to Be Free," *Paris Review*, June 11, 2020, and "Feeling That Motley We," *Audio QT*, January 19, 2021.
35. Stefano Harney and Fred Moten, *The Undercommons: Fugitive Planning and Black Study* (Brooklyn: Autonomedia, 2013), 74.
36. *Something Queer Happened Here*, 21, 20.
37. *Something Queer Happened Here*, 9.
38. *Something Queer Happened Here*, 8, 21, 3, 4.
39. *Something Queer Happened Here*, 2. Two references to "crazy" also occur in Omi Osun/Dr. Joni Jones, "Six Rules for Allies," *Something Queer Happened Here*, 10–12.
40. *Something Queer Happened Here*, 5.
41. *Something Queer Happened Here*, 4.
42. *Something Queer Happened Here*, 32.
43. *Something Queer Happened Here*, 15.
44. Interview with Joshua by Perry Zurn, July 10, 2020.
45. Interview with Blake by Perry Zurn, February 12, 2021. See also Williams v. Kincaid 2022, 45. F.4th 759, 763 (4th Cir. 2022).
46. Cavar, "Toward transMad Epistemologies: A Working Text," *Spark: A 4C4Equality Journal* 4 (2022): https://sparkactivism.com/toward-transmad-epistemologies/; Megan Burke, "Cis Sense and the Habit of Gender Assignment," *Journal of Speculative Philosophy* 36, no. 2 (2022): 206–18.
47. Cavar, "Keeping It Surreal: Writing transMad Poetic Realities," presentation at Midwest Modern Language Association, November 16–21, 2022, Minneapolis.
48. Cavar, "In Praise of -Less: [transMad Shouts from Absent (Pl)aces]," *AZE Journal* (August 7, 2022): https://azejournal.com/article/2022/8/4/in-praise-of-less-transmad-shouts-from-absent-places.
49. T-SWAG (Trans Studies Working Group), 2018–2019.

50. Sonny Nordmarken, "Becoming Ever More Monstrous: Feeling Trans-gender In-Betweenness," *Qualitative Inquiry* 20, no. 1 (2014): 37–50; Sonny Nordmarken, "Queering Gendering: Trans Epistemologies and the Disruption and Production of Gender Accomplishment Practices," *Feminist Studies* 45, no. 1 (2019): 36–66.

51. Sonny Nordmarken, "Contesting Lyme," in *The Oxford Handbook of the Sociology of the Body and Embodiment* (Oxford: Oxford University Press, 2020), 431–46.

52. Nordmarken, "Contesting Lyme," 437.

53. See also Jennifer Nash, "Citational Desires: On Black Feminism's Institutional Longings," *Diacritics* 48, no. 3 (2020): 76–91.

54. Perry Zurn, preface to *Curiosity and Power: The Politics of Inquiry* (Minneapolis: University of Minnesota Press, 2021), x.

The Racializing Work of Biological Sex

Marie Draz

The concept of biological sex continues to be a cornerstone of anti-trans politics. Evidence of this can be found across a wide range of institutions, from education and the military to health care and housing. Recent examples include state legislative attempts to mandate that students should only have access to sports and bathrooms that align with their biological sex, not their gender identity; a policy explicitly requiring military members to serve in their biological sex; and a leaked 2017 memo by the Department of Health and Human Services (HHS) proposing a federal definition of *sex* as established "on a biological basis."[1]

Despite the confidence with which such legislation is often proposed, the question of what exactly biological sex is remains far from answered. The 2018 military policy, for instance, defines it as "chromosomes, gonads, hormones, and genitals," while the HHS memo reportedly states that it means individuals are established as "either male or female, unchangeable, and determined by the genitals that a person is born with" and "based on immutable biological traits identifiable by or before birth."[2] In 2016, a federal judge in Texas overturning an Obama-era recommendation allowing trans students to use the bathroom associated with their gender identity stated that the "plain meaning of the term sex" (a meaning that "cannot be disputed") referred to "biological and anatomical differences between male and female students as determined at their birth."[3] Other state legislative attempts quickly move to the birth certificate as the final arbiter of what sex is, as in North Carolina's bathroom bill (H.B. 2): "biological sex—the physical condition of being male or female, which is stated on a person's birth certificate."[4]

Following the U.S. Supreme Court June 2020 ruling in *Bostock v. Clayton County*, which declared that discrimination against LGBTQ people is prohibited under Title VII's sex discrimination clause, many trans advocates thought that perhaps the tide was turning on what had been widely reported as a rollback of trans rights.[5] However, while there have been important examples of overturned policy, such as in the case of the 2018 military requirement to serve in one's biological sex, the early days of the Biden administration also brought with them a record number of states rushing to one-up each other with evidence to the contrary. The concept of biological sex has remained steadily at the core of these intensifying efforts. To offer just a few examples, in 2021 the governor of Tennessee signed an antitrans sports bill, an antitrans bathroom bill, and an anti-LGBTQ education bill, all of which cite biological sex.[6] In Alabama, H.B. 391 uses the language of "biological males and biological females" to justify an antitrans sports ban.[7] And in Arkansas, a bill banning gender-affirming medical treatment for people under eighteen states that "'biological sex' means the biological indication of male and female in the context of reproductive potential or capacity."[8]

These legislative attempts have been widely reported as trying to legislate trans people "out of existence," a point that echoes Eva S. Hayward's more theoretical reflections on how trans people are denied ontological substance.[9] Across their efforts, a set of views about sex repeatedly emerges: sex is rooted in the body, sex is binary, sex is determined at birth, and sex should be recorded in a document. While these more recent actions can certainly be chalked up to a desire to stoke a culture war in response to losses in the 2020 U.S. presidential election, they—and their very real effects on people's lives—nevertheless deserve careful attention and committed resistance. This is especially true when it comes to the concept of biological sex, the use of which is certainly not restricted to the legislative realm: this line of thinking about biological sex has regularly been amplified by trans-exclusionary or gender-critical feminists.

Within antitrans feminism, one of the more prominent examples of the use of sex is Sheila Jeffreys's *Gender Hurts,* which
argues that trans people (and, it follows, the gender studies scholars who listen to them) are dangerously disrupting the idea of sex
as a universal, unchanging, and biological category and, as a result, harming feminism and disallowing women (and lesbians in
particular) a stable identity rooted in sex.[10] In the United States,
the alliance between conservative, right-wing projects and radical feminists is nowhere more apparent than in the appearance
of a group of self-proclaimed feminists at an event hosted by the
Heritage Foundation in 2019.[11] The Heritage Foundation is a think
tank that espouses conservative, right-wing ideas, including that
the sex/gender distinction and "transgender theories" are the root
of the destruction of the family and the end of the idea of man and
woman.[12] Republican Senator James Lankford cited J. K. Rowling's
now infamous remarks on the immutable reality of biological sex
and the need to maintain biological sex as a central political category as part of an argument against the Equality Act, which would
amend the Civil Rights Act of 1964 to include antidiscrimination
protections on the basis of sexual orientation and gender identity.[13]

In this chapter, I argue that decolonial feminist methodology
offers a crucial lens for understanding the use of biological sex in
antitrans politics. I use the work of decolonial feminist philosopher María Lugones to illuminate the abovementioned legislative
and feminist moves as not only antitrans but also fundamentally
colonial and racist. I do this by placing Lugones into conversation with trans studies scholar Paisley Currah's argument that
we should focus on what sex does, not what it is. The conversation sharpens the need to think the racialized material history of
the category of biological sex alongside its persistence in antitrans
politics today. I use Lugones's work to point to the insufficiency of
common points of trans advocacy, including some forms of trans-
affirming feminism, and the need for simultaneously trans and decolonial analyses of the use of biological sex. While Lugones does
not engage explicitly with trans thought, I show that this conversation enriches not only trans thought but also Lugones's decolonial
feminism, as the cisgender commitments of what Lugones calls
"the colonial/modern gender system" are brought into sharper

focus.[14] In closing, I reflect on how philosophical resources such as Lugones's decolonial feminism may illuminate trans experiences without being accountable to those experiences, and I speculate about what it takes to make philosophical frameworks both illuminative and accountable.

What Sex Does

The appeal to "common sense" about biological sex pervasive in antitrans legislation echoes what Talia Mae Bettcher, referencing Harold Garfinkel, summarizes as the "natural attitude" about sex: "the view that genitalia are the essential determinants of sex," a view that remains "deeply entrenched in the dominant cultural mainstream" despite its reductive simplicity.[15] In Bettcher's words, the natural attitude offers a "kind of pretheoretical common sense about sex," one that does not seem to be disrupted by evidence to the contrary.[16] Along similar lines, Paisley Currah writes that despite decades of feminist and trans scholarship and activism, sex continues to operate as a "'common sense' universalizing backdrop," a point that echoes the abovementioned Texas judge's comment about how the "plain meaning" of sex "cannot be disputed."[17] Currah calls this commonsense view about sex the "traditional view," which is that sex is fixed at birth, that it is binary, and that it cannot be changed.

While acknowledging the power that this view continues to have, as evident in the previous examples of legislative and feminist views, Currah also outlines other theories of sex and their corresponding positions on sex (re)classification, all of which have put an increasing amount of pressure on the traditional view over the last several decades. The first view states that sex is constituted by genitals but can be changed, thus allowing for sex reclassification based on medical reassignment. This view is associated with mid-twentieth-century sexology, yet it also continues to powerfully resonate with commonsense views that gender is about genitalia and that biological sex marks that connection. Second, there is the view that sex should be replaced with gender identity and that the assignment of a female, male, or nonbinary marker should follow from one's self-identification. This is the position adopted by most mainstream trans rights experts and organizations, including an increasing number of medical organizations, who argue that there is no one medical definition of *sex* that allows it to be a quick and easy arbiter of legal classification. In the face of what once felt like an immoveable marriage of the law and medicine on the fixed nature of sex, Joanne Meyerowitz details how many medical professionals instead came to believe that the strongly felt sense of one's own gender was "less malleable than the body."[18] It is worth noting that this latter view (emphasizing gender identity over sex) also mirrors the movement of trans-affirming (or at least trans-neutral) feminism, which has, for several decades now, used the language of *gender* over that of *sex*. Finally, the third view states explicitly that sex is an effect of gender norms and that sex classification should be ended.[19] This view is more closely related to work by feminist theorists such as Judith Butler (and is, along with the second view, also a central target of antitrans feminists invested in the category of biological sex) and Anne Fausto-Sterling.[20] While distinct in its argument that sex classification should be ended, it remains connected to the second view through its critique of how gender is naturalized by way of discourse around biological sex differences.

My argument is that the second and third views, which are arguably the most popular trans-affirming alternatives to the view that sex is immutable, binary, and fixed at birth, both miss the racializing work of sex.[21] By referring to the "work" of sex, I am drawing on Currah's argument that we should focus less on what sex is (battles over definitions of *sex,* pointing out the insufficiencies of various definitions, etc.) and more on what sex does.[22] By focusing on what sex does, Currah directs our attention to the effects of sex: How is *sex* used by different institutions? How do the definitions of *sex* shift depending on those different uses? As evidence for this necessary shift in focus, Currah cites how often state officials exhibit a concern over the consequences (both intended and unintended) of various decisions about sex classification. For example, in debates around sex classification on birth certificates in New York City, policymakers were most concerned about the effects of changing definitions of *sex,* not necessarily with what sex is.[23] This was in marked contrast to trans advocates, who dealt in the "register of expertise and truth," expecting rationality and correct definitions of *sex* to win.[24] By contrast, Currah gives several examples of officials responding with concerns about "ramifications"—for example, those who distributed benefits were worried about how it may complicate their work, while those involved with identity management were concerned with the correct match between an individual and their records. Other possible effects for "schools, housing, workplaces, and prisons" were also noted. "In the syntax of the City's structures of governance," Currah writes, "sex was a mobile property—dependent not on what it is, but what it does."[25] This is why Currah defines *sex* as "what is recorded after a decision has been made by state bureaucracies and judges," "ink shapes on paper, the electrical on/off pulses of binary codes in administrative records": to focus on what sex does, rather than what it is, means to ask how different agencies put sex to work, such as in the regulation of families, tracking of births and deaths, administration of identity documents (and what those documents do), etc.[26] "Fixating on what sex 'really is,'" Currah writes, "hinders our ability to understand why sex is operationalized differently in particular circumstances."[27]

Letting go of the *what*ness of sex, seeing it as the "mobile property" it is, challenges common trans advocacy focused on showing misclassifications (sex has been gotten "wrong") or contradictions (showing that the rules of different institutions do not agree with each other about what sex is). Instead, Currah argues that we should prioritize the questions: What is produced by sex in particular contexts? What does it accomplish?

I turn now to the "racializing" part of my claim about the racializing work of sex that can be missed in both mainstream trans and feminist arguments about sex. While Currah focuses on what sex does in distinct institutions, I argue that within Lugones's decolonial feminist philosophy there is a different account of what sex does, one that offers a crucial vantage point from which to situate and understand antitrans uses of biological sex and their implicit commitments in a broader historical framework. Keeping Currah's focus on what sex does in mind, looking at sex through a decolonial feminist framework emphasizes the racializing and colonial work of sex, both historically and today. As I will explore, this account has important implications for understanding at least some of the animating force behind the persistence of the category of biological sex today.

The Racializing Work of Sex in the Colonial/Modern Gender System

In "Gender and Universality in Colonial Methodology," Lugones builds on her earlier writing on decolonial feminism to question the universality tied to the concept of gender, arguing instead for an understanding of gender as a colonial conception.[28] It is this understanding of gender that I argue should be brought to bear on antitrans uses of biological sex today. Against a colonial methodology that reads gender across all temporal and spatial frameworks (a reading that Lugones links to "feminism in its universal face"), Lugones argues for a decolonial feminist methodology.[29] This methodology resists an "attachment to gender." *Gender* carries a specific meaning here: the "attachment" Lugones critiques is to the coloniality of gender, or to the ongoing effects of colonialism in the way gender is theorized, lived, and perceived.

In Lugones's earlier work on the topic, she draws on Black feminist theories of intersectionality (Patricia Hill Collins, Kimberlé Crenshaw) and decolonial theorist Aníbal Quijano's account of the coloniality of power to develop the concept of the colonial/modern gender system.[30] The coloniality of power describes the lasting impact of the colonial imposition of biologized racial categories on modern geocultural identities coded as inferior and superior (as well as primitive/civilized, traditional/modern, irrational/rational) and the use of those identities in global capitalism. Following Quijano, we can witness the ongoing effects of racial categories forged in colonialism in the racialized valuation of labor today, such as in the processes by which colonized parts of the globe become coded as "cheap labor" while other parts become the beneficiaries of that labor. While Lugones agrees with Quijano that the coloniality of power and modernity suffuse human existence today, and also includes class and capitalist logics as places where we can see these ongoing effects, she critiques Quijano for failing to subject the concept of gender to sufficient critique.

The role of sex reemerges at this point. Lugones argues that although Quijano's account of coloniality rightly includes the ways that modern, biologized concepts of race emerged through colonization, his understanding of coloniality and gender is limited. While Quijano sees coloniality as structuring gender, he sees gender as a way of organizing "sex, its resources and products."[31] For Lugones, this account of gender makes the mistake of taking for granted the preexisting nature of that which it is organizing: a biologically deterministic notion of sexual dimorphism. Using African anticolonial scholar Oyèrónkẹ́ Oyěwùmí's work on pre-colonial Yoruban understandings of gender and Native (Laguna Pueblo) feminist scholar Paula Gunn Allen's work on the impact of colonization on Indigenous organization of social life, Lugones argues that the modern understanding of gender (as binary and grounded in biological attributes) should instead be understood as a colonial imposition.[32] As she writes in "Toward a Decolonial Feminism," this is not about "adding" a gendered reading to a raced reading of colonialism but rather about "re-reading" capitalist colonial modernity, "a lens which allows us to see that which is hidden" in understandings of both race and gender.[33]

That which is hidden, according to Lugones, is the "light and dark side" of the colonial/modern gender system. When hidden, it is the light side that travels under the name of "gender." Sexual dimorphism is crucial to the light side, as it serves as the basis for the dominant ordering of gender and sexual norms. By contrast, those on the dark side of the system are regularly portrayed as sexually aberrant (e.g., nonheterosexual) and as nondimorphic.[34] They are associated with sex, rather than gender, and subsequently barred from normative gender categories of "man" and "woman." Sex and gender therefore become a generative source of difference between the light and dark side; gender is denied to the colonized, who are portrayed as trapped at the level of sex while still being judged according to the very gendered norms they are denied access to. As a result, Lugones argues that one of the most important elements of the coloniality of gender, or the ongoing effects of colonialism on the way gender is lived today, "is the dehumanization of colonized and African-diasporic women as lacking gender, one of the marks of the human, and thus being reduced to labor and to raw sex, conceived as non-socializable sexual differ-ence."[35] Class and labor reemerge here as important concepts, as animated not only by racial categories forged in colonialism (as we saw in Quijano's argument) but also by sex and gender. In Xhercis Méndez's words, Lugones shows how "the existence of and later further introduction of physiognomically distinct laboring bodies become produced as the constitutive outside of 'gender.'"[36] Or, as Françoise Vergès puts it, in reference to Lugones's work, "The his-torical experience of colonized women is not only that of racial devaluation . . . but also of sexual assignment."[37]

The production of the concept of biological sex ("conceived as non-socializable sexual difference") is crucial to Lugones's account because it is through the separation of sex and gender that the ra-cialization occurs. Sex and gender, in other words, function in dis-tinct ways; it is not simply that gender needs the biological sub-stratum of sex to retroactively justify its norms but rather that the gender system needs the very idea of biological sex as an entirely separate matter to accomplish its racializing function. The idea of biological sex, in other words, is needed over and beyond the ways it secures and grounds the concept of gender; in Lugones's account, the concept of gender as the socialization of sex differ-ences is an insufficient way of understanding what the sex/gender underpinnings of the colonial/modern gender system does. "If I am right about the coloniality of gender," Lugones writes, "sex has to stand alone."[38] Insofar as gender is a "mark of the human," being denied gender means being barred not only from the categories "man" and "woman" but also from humanity itself. The denial oc-curs through the separation of sex and gender: gender grounded in sexual dimorphism is an achievement reserved for the light side; those on the dark side are used to represent sex, or the ideal of a biological substratum, but are blocked from gender. The cognitive needs of colonialism require the colonized to be associated with sex as a division between male and female bodies (and therefore the possibility of normative gender grounded in sexual dimor-phism for the light side) while simultaneously being portrayed as nondimorphic and therefore incapable of accessing normative gender.[39]

This brings us back to the second primary target of Lugones's analysis: feminist theory that fails to take seriously the colonial/

modern gender system. Lugones's critique of white Anglo-American feminist accounts of gender becomes more pronounced in "Toward a Decolonial Feminism," where Lugones critiques a tendency to see gender as socializable sexual difference.[40] This critique re-emerges as a central tenet of decolonial feminist methodology in "Gender and Universality in Colonial Methodology." A colonial methodology understands gender as the social organization of sex, thereby obfuscating the very way the dark side of the gender system is produced. To reiterate, the problem is that this understanding of sex and gender as mutually constitutive, or the replacement of sex with gender—commonly seen in both trans and feminist accounts—cannot account for the racialization accomplished by the separation of the concepts. Lugones's intervention is therefore twofold: against decolonial theories that do not take seriously the role of gender in colonization and against feminist theories that do not take seriously the impact of colonization on understandings of gender today. Both accounts of gender are only capable of theorizing what she calls the "light side of gender." Instead, Lugones allows us to hear the persistence of the idea of biological sex as grounded in racist and colonial pasts and presents.

I turn now more explicitly to the question of how Lugones's decolonial feminist approach to sex and gender illuminates anti-trans uses of biological sex. I then explore the question of what it means for theories to be not only illuminative of but also accountable to trans experiences: while Lugones's decolonial feminist methodology may be useful for trans philosophical accounts of sex and gender, and the racialized material history behind the sex/gender distinction, it is also important to acknowledge its limitations. I therefore conclude with reflections on how to build a decolonial, trans, feminist philosophy by drawing on another aspect of Lugones's methodology: the emphasis on seeing decolonial feminism as a praxical task.

On Illumination and Accountability

In J. R. Latham's autoethnographic study of Latham's own experience as a trans patient, Latham traces the multiple meanings of *sex* that emerge in clinical practices of trans medicine.[41] Here is an incomplete list of "what sex is" produced by Latham's analysis: sex is self-determined, sex is not permanent, sex is assigned at birth, sex is breast prominence, sex is testosterone levels in the blood, sex is hormones, sex is genitals, sex is feeling, sex is a believable narrative linking past-sex, present-sex, and future-sex, sex is dress, sex is gait, sex is mannerism, sex is facial features, sex is height, sex is body build, sex is diagnosable, sex is nipple size, sex is nipple position, sex is chest shape, sex is the most important aspect of a person's life. Sex, Latham theorizes, is multiple: as one moves through the clinic, the "target" of sex shifts constantly; as soon as you meet one goal, another emerges.

In resistance to antitrans uses of sex, it is common to point to examples such as the ones given by Latham to show the actual mutability of sex. This approach is tied to the larger strategy of martialing both science and rationality to show the fundamental incoherence of the way that sex is used: to show the reductive simplicity of treating sex as if it were binary, fixed, singular, and the kind of thing that could be assessed and recorded in a document once and for all. As Lugones's work helps us to see, however, when theorized through the lens of the colonial/modern gender system, the significance of this mutability of sex shifts; it is the mutability of sex that enables its racializing work.

In "Gender and Universality in Colonial Methodology," Lugones writes that the "new thinking about gender" that has "accompanied the critique of the binary by focusing on intersexuality, transgender, transsssexuality, and the introduction of 'queer' as a nonbinary understanding of gender" has not sufficiently interrogated the connections between the gender binary and colonization or the "relation between colonization, race, and gender."[42] This is an intriguing moment given that it is Lugones's first explicit mention of trans understandings of gender in her writing on decolonial feminism. When read in the context of her larger body of work on decolonial feminism, the critique in this passage is sharpened: given that only the light side of the colonial/modern gender system has ever been treated as binary, critiques of binaristic thought about sex and gender that do not acknowledge its racialized history are insufficiently prepared to understand the racialized stakes of its mobilization. Likewise, it is precisely the mutability of sex, or its lack of any solid identifiable foundation, that has allowed it to be such a mobile source of racializing power. Sally Markowitz, in her work on nineteenth-century sexology, puts the point as follows: "An ideology that considers sexual dimorphism to be embodied only in European 'races' has already, in a sense, thought beyond it [the binary]—hardly, it starts to seem, a revolutionary accomplishment."[43] This point echoes Lugones's analysis that the critique of the binary has not been accompanied by sufficient attention to the role of the binary in establishing the colonial/modern gender system. Insofar as Lugones argues that a binary dimorphic sex has never been applied to the dark side of the gender system, the critique of binary gender must be accompanied by an acknowledgment that the achievement of normative gender grounded in binary sex is already a racial accomplishment.

Lugones's decolonial feminism directs our attention to the racializing work of sex. Recall that the work of sex, on Currah's account, refers to a focus on what sex accomplishes for various institutions. However, as Currah also notes, long-standing forms of state-sanctioned institutional gender discrimination has lessened over previous years; as a result, the consequences of altering sex-classification rules arguably matters less now precisely because such classifications are no longer used to ban same-sex marriages, control property and inheritance allocations, and so on.[44] And yet, sex remains baked into both legal architectures and common sense, as well as a seemingly endless source of grist for the culture war mills. Lugones's decolonial feminist methodology offers another way of thinking about the persistence of the concept of biological sex and why it is not easily refuted with science and rationality, as in efforts to show that sex is not fixed, binary, or singular, or easily replaced with the concept of gender identity, as has been the preferred approach of mainstream trans advocates for many years now. And while the Butlerian view that sex has been gender all along, and is produced by gender norms, has fueled much important resistance to antitrans politics, Lugones also shows that this view often does not do enough to consider how racism and colonialism fuel the very distinction between sex and gender, as well as the history of racial investment in their persistence as categories of knowledge.

A related dimension of antitrans uses of sex illuminated by

Lugones's analysis is the emphasis in antitrans rhetoric on "protecting women" by saving the category of biological sex. For example, the group Hands Across the Aisle explains their platform as follows (under the heading "Gender Identity Harms Women"): "We are a politically diverse group of women who are choosing to stand together to reclaim the definition of sex as a binary concept that refers to one's biological status as male or female."[45] As illustrated in the opening of this chapter, such groups have increasingly joined forces with conservative groups around the legal codification of sex as a biological binary. Lugones's analysis shows not only that this is the outcome of a system that depends on biological sex to prop up normative gender but also that it is white womanhood being protected; the racializing work of sex allows for the category of "woman" to emerge. Emi Koyama's "The Transfeminist Manifesto," written in response to trans-exclusionary feminism, captures this point well.[46] Koyama writes that trans exclusion should be seen as a failure to form a coalitional politics, one that would reach across diverse forms of oppression to "stand up for each other."[47] As such, trans exclusion should be thought alongside an inability to situate the problem of sexism amid "other oppressions such as racism and classism"; in other words, it is a commitment to a politics in which "women from different backgrounds stand up for each other, because if we do not stand up for each other, nobody will."[48] As Kevin Henderson points out in an analysis of the white supremacist history of the concept of biological sex, trans-exclusionary feminists ignore the rich history of feminism as countering precisely the kinds of biological essentialism prevalent in their views.[49] The Combahee River Collective, Henderson reminds us, offers one example of how Black feminists explicitly critique biological determinism; in their 1977 statement, they write: "We know that there is such a thing as a racial-sexual oppression which is neither solely racial nor solely sexual. . . . As Black women we find any type of biological determinism a particularly dangerous and reactionary basis upon which to build a politic."[50]

While I have focused so far on the relevance of Lugones's decolonial feminist account for illuminating trans experiences of the category of biological sex, it is important to note some limitations. First, while I have focused on sex, gender, and race in this chapter, class and sexuality have also made appearances as important threads in Lugones's decolonial feminist writing. One omission, however, is a direct engagement with disability. And yet, there are many signs that a disability justice framework is necessary for a more layered understanding of antitrans legislation from a decolonial perspective. Consider, for example, how colonization involves a differentiation of capacities between the colonized and colonizer, including whether one is perceived to possess reason or be capable of rationality, a judgment that is in turn tied to the type of labor one could perform. Given the strong narrative of trans people as "mentally ill" or unstable in antitrans politics, and the way that biological sex is regularly portrayed in contemporary debates as returning us to both sanity and whiteness, there is a great need for more analysis of antitrans rhetoric that takes seriously both disability justice and the decolonial frameworks identified in this chapter.

Second, Brooklyn Leo highlights the erasure of two-spirit and trans of color lives in Lugones's writing on decolonial feminism, pointing out that Lugones consistently fails to mark the specific targeting of these groups in colonial violence and to explicitly identify the light side of the colonial/modern gender system as normatively cisgender, or as holding the view that "gender is static, indexed to one's sex at birth, and dimorphic."[51] Lugones, in Leo's words, does not go far enough in examining "how cisgender privilege is intimately tied up in colonial structures."[52] As Leo shows, the work of Hortense J. Spillers and C. Riley Snorton also furthers the significance of marking the cisgender commitments of the colonial/modern gender system. Focusing on the context of the Atlantic slave trade, Spillers shows that the conditions of enslavement worked to reduce the captive body to "a thing, becoming *before for* the captor" through the constitution of Black flesh as genderless, nonhuman, and fungible; dovetailing with Lugones's analysis of colonialism, Black feminist scholarship such as that by Spillers shows it is the denial of gender and the assignment of sex that enable the racialized justificatory narratives of enslavement and captivity.[53] In *Black on Both Sides,* C. Riley Snorton builds on Spillers's work by showing that this genealogy offers a critical framework for thinking trans experience today, arguing that modern transness is rooted in how chattel slavery "gave rise to an understanding of gender as mutable and as an amendable form of being."[54] Leo points out that both Spillers and Snorton offer ways of thinking about how "fungibility makes fugitivity possible— moments of flight, escape, and perhaps even liberation," such as in Snorton's exploration of the phenomenon of Black persons "cross-dressing" to escape captivity.[55] Insofar as Blackness is figured as outside of the gender differentiation reserved for whiteness, that very production of "indefiniteness" becomes a source of a "critical modality of political and cultural maneuvering."[56] The mutability of sex/gender not only enables their racialization but also contributes to an understanding of sex/gender as that which can be reconfigured for more liberatory purposes. As such, that which was imposed becomes a condition of escape.

While the bulk of Lugones's writing on decolonial feminism does not attend to what Snorton may call "moments of escape" ("loopholes") from the coloniality of gender, focusing instead on explaining how the colonial/modern gender system works, Lugones does emphasize the question of resistance more strongly in "On Gender and Universality in Colonial Methodology." In this text, she again cites Sojourner Truth as a foundational example of what it means to recognize that *woman* is not a universal term, but she goes on—unlike in her previous mention of Truth—to say that Truth's question ("Ain't I a Woman?") calls for a "new meaning" of *woman*, one "distant from" and "at odds with" the category through whiteness.[57] Lugones connects this call to Frantz Fanon's interrogation of the category of the human and the ways he asks if he—as a Black man—can or should lay claim to the category of the human, given the many ways the category has been constructed to exclude him.[58] Following Truth and Fanon, Lugones calls across this essay for "new men and women," the first time in her writing on decolonial feminism she has made such a call.[59] Moreover, although Lugones does not directly engage with trans resistance to the colonial/modern gender system and its cisgender commitments, work in trans philosophy has certainly engaged with Lugones on the question of resistance.[60] An especially generative example is Talia Mae Bettcher's use of Lugones's work in *Pilgrimages/Peregrinajes* on multiple worlds of sense to theorize how the meanings of *man* and *woman* that circulate in trans communities do not simply reflect the meanings that circulate in dominant, nontrans communities but rather are shaped in and through trans worlds of sense.[61] Such connections could bring us to explore the significance of figuring trans resistance to cisgender logics as resistance to the colonial/modern gender system, questioning when and how these nondominant meanings circulate, a point that would ultimately deepen both trans and decolonial accounts of sex and gender.

Across her work, Lugones repeatedly states that her goal is to make visible the colonial difference. She wants to make visible what was hidden through the illusion of a break between the colonial and the modern and how colonial narratives both relied on and transformed a number of dichotomous hierarchies such as civilized/uncivilized, gender/sex, culture/nature, and man/woman now taken as common sense.[62] She also acknowledges that what she is saying about gender may be said by some to not be "new," a point that she responds to by saying she doesn't see this as a problem.[63] Instead, she invites us to see her work as a call to incorporate this knowledge, however new or old it may be, more deeply into our embodied and perceptual frameworks, into how we perceive and live in the world. How does the attachment to (the coloniality of) gender, as Lugones puts it, keep us from witnessing the use of biological sex outlined in this chapter as not only anti-trans but also racist and colonial? How do various understandings of race, gender, class, disability, and sexuality exhibit complicity with the coloniality of power? The point is not to be entirely free of such complicity but to be able to perceive it and move against it in whatever ways are possible. As Linda Martín Alcoff puts it in an essay on Lugones, "Liberation is defined, then, as changing perceptual and analytical practices so that multiple worlds of sense can be revealed."[64]

In this chapter, I have sought to demonstrate nondominant worlds of sense about the concept of biological sex. I have done this by outlining some of the contributions Lugones makes to understandings of the category of biological sex. By attending to the racialized material history of sex and gender, Lugones offers a philosophical resource that illuminates the persistence of the concept of biological sex despite its incoherence and waning structural influence; what other frameworks might illuminate its ongoing impact on trans lives?

In their introduction to a journal special issue on the work of Lugones, Emma Velez and Nancy Tuana note that Lugones's challenge is "especially important for those interested in liberatory philosophies, broadly, and the critical philosophy of race and feminist thought, specifically."[65] While it has been most common for Lugones's work to be brought to bear on Anglo-American feminism, I have sought to show here that Lugones's work should also be of interest to those interested in trans philosophy and that trans thought should also be seen as a crucial interlocutor for decolonial feminist philosophy. Without the voices, perspectives, and arguments of trans writers, thinkers, and activists, critical elements of the intermeshed systems of categories of difference, such as race and gender, are overlooked. Decolonial feminism is strengthened through a consideration of the cisgender commitments of the colonial/modern gender system and the possibilities of coalitional resistance (trans, feminist, decolonial) to that system. Work at this intersection takes seriously both decolonial feminist and trans insights on the formation and impact of categories such as sex, gender, and race. Doing so requires simultaneously pushing both fields—in the case of decolonial feminism, attending to the interconnections of cisgender and colonial structures; in the case of trans studies, resisting the historical tendency of the field to privilege white, Western theoretical frameworks for thinking sex and gender.

In conclusion, even theories that illuminate trans experiences carry with them potential omissions and unintended consequences. As trans philosophy develops, it is important to think about how illumination and accountability do not always coincide. Philosophers who are invested in undoing white supremacy and colonial structures should see the history of biological sex, and the cisgender commitments of whiteness, as part and parcel of that undoing. Likewise, the field of trans philosophy should interrogate both trans-exclusionary and trans-affirming frameworks for thinking sex and gender, as elements of those frameworks will need to be rethought as part of developing simultaneously trans, decolonial, and feminist insights about the operations of embodiment and power.

Notes

1. Lola Fadulu, "Trump's Rollback of Transgender Rights Extends through Entire Government," *New York Times,* December 6, 2019.
2. "5 Things to Know about DoD's New Policy on Military Service by Transgender Persons and Persons with Gender Dysphoria," U.S. Department of Defense, February 14, 2019, https://www.defense.gov/News /News-Stories/article/article/1783822/5-things-to-know-about-dods -new-policy-on-military-service-by-transgender-perso/; Erica L. Green, Katie Benner, and Robert Pear, "'Transgender' Could Be Defined Out of Existence under Trump Administration," *New York Times,* October 21, 2018.
3. Preliminary Injunction Order, State of Texas et al. v. United States of America et al., No. 7:16-cv-00054-O (U.S. Dist. Ct. for the Northern District of Texas), August 21, 2016, at 31, https://www.txnd.uscourts.gov /sites/default/files/documents/716cv54Doc58.pdf.
4. An Act to Provide for Single-Sex Multiple Occupancy Bathroom and Changing Facilities in Schools and Public Agencies and to Create State-wide Consistency in Regulation of Employment and Public Accommodations, H.B. 2, North Carolina General Assembly, Second Extra Session 2016, https://www.ncleg.gov/Sessions/2015E2/Bills/House/PDF /H2v3.pdf.
5. Bostock v. Clayton County, 590 U.S. 209 (2020).
6. S.B. 228, Tennessee General Assembly, 2021, https://wapp.capitol.tn .gov/apps/Billinfo/default.aspx?BillNumber=SB0228&ga=112; H.B. 1233, Tennessee Accommodations for All Children Act, 2021, https://wapp.capitol.tn.gov/apps/Billinfo/default.aspx?BillNumber =HB1233&ga=112; S.B. 1229, Tennessee General Assembly, 2021, https:// legiscan.com/TN/bill/SB1229/2021.
7. H.B. 391, Alabama General Assembly, 2021, https://legiscan.com/AL /text/HB391/id/2286056.
8. H.B. 1570, Save Adolescents from Experimentation Act, at 5, https:// www.arkleg.state.ar.us/Bills/Detail?id=HB1570&ddBienniumSession =2021%2F2021R.
9. Green, Benner, and Pear, "'Transgender' Could Be Defined out of Existence"; Eva S. Hayward, "Don't Exist," *TSQ: Transgender Studies Quarterly* 4, no. 2 (2017): 191–94.
10. Sheila Jeffreys, *Gender Hurts: A Feminist Analysis of the Politics of Transgenderism* (Abingdon, U.K.: Routledge, Taylor & Francis Group, 2014). For a response to this line of thinking, see Susan Stryker and Talia M. Bettcher, "Introduction: Trans/Feminisms," *TSQ: Transgender Studies*

Quarterly 3, no. 1–2 (2016): 5–14. See also Cameron Awkward-Rich, "Trans, Feminism: Or Reading like a Depressed Transsexual," *Signs* 42, no. 4 (2017): 819–41. For an extended analysis of the narrative so often cited in transphobic feminism that the category of "lesbian" is in danger of being erased, see Mairead Sullivan, *Lesbian Death: Desire and Danger between Feminist and Queer* (Minneapolis: University of Minnesota Press, 2022). For a foundational analysis of feminist transphobia in the United States, see Emi Koyama, "Whose Feminism Is It Anyway?," in *The Transgender Studies Reader,* ed. Susan Stryker and Stephen Whittle (New York: Routledge, 2006), 29–50.

11. Tim Fitzsimons, "Conservative Group Hosts Anti-Transgender Panel of Feminists 'from the Left,'" NBC News, January 29, 2019, https://www.nbcnews.com/feature/nbc-out/conservative-group-hosts-anti-transgender-panel-feminists-left-n964246.

12. Scott Yenor, "Sex, Gender, and the Origin of the Culture Wars: An Intellectual History," Heritage Foundation, accessed July 2, 2021, https://www.heritage.org/gender/report/sex-gender-and-the-origin-the-culture-wars-intellectual-history.

13. Tim Fitzsimons, "GOP Senator Quotes J. K. Rowling while Blocking Vote on LGBTQ Bill," NBC News, June 19, 2020, https://www.nbcnews.com/feature/nbc-out/gop-senator-quotes-j-k-rowling-while-blocking-vote-lgbtq-n1231569.

14. María Lugones, "Heterosexualism and the Colonial/Modern Gender System," *Hypatia* 22, no. 1 (2007): 186–209.

15. Talia Mae Bettcher, "Evil Deceivers and Make Believers: On Transphobic Violence and the Politics of Illusion," *Hypatia* 22, no. 3 (2007): 48.

16. Bettcher, "Evil Deceivers and Make Believers," 49.

17. Paisley Currah, *Sex Is as Sex Does: Governing Transgender Identity* (New York: New York University Press, 2022), 38.

18. Joanne Meyerowitz, *How Sex Changed: A History of Transsexuality in the United States* (Cambridge, Mass.: Harvard University Press, 2002), 99.

19. A more detailed analysis of these views can be found in Currah, *Sex Is as Sex Does,* 42–48.

20. See, for example, Judith Butler, *Gender Trouble: Feminism and the Subversion of Identity* (New York: Routledge, 1990); Anne Fausto-Sterling, *Sexing the Body: Gender Politics and the Construction of Sexuality* (New York: Basic Books, 2000).

21. This argument resonates with work by queer of color theorists about how Butler's early work on sex as an effect of gender misses the racialization of sex. See, for example, Michael Hames-García, "Queer Theory Revisited," in *Gay Latino Studies,* ed. Michael Hames-García and Ernesto Javier Martínez (Durham, N.C.: Duke University Press, 2011).

22. Paisley Currah, "The State," *TSQ: Transgender Studies Quarterly* 1, no. 1–2 (2014): 197–200; Currah, *Sex Is as Sex Does.*

23. Paisley Currah and Lisa Jean Moore, "'We Won't Know Who You Are':

Contesting Sex Designations in New York City Birth Certificates,"
Hypatia 24, no. 3 (2009): 113–35.

24. Currah, *Sex Is as Sex Does*, 35.

25. Currah, 36.

26. Currah, 32.

27. Currah, 32.

28. María Lugones, "Gender and Universality in Colonial Methodology,"
Critical Philosophy of Race 8, no. 1–2 (2020): 25–47.

29. Lugones, "Gender and Universality in Colonial Methodology," 28. For
a longer introduction to the project(s) of decolonial feminism and
connections to women of color feminism, postcolonial feminism, and
anticolonial movements more broadly, see Breny Mendoza, "Coloniality of Gender and Power: From Postcoloniality to Decoloniality,"
in *The Oxford Handbook of Feminist Theory*, ed. Lisa Disch and Mary
Hawkesworth (New York: Oxford University Press, 2015), 100–21.

30. Lugones, "Heterosexualism and the Colonial/Modern Gender Sys-
tem"; María Lugones, "Toward a Decolonial Feminism," *Hypatia* 25,
no. 4 (2010): 742–59; Patricia Hill Collins, *Black Feminist Thought* (New
York: Routledge, 2000); Kimberlé Crenshaw, "Mapping the Margins:
Intersectionality, Identity Politics, and Violence against Women of
Color," in *Critical Race Theory: The Key Writings That Formed the Move-
ment*, ed. Kimberlé Crenshaw, Neil Gotanda, Gary Peller, and Kendall
Thomas (New York: New Press, 1995); Aníbal Quijano, "Coloniality of
Power, Eurocentrism, and Latin America," *Nepantla: Views from South*
1, no. 3 (2000): 533–80.

31. Lugones, "Heterosexualism and the Colonial/Modern Gender System,"
193.

32. Oyèrónkẹ́ Oyěwùmí, *The Invention of Women: Making an African Sense
of Western Gender Discourses* (Minneapolis: University of Minnesota
Press, 1997); Paula Gunn Allen, *The Sacred Hoop: Recovering the Feminine in American Indian Traditions* (Boston: Beacon Press, 1986).

33. Lugones, "Toward a Decolonial Feminism," 742.

34. For a more detailed analysis of this portrayal, see Anne McClintock,
Imperial Leather: Race, Gender, and Sexuality in the Colonial Contest
(New York: Routledge, 1995).

35. Lugones, "Gender and Universality in Colonial Methodology," 33.

36. Xhercis Méndez, "Notes toward a Decolonial Feminist Methodology:
Revisiting the Race/Gender Matrix," *Trans-Scripts* 5 (2015): 43.

37. Françoise Vergès, *A Decolonial Feminism*, trans. Ashley J. Bohrer (London: Pluto Press, 2021), 27.

38. Lugones, "Toward a Decolonial Feminism," 744.

39. See Marie Draz, "Retro-Sex, Anti-Trans Legislation, and the Colonial/
Modern Gender System," *philoSOPHIA* 11, no. 1–2 (2021): 26–48.

40. For a more sustained analysis of how Lugones's account of the coloniality of gender challenges white Anglo feminist philosophical

accounts of sex and gender, see Draz, "Retro-Sex, Anti-Trans Legislation, and the Colonial/Modern Gender System."

41. J. R. Latham, "(Re)Making Sex: A Praxiography of the Gender Clinic," *Feminist Theory* 18, no. 2 (2017): 177–204.
42. Lugones, "Gender and Universality in Colonial Methodology," 30.
43. Sally Markowitz, "Pelvic Politics: Sexual Dimorphism and Racial Difference," *Signs* 26, no. 2 (2001): 391.
44. Currah, *Sex Is as Sex Does*, 21–22.
45. "Gender Identity Harms Women," Hands Across the Aisle, accessed July 2, 2021, https://handsacrosstheaislewomen.com/.
46. Emi Koyama, "The Transfeminist Manifesto," in *Catching a Wave: Reclaiming Feminism for the 21st Century,* ed. Rory Dicker and Alison Piepmeier (Boston: Northeastern University Press, 2003), 244–54.
47. Koyama, "Transfeminist Manifesto," 245.
48. Koyama, 245.
49. Kevin Henderson, "J.K. Rowling and the White Supremacist History of 'Biological Sex,'" *Radical History Review Blog,* July 28, 2020, https://abusablepast.org/j-k-rowling-and-the-white-supremacist-history-of-biological-sex/.
50. Combahee River Collective, "A Black Feminist Statement," in *This Bridge Called My Back: Writings by Radical Women of Color,* ed. Cherríe Moraga and Gloria Anzaldúa (New York: Kitchen Table Press, 1981), 217.
51. Brooklyn Leo, "The Colonial/Modern [Cis]Gender System and Trans World Traveling," *Hypatia* 35, no. 3 (2020): 467.
52. Leo, "Colonial/Modern [Cis]Gender System," 456.
53. Hortense J. Spillers, "Mama's Baby, Papa's Maybe: An American Grammar Book," *Diacritics* 17, no. 2 (1987): 64.
54. C. Riley Snorton, *Black on Both Sides: A Racial History of Trans Identity* (Minneapolis: University of Minnesota Press, 2017), 57.
55. Leo, "Colonial/Modern [Cis]Gender System," 457; Snorton, *Black on Both Sides.*
56. Snorton, *Black on Both Sides,* 56.
57. Lugones, "Toward a Decolonial Feminism," 745; Lugones, "Gender and Universality in Colonial Methodology," 36.
58. Lugones, "Gender and Universality in Colonial Methodology," 36; Frantz Fanon, *The Wretched of the Earth,* trans. Richard Philcox (New York: Grove Press, 2005).
59. Lugones, "Gender and Universality in Colonial Methodology," 36.
60. In addition to Leo, discussed above, see also PJ DiPietro, "Hallucinating Knowing: (Extra)Ordinary Consciousness, More-Than-Human Perception, and Other Decolonizing Remedios within Latina and Xicana Feminist and Queer Theories," in *Theories of the Flesh: Latinx and Latin American Feminisms, Transformation, and Resistance,* ed. Andrea J. Pitts, Mariana Ortega, and José Medina (New York: Oxford Uni-

versity Press, 2020), 220–38; Hil Malatino, "Tough Breaks: Trans Rage and the Cultivation of Resilience," *Hypatia* 34, no. 1 (2018): 121–40.

61. Talia Mae Bettcher, "Trapped in the Wrong Theory: Rethinking Trans Oppression and Resistance," *Signs* 39, no. 2 (2014): 383–406; María Lugones, *Pilgrimages/Peregrinajes: Theorizing Coalition against Multiple Oppressions* (Lanham, Md.: Rowman & Littlefield, 2003).

62. Lugones, "Gender and Universality in Colonial Methodology," 8.

63. Lugones, "Heterosexualism and the Colonial/Modern Gender System," 208n15.

64. Linda Martín Alcoff, "Lugones's World-Making," *Critical Philosophy of Race* 8, no. 1–2 (2020): 209.

65. Emma Velez and Nancy Tuana, "Editors' Introduction: Tango Dancing with María Lugones: Toward Decolonial Feminisms," *Critical Philosophy of Race* 8, no. 1–2 (2020): 1.

Latin American
Travesti/Trans Theory

Marlene Wayar
Translated by Rocío Pichon-Rivière

The travesti/trans community in Latin America has disrupted
persistent political practices. The denunciation of compulsory
heterosexuality as a core construct that sustains the oppressions
against our bodies points to patriarchy and its role imparting violence, discrimination, and death. It also makes visible the ways
in which the LGTTTBIQ+ and women's movements, the feminist
spaces, the Left, and academia sustain patriarchy inasmuch as they
sustain the sex/gender binary and impose upon the travesti/trans
community an agenda born from that colonial logic.[1] The emerging presence of travesti/trans people in public spaces has been and
still is resisted with egregious vehemence. Yet the force of our demands has opened cracks in and infiltrated languages, with our
perspectives and modes of intervention contributing to spaces
such as public policy. Today it is impossible to think about gender,
identity politics, and the idea of humankind without the contribution of the travesti/trans people territorialized in Latin America.
However, the practices of invisibilization of our bodies and what
they elicit are pervasive. One aspect that is often invisibilized is
that these forms of knowledge have their root in Latin America
and often in a situation of sex work. There are also practices of
extraction and exclusion that come from the feminist sector. For
some people, extractivism allows them to present themselves as
progressive and, for feminists on the TERF spectrum, exclusion is
an opportunity for producing pseudo-biological arguments.

There continues to be a barrier blocking real incorporation of travesti/trans perspectives, one that could transcend borders and unify different gazes into one overarching plan of action. This is due to a number of reasons, including the lack of effective understanding of the complexity offered by travesti and trans people's perspectives, the difficulty of feeling empathy toward such life experiences, or the ways in which feminist practices have surreptitiously mimicked passé discourses regarding politics, art, the experience of colonization, diaspora, strangeness, and migration. It is not enough to include the prefix *trans* in political proposals; rather, one must recognize the limits of one's own conceptualizations, increase the capacity to listen, and produce collective actions and interventions.

This Latin American travesti theory in transformation is an invocation, inviting those *identidades cloacalizadas* [literally, "gutterized identities"], who have not yet been conceived as agents of knowledge-power, to join the conversation and construct a theoretical corpus that shows without euphemisms the world through their gaze.[2] From a sex-working perspective, we complicate the theoretical framework with a series of epistemological interventions: converging, nomadic *[transhumante],* and eclectic epistemologies, each with a depth of its own, grounded in our experiences. A break from colonial order implies thinking (of oneself with) autonomy, not just emancipation from coloniality. It demands an ethics not to colonize, which is why this invitation is to collectively construct, using as a point of departure some first intuitions. In this essay, I propose two concepts to be revised: one of them contemporary ("sexual/gender dissidence") and the other historical. I present the latter, "travesti," in a pedagogical vein to interrogate how we can create a theory that responds to the precept of not objectifying subjects in order to study them and, quite to the contrary, how we can create a theory for listening to all those who have been made mere objects. This is an invitation to hold space where the formerly marginalized can have the agency to produce knowledge without having to abandon their own vernacular, to confirm and correct any proposition, and to reach conclusions and consensus. From the clarity that emerges from this failed world of hate and unwell-being, I propose *A Good Enough Theory* to search for alternative strategies for existing and for being in the world.[3]

The proposal is to recuperate some key concepts that travesti/ trans bodies have generated and, from there, to acknowledge the presence of the realities they do and have named, ever since the conquest. These realities flourished first in the silence imposed as sexual dissidences were thought of as a "cardinal sin" *[pecado ne-fando]* and, later, in the ways in which criminalization and patholo-gization were to become entangled in nation-state formations. In recent decades, through different mediums—such as spoken speech, theories, literature, interviews, manifestos, testimonies, artwork, and performances—these ideas came together to build the matrix of a Latin American travesti/trans theory, despite the enormous difficulties that are implicated in the unification of such diverse sociogeographical experiences.

Sexual/Gender Dissidence

The expression "sexual/gender dissidence" encompasses several diverse identities, collectives, and communities. It is risky to at-tempt an enumeration expecting it to be exhaustive. Perhaps the terms *maricas, lesbianas, tortas,* travestis, trans, *sapatão, veado, putxs, no-binarios* are the most extended and politicized.[4] These came to-gether as a sociopolitical movement that does not align itself with heteronormativity, while also differentiating itself from homonor-mativity. The concept has been affirmed since the early first de-cade of the 2000s as a critique of the descriptive, ahistorical, and depoliticized term *sexual diversity.* While the latter seems to be rooted in taxonomic criteria that could even include heterosexual-ity, sexual/gender dissidence by contrast refuses to think of iden-tities as discrete notions around which people adjust themselves in stereotypical ways. Affirming instead that we are identitarian constructs of extremely personal, open, and moving features, under constant construction as expressed in the gerund *[gerundio] becoming.*[5] Its meaning is a rejection of terms devoid of political potential, where governments can account for a bare minimum of representation to clean up their political image (e.g., pinkwash-ing). The strategy is to become untokenizable and to democratize spaces, understanding that these are shared spaces of shared be-longing. To refuse to allow a hegemony that is protecting its formal power and privileges to offer the pretense of generosity or charity by way of managing and extending inclusion rates with their exclusive discretionary power. Dissidence is understood as a practice: that of refusing the doctrine, beliefs, or conducts dictated and demanded by heteronormality. The hegemony has regimented the spaces of circulation, aesthetics, roles, types of relationality, ways of interpellation, modes of expression, and, above all, manners and positionalities in the political negotiation that do not account for intersectionality regarding racialization, class, and colonization. In other words, decolonial efforts should not only be attuned to geopolitical and economic power differences but also address the entire colonizing combo that has imposed a culture, language, religion, social/relational organization (e.g., forms of familiarity, paternity, and maternity, among others), and, above all else, an exclusionary concept of humanity (i.e., man/woman as engenderization).

If people in general are situated in alignment with patriarchal order, so too are the diversity movement and institutional LGTTTBIQ+ discourses. The LGTTTBIQ+ movement has economic power of its own in addition to absorbing international funds coming from nonprofits, which increases its power to impose an agenda, a way of naming, and a style of negotiation with patriarchy. Latin American/Abya Yalan travesti theory hopes to account for identities in diverse contexts and from the perspective of converging epistemologies: that of First Nations, Afro-descendants, popular educators, art, masculinities, and trans childhoods free of violence. That is, revisiting Marxist, feminist, and queer currents of thought but territorializing them—in the local contexts of our continent with the purpose of making sense and explaining such knowledge formations as a colonialist tool that historically had extractivist manners. They often strip dissident identities of their knowledge and use them in institutional contexts in ways that deform and ignore the reality that they emerged from, with the excuse of making them legible and of legitimizing their existence. In the process of universalization, privileges are conserved, and the sexual diversity paradigm gets reinforced with a homogenizing effect. To make these modes of knowing intelligible is to reformat them in heteronormativity's own image. Dissidence makes visible

the violence of the stigmatization, criminalization, pathologization, and hierarchization that results from all this.

Human people are born in a situation of extreme precarity,
with mortal bodies, vulnerable, highly dependent, and with a need
for love, care, and also a state capable of protecting their human
rights. The birth of intersex children allows anyone to see with
crudeness the violence that is currently exercised. If these vulnerable bodies are not born with supposedly intelligible genitality
[genitalidad] according to medical/scientific expected parameters,
their original precarity is paired with more precarity. Medicine
and juridical science in synergy with religious fundamentalism
and educational devices of submission come together to enforce
surgical adaptation in that body with the purpose of turning it intelligible, adjusting it, and making it apt for heteronormative function. This incapacity for recognition, respect, and unconditional
care for that life violates personal rights in a flagrant and radical
fashion while at the same time concealing the criminal act thus
implied (a crime committed by institutions, the family, and the
state). The classification, the delimitation, and the "adjustment"
kills; heteronormativity kills. Homonormativity is an accom-
plice and contributes with its own system of legitimation. Latin
American travesti theory's framework confronts these forces in
self-defense.

Sexual/gender dissidence refers to the action and effect of sepa-
rating and distancing oneself from the norm as mandatory heterosexuality. Dissident activism rejects the politics of inclusion—
"We include you as long as you fit our stereotypes"—and demands
transformative action. The affirmation is: "We no longer want to
be this humanity." What are we then? Where is the certainty? We
are identity constructions, permanently under construction. The
way of expressing it is always in a simple gerund: I am being—
transiting/transitioning. As rigid as our personality may be regarding convictions, beliefs, or morals, there are aspects such
as age that it is necessary to account for: growing up, aging. And
therefore, our identity is transformed. There are events that can
change us abruptly, unexpectedly, and quickly, such as becoming
a widower or migrating, but in general they are gradual and progressive processes. If we understand identity as built by respon-

sible actions of an affirmative and negative nature, not in moral terms but rather in terms of an ethics and an aesthetics, we can see it built by actions of identification/disidentification. Thus, the uncertainty about the affirmative caused by the gerund obtains a counterpart of firmness through what each person (dis)identifies with. These negative actions constitute us much more decisively and influence our political relations in a substantial way. Much emphasis is then placed on the (dis)identification regarding the regime of the mandatory heteronorm. Let's see examples: we are born; we are assigned a name, sex, and gender; and as we grow, we experiment, we inform ourselves, we share experiences, and perhaps we may affirm these heteronormal decisions, or maybe we start identifying ourselves from other more fluid proposals. This should not affect our relationships substantially. Now, if we affirm negatively—"I am not fascist, xenophobic, racist, discriminatory, sexist, a rapist, etc."—these issues that negatively constitute identity (through "I am not") have a more solid, defining character and entail greater responsibility that for the rest of us matters more, in a substantial way, and therefore they are of radical interest in political relations. There, yes, we demand firm and clear certainties and definitions because they are of vital importance: we are survivors of these. A body is not only volume; it is defined by its voids, its sinuousness, its textures and tones, just as music is built not with the mere sum of sounds but also with its silences, rhythms, and vibrations, its cadence and fluctuating volume.

So, we affirm ourselves as complex identity constructions with a historicity and in transit: we are being (gerund) lesbians, queers, travesti/trans. With a territoriality: *sapatão* (Brazil), 108 (Paraguay), *muxe* (Oaxaca, Mexico). With a time stamp: homosexual/ Sapphira (ancient Greece), *marika* (contemporary), genderfluid (contemporary). And with a cultural belonging: *kakcha* (Aymara), *chinaku* (Quechua), *weye* (Mapuche). With a class membership: *torta* [slang for lesbian], *puto* [slang for gay], *trava* [short for travesti] (Argentina in popular sectors); lesbian, gay, trans man or woman (Argentina in middle/high sectors). These identities are becoming increasingly fluid and elusive with their cultural practices, their sexual-affective relationships, their expressions of gender, and even their objects of desire. These forms of sociopolitical confrontation are increasingly free, breaking the limits imposed by the heteronorm and the homonorm of lesbian, gay, bisexual, and trans (male/female) in identity, class, ethnicity, age, territoriality, historicity, corporal abstraction, and so on. The paradigms of monogamy as a foundation of the family, based on sex-genitality, consanguinity, or romantic love, are being broken while we resist with friendship, community, and group relationships that are more open.

In the face of the hegemonic proposal of opposing the concept of otherness to the self, the Latin American/Abya Yalan travesti theory provides the concept of "Ourness" *[Nostredad]*, through which the nonself can be conceived as part of the self, part of the community body, part of its affective and mutual networks of care that are sustained over time. Thus, the predesigned and always threatening quality of otherness is stripped bare, exposing a cultural imaginary and its effectivity where we would find ourselves in alienating relationships and loneliness, even in micropolitical systems such as the nuclear family, where even today we dissidents must maintain silence for fear of conversion pedagogies aimed at reconducting us to the norm. We demand instead a pedagogy that guides us in the construction of a first art object, a unique Self, therefore different, and to endow that difference with real legal equity in the collective self, which we conceive of being Ourness *[Nostredad]*.

If we go back to identification and disidentification as constitutive actions of the Self and therefore of Ourness, we see that identification loses relevance while disidentification emerges as vital, revealing the exercise of differentiation imposed by hegemony—a differentiation emerging in the exercise of violence toward that otherness that has been erected as a paradigm and threat. It is based on racialization, nationality, gender, religion, ethnicity, age, bodily characteristics, cognitive ability, socioeconomic status, etc. We are conditioned with two basic fears of all otherness: fear of being attacked and fear of loss. And in order supposedly to protect us, this hegemony validates its exercise of state violence constituted and sustained by men and women in hetero-centered relationships. This indicates to us that with which we should disidentify: manhood and womanhood *[lo hombre y lo mujer]*, the factory of all violence.[6] If the proposal is one of inclusion, questions arise: To include us where? In the binary? Its institutions, logics, and social dynamics? Their relational modes? Their productive structures? Their ways of reproduction?

From the perspective of Latin American travesti theory, we observe the effects of these discourses (and their narrative capacity to influence public policies via their access to mass media) as a negotiation problem. From a monolithic discourse, they negotiate how to share the funds available for political action, thus limiting to the binary what is deemed financeable. All this creates the conditions in which projects of instituting force that yet lack formal structures, lobbying power, mass media for their protests, etc., become brittle. The proposal is not to discard the traditions of academic studies but to territorialize them in the Abya Yalan context, to resist the universalization that strengthens the colonialist sense of the production of patriarchal/Western knowledge. It is a challenge to understand the complexity of the territories and to be able to escape from the common sense of North–South geopolitics. Facing these challenges is the condition of possibility for new virtuous North–South articulations. And for this, it is important to understand the extractivist practices that diversity, feminism, and progressivism carry out through subtle extraction movements when they photograph themselves with the dissidence and through microphone extractions when they invite dissidence with a gesture of equality to negotiation forums that are constituted by an overwhelming inequity.

Returning to the point of identity—understood as a heteroproduced taxonomy emerging from religious, medical, and legal discourses and as the strategy adopted by the diversity movements of supposed inclusion—optical illusions are built by including gays, lesbians, and trans people in different spheres inasmuch as they remain heteronormative. From their economic/financial logics, it generates a self-demand for the attachment to what might be intelligible by the norm and reassuring of the sex/gender binary. Overadaptation is required, and the binary paradigm proposed by patriarchy is left unshaken where "man" constitutes the privileged subject of humanity with a greater or lesser willingness to grant rights to dehierarchized subjects.[7] Thus, inclusion will be for so-called intelligible bodies. That intelligibility is a euphemism for not attacking their prerogatives, privileges, and hierarchies. What does this inclusive proposal entail as a risk? It makes invisible the violence of a system that in its differentiation and hierarchization permanently and actively produces precarity and pre-charity ["precariedad y pre-caridad"], as well as a refusal to recognize its absolute failure in maternal-paternal functions. The impoverishment of the concrete life conditions of dissident people starts with stripping them of the human ideal, in flagrant violation of the legal system of human rights, if that humanity remains unrecognized in its difference. The family is the first executing entity through pedagogies that train us with learning matrixes in two sole positions: domination and submission. This training produces subjectivity in those positions to negotiate coexistence.

The human person is born in a situation of extreme precariousness, with a mortal body, vulnerable, dependent, and in need of someone fulfilling material responsibilities of care and subjective desire and love, as well as a state apparatus that guarantees certain minimum contextual conditions of subsistence through their family, schooling, and other institutions. At birth, the plexus of human rights is inextricably inalienable. However, in the infant experience of dissidences this does not occur. Growing up through that precariousness, maximized precarity will be additionally imposed on them if they do not show attachment to the canons of masculinity and femininity. The narratives of medicine and legal sciences demand normalization that will be carried out with violence in the family as well as in school by adults and among peers. In order to adapt to this heteronormative fictional system seemingly based on assumptions of truth and objectivity, all forms of violence are used, including psychiatrization. This is also the mode of negotiation and inclusion of the patriarchy in a dominant position. A series of surgical, pedagogical, psychiatric, coercive, and punitive legal devices are superimposed on trans childhoods or all those childhoods that do not conform to those heteronormal ideal constructs with training purposes. And so, the violation of human rights is flagrant and radical in the familial, social, and state dimensions. The inability to recognize, safeguard, and unconditionally respect that humanity itself shakes all the precepts of humanity and legality. And in the face of these criminal acts there is a denial of the joint failure of the micro and macro political paternal-maternal functions of the entire state apparatus. This whole complex web has severe tangible and intangible consequences that we can conceptualize as the impoverishment of the concrete conditions of life. Sexual-gender dissidents will see their human, civil, social, political, economic, legal, and cultural rights profoundly undermined. These can be reflected in statistics such as the average life span of the travesti/trans femme Latina community (approximately thirty-five years of age);[8] the very high case numbers of hate crimes; the constant supposedly corrective sexual assaults on lesbians and trans men; prostitution of (children, adolescents, and adult) travesti persons (79 percent);[9] expulsion from school; the high number of suicide attempts and youth suicides; the constant migration away from contexts of violence; school bullying and cyberbullying; and the high rate of incarceration without due process and deaths from institutional violence, among the most serious.[10] These are the modes of training and negotiation for existence: the response of those who negotiate on our behalf seems unacceptable to us. As members of this dissidence, we refuse to connect from a place of humiliation.

When we talk about homonormativity, we are denouncing the political action by which all of us are subjected to the exercise of following a script to enter a taxonomy built in a colonized way and with the political purpose of assimilation, a heterosexual promise of not being vulnerable to inequality, of not losing rights. This promise is abstract and extended as a canon for masculinity and another for femininity. What are expected are bodies without social noise, attuned to the logic of masculine domination, subordination of unmanliness, and monogamy as the only relational form within the statute of marriage or civil union, and without public demonstrations of affection that may offend that heterosexuality. This is well expressed in the formulas "men who have sex with men," "women who love women," and "woman trapped in a man's body." This stems from a clear pathologizing root that comes from the dawn of modernity, creating a resistance to disidentify from the power that the word *man* grants to gay men, as well as the negotiation force of the word *woman* and the convenience of an image adapted to make demands in the field of civil rights while, in contrast, the dissidence denounces the violation of human rights. The homonorm does not go beyond gender but reproduces it, contributing to the essentialization of identities and making them mandatory. The sine qua non condition for intelligibility is based on this, which is necessary for the rigidity of thought that defines fundamentalisms. Intelligibility is everything endowed with coherence and rationality in the heterosexual fiction of the constrained concept of "humanity." Hegemony continues to establish relations of apprehension of reality in a unidirectional way: subject → object. We denounce the epistemic and hermeneutical violence on our lives through the status of nonhumanity. Absolute fallacy: nothing nonhuman arises from the human.

Travesti

Travestis are subjectivities who self-determine breaking free from the supposed logic of sex/gender correspondence and who were assigned at birth to a gender based on their genitality and yet constructed themselves in their own gender departing from the adjudicated one, changing their name, the pronouns they choose for themselves, adopting clothing, gestural modes, and body modifications not congruent according to the standards of their social context. They do not consider among the interventions those of genital alteration; they choose instead to resignify genitalia symbolically and to accept and enjoy them. Travesti is also the identity mode of recognizing oneself in the difference for a group that deidentifies from "manhood" and "womanhood" [lo hombre y lo mujer] as the sole subjective and collective categories legitimized in this Western/modern sex/gender system. Within the binary and heterocentric thought system, travestis are thought of as men who dress as women and women who dress as men, the result of a successful colonization process imposed by the Western Christian invasion with great force from the liminal times between the Middle Ages and modernity. However, travesti is much more complex and has a greater historicity.

In Argentina at the end of the twentieth century (1990–1996), collective organization movements were formed that would delineate the travesti identity as a civic and political identity. Three organizations were formed— Association for the Struggle toward a Travesti Transsexual Identity (ALITT), Organización de Travestis y Transexuales de Argentina (OTTRA), and Futuro Trans—making their activism more complex with strategies that go beyond the struggle in reaction to police/institutional violence to advance their own agendas. These organizations used tools from feminism and the field of human rights to think about their own being and becoming in the world. This is evident in the name of ALITT, understanding the term *travesti* as an identity and fighting to be included in the concept of citizenship. In 1995, they actively participated in lobbying in the Constitutional Convention that procured a constitution for the Autonomous City of Buenos Aires in order to include "sexual orientation" as grounds for discrimination (if only to immediately realize that, strictly speaking, it was not a category that contemplated this collective's identity). This meeting between local feminists and the travesti movement would be fruitful in the sense that it sped up self-reflection and survival for a group with a life expectancy of thirty-two years of age. Lohana Berkins, president of ALITT, ceased to endure prostitution and that gave her time to participate in the feminist movement and its political discussions, and Berkins, together with Nadia Echazú (OTTRA) and Marlene Wayar (OTTRA-Futuro Transgenérico), confronted the gay and lesbian movement first and imposed the three *T*'s (travesti, transsexual, and transgender). Later they confronted the human rights movement and from 2003 to 2004 they drew conclusions in the cycle of talks "Inescapable Bodies" ["Cuerpos Ineludibles"] organized by the feminist group Ají de Pollo, which compiled and edited them in a homonymous book.[11]

If the human experience continues to be understood in terms of the male/female binary, the travesti movement declares itself free from these heterocentric limits and proposes self-determination in its identity construction, which is characterized by the contradiction between the social interpretation that is made of these people at birth based on their sexuation and self-perception. In this self-perception, there is an evolution since childhood according to the context and lexical reality: a language constructing a reality. Language is a battlefield for the travesti community, which constructs a narrative based on the redefinition of the insult. These often are violated childhoods, as each one of those childhoods is born in a hostile context that does not name them, does not understand them, denigrates them, stigmatizes them, pathologizes them, and criminalizes them. Each travesti childhood must face the threat of family rejection and social harassment. In search of acceptance, hegemonic discourses have had a great impact regulating a subjectivity that claims freedom to build itself in its own way, in the face of the social offer of building according to the stereotypes that strengthen the binary idea of humanity, its paradigms of sex/gender coherence, and relationships limited to romantic love for the purpose of procreation. The organization Futuro Transgenérico assessed itself as colonized by pathologizing discourses and later returned to the self-affirmation of *travesti,* reimagining its concept. And it dared to change its name to Futuro Trans, understanding *Trans* not as an apocope of *transgender* but as a linguistic umbrella that includes all the *T*'s identities. *Trans* affirms that we must also understand ourselves from an aesthetic perspective, most especially during childhood. Education is a time/territory to create ourselves as our first art object, a self aesthetically conceived and hence beautiful for oneself and that can be appreciated by other people.

Children have a right to build themselves freely by choosing for themselves what gives them fulfillment and brings them closer to happiness. The hegemonic pedagogical processes encourage a standardization seeking to equalize for an overadaptation to the conditions of a system based on dynamics of power >< disempower [power-over instead of power-with]. Childhood is recognized with instituting force, in [Cornelius] Castoriadis's terms.[12] Travestiness demands to construct itself free from adult-centric power.

Travestiness imposes the first break in linguistic logic, the use of the feminine article for travesti femininities, and thus manages to show bad faith and discrimination against those who insist on using masculine pronouns, articles, and adjectives for them, especially in the press. Travestiness declares itself to society as a subjective construction that has its own substance and derives from the labor of meditating on identity, and I express it by reformulating [Friedrich] Nietzsche: "The human person is a rope stretched between the beast and the trans person."[13] Travestiness understands the action ([Hannah] Arendt) not as a mere practice and banishes the use of *transvestism [travestismo]* while affirming instead *travesticity [travestidad]* in equity with *masculinity [masculinidad]* and *femininity [feminidad]*.[14] All this with unrelenting freedom to manifest oneself in public and private in one's travesticity.

Although transvestism historically has been a much more visible movement, "the travestis" [with feminine article and grammar: *las travestis*] should not be understood necessarily as feminine, for there are extensive and well-known cases of travesti masculinities, and many of them did not come to light until the moment of death. In existing surveys there are always masculinities that identify themselves as travestis. An important turning point was achieved after ALITT won its lawsuit against the General Inspectorate of Justice in the Supreme Court of Argentina, getting the court to issue a ruling in its favor and stating: "The definitive restoration of the democratic and republican ideal that shaped the constituents of 1853 and deepened those of 1994, calls . . . for national unity, in freedom, but not for uniformity or homogeneity. The meaning of democratic and liberal equality is that of the 'right to be different,' but it can never be confused with 'egalitarization,' which is a totalitarian ideal and therefore is precisely the most complete negation of the former, since it makes no sense whatsoever to speak of the right to equal treatment if, previously, we were all forced to be equal."[15] It recognizes the civic status of travestis and transsexuals as such.

Futuro Trans becomes a node of thought for the coalition of trans organizations and begins to question society regarding childhood, territoriality, and intersectionality. These conversations emerged in the Casa Caracol circle with Maite Amaya, a leading force in the city of Córdoba, and gradually the need became clear to analyze two essential points: childhood and ethnicity, two themes that strengthen the construction of subjective and collective identity. In childhood, the family, schooling, and the psychological sciences oversee the violation of the right to self-determination, to freely know oneself and to interpret one's own being. Studying ethnic diversities after the conquest, one can observe the uniformity of a mandatory heterosexuality as one of the most profound forms of colonization, more so than political or economic submission (which at least is visible and recognized). As we root ourselves in contemporary times, we see how deeply modified are what used to be different experiences of gender multiplicity in pre-Hispanic cultures, where no identity used to be demonized, a reality that is today buried. There are few resources except for the prolific chronicles written by the conquerors who have no shelter from their own cruelty. From the reconstructions, we can affirm that gender diversity was a reality that had its own characteristics from culture to culture, but in all there existed something beyond manhood and womanhood. A community stigma was created based on cannibalism and sodomy, as they forayed into the continent, to justify cruelty. There are three types of chronicles: those of military power, those of the church, and those of the civil society. The Spanish clergyman Bartolomé de la Casas wrote in his chronicles: "Certain Spaniards found in a certain corner of one of the said provinces three men dressed in women's habits, whom just by seeing what they judged to be corrupted by that sin [sodomy], and without further proof they threw them to the dogs they had, which tore them to pieces and ate them alive, as if they were their judges."[16] As for the military case: "So, what I have said about these people on the island and in the regions is very public, and even on the mainland where many of these Indians were sodomites, and it is known that there are many of them."[17] And from the civil sphere as a historian: "In the royal habit of a woman, because not only in the suit, but in everything, except in giving birth was not female. . . . Balboa dogged 50 faggots that he found there, and later he burned, first informing of their abominable and dirty sin. As it became known in the region this victory and justice, they brought him men of sodomy so that he could kill them."[18]

There are some material remains, pictograms, and ceramics that invite a great pending task for our own readings about the reality of sexual/gender dissidence in Abya Yala. They account for the existence and coexistence in different ways of another human reality more complex than the Western binary. They had their social roles assigned according to their social status and capabilities, and that feeling was respected by their social context based on a performativity not dependent on current gender technologies but simply by self-perception that drives and guides sociopolitical recognition.

In relation to this historicity in self-construction, the travesti movement is demanding many measures of recognition, compensation, and redistribution on the part of society and the state. The priority is for reparations, since a travesti person is considered as a community victim and survivor of genocide and crimes against humanity based on international criminal law and the different regulations and international and national agreements. The Rome Statute of the International Criminal Court says: "Article 6: Genocide. For the purposes of this Statute, 'genocide' shall mean any of the acts mentioned below, perpetrated with the intention of totally or partially destroying a national, ethnic, racial, or religious group as such."[19] It is necessary to perform a hermeneutics of the letter of the legal text and to deepen its spirit. In reference to the term *group,* the travesti community is understood to be included in the concept and thus protected by the law, since travestiness can be understood as a group based on gender. Not only do travestis perceive themselves as a group, but the social body understands it this way as well, and it is reflected in the infracriminal regulations that persecute them, as well as in a social practice that names them, identifying these people as a specific group, as seen in the press and in numerous academic papers and in the National Supreme Court ruling referred to above.[20]

Hence, travestis are a group united by their gender identity and the conditions of existence to which they are exposed by it, which is why they propose the category of "Identicide" based on the specificity of the criminal act. The concept of identicide is built upon the categories of "genocide" and "crimes against humanity" [*crímenes de lesa humanidad*] as defined by the Rome Statute of the International Criminal Court. This social and state terrorism in relation to the travesti community is expressed in the killing of members of the group with the witness case raised by Amnesty International regarding *Vanesa Lorena Ledesma vs. the Police of the Province of Córdoba.* There are numerous cases of travesticide that are not investigated and go unpunished, with the only exception of the first ruling in favor of classifying as travesticide the murder of Diana Amancay Sacayán, in which justice understood it in its specificity as a form of gender-based hate crime.

The travesti identicide includes in a systematic way "serious injury to the physical or mental integrity of the members of the group" and "intentional subjection of the group to conditions of existence that will lead to its physical destruction, in whole or in part," systematic police persecution and subjection to unsanitary housing conditions in police stations and prisons, denial of health services, denial of medication and prescribed medical treatment, denial of the right to school, denial of the child support that is available for boys and girls in a situation of abandonment, the creation of criminal cases without legal basis, and the lack of any protection against the situation of prostitution.[21] These, among other indicators, mark how they are subjected to degrading conditions of existence for their physical condition, which ends with the result of an average life span of thirty-two. And we must emphasize as well that from the statistics it emerges that the age of entry into prostitution is between eight and thirteen.[22] This is the "forcible transfer of children from one group to another group."[23] At this point, a hermeneutical exercise is also needed, since it must be understood that the travesti childhood is transferred by violence and abandonment of the heterosexual family to the street situation, where they are generally forced to move to areas of prostitution and follow schedules established by use for this matter, which configures open-air concentration camps.[24]

Regarding the category of crimes against humanity, as defined by the Rome Statute of the International Criminal Court, the justification is reiterated and exceeds the brief length of this essay, but it is simple to verify.[25] "Incarceration": here it is observed that the regulations that were used to justify imprisonment are of an infracriminal nature and that they are unconstitutional and contrary to the internal legal order and the international order.[26] "Torture": both in institutionalized cases and in civil cases, this is demonstrated while at the same time it supports the specificity of the hate crime, travesticides, and is expressed in bodies subjected to sexual violence, burns, mutilations, cuts, and suffocation and in the sites and ways in which they are found dumped without any qualms. "Rape, sexual slavery, and forced prostitution": these are common to all the stories of police abuse—rape by police personnel, prison personnel, and subjection to prostitution with other prisoners in police stations and jails. All this without any contemplation of the fact that their condition of abandonment is between eight and thirteen years old and marks the entry into prostitution to subsist and therefore is forced. "Persecution": as defined in paragraph 3, this is mostly based on a gender issue, but other issues are also involved, including of a religious, moral, political, racial, and cultural nature. "Forced disappearance of persons": there is no investigation and there is no record either, and the situation is more complex because the only people authorized to initiate the process are relatives and not the group to which they belong. Since the recognition of identity by the state is denied, it is the state that prevents the production of statistics, making this group taxonomically invisible. "The crime of apartheid": being thrown into prostitution implies that they must restrict their movements to the red zones and only at night, while access to housing is also highly conditioned. "Other inhumane acts of a similar nature that intentionally cause great suffering or seriously threaten physical integrity or mental or physical health": these are explained at various points, but above all in institutional violence such as in the fields of police forces, health care, and education. With this succinct analysis, I believe that the travesti community is explicitly a victim of crimes of genocide and crimes against humanity, that our collective condition is such that there is a historical debt that calls for reparations, to begin to face a discussion for which currently there is no political or economic support or access to justice. The extermination has been successful to the highest degree. I affirm in numerous texts and public presentations: The reason we continue to exist is basically because we continue to be born and some of us exceptionally survive.

Travesti/trans people (I appropriate the term inasmuch as this is a shared identity with common characters such as its culture, history, and institutions) have been the target of a continuum of violence with distinctive characteristics in different historical periods, resulting in a shorter life expectancy due to avoidable causes of death that are perpetrated by the socius both formally through the state and informally via civil society and its deadly social fabric: a threading of ubiquitous targeted violence. The foundational colonization act of binary gendering Amerindian bodies that founds the fiction of a universal humanity understood generically in terms of man/woman produces the foundational myth of the sodomite demon. This stigma is a historical imbrication of criminalization and pathologization, providing a practice and an ethics of dehumanization that destroys a people even before it can be constituted as such. The interruption, dissemination, and permanent attack on vital projects, the deprivation of educational opportunities, and thus access to formal critical thinking, are conditions that need to be analyzed as a people subjected to life conditions such that its social relations are thwarted. Both the relations with other communities as well as intracommunity bonding possibilities are permanently broken by these life conditions. This rupture in the conditions of social bonding not only makes it impossible to think of ourselves as a people and thus be able to envision a future for its members but also makes its members poor. Structural poverty should be analyzed as an aggregate of vital, political, and economic poverty in comparison with others. Our lives are decimated, deprived of the vitality that is necessary for the exercise of power as a capacity to cocreate, deprived of hope and confidence in ourselves and, of course, in our community. We don't have political representation, making it impossible to have equity and true autonomy in the exercise of politics. Finally, economic poverty makes it impossible for us to accumulate enough capital for the production of a shared life, the production of culture, decisions about mutuality, institutions that we can call our own, political leverage, freedom for the construction and dissemination of knowledge, the preservation of our collective memory, and the construction of our history.

There is an imperative of resistance within the sexual/gender dissidence community, only holding space for us inasmuch as we are enacting oppositional resistance to patriarchy, but thus far it has failed to hold that space as a nucleus of community building where to rest, resolve, and preserve our vital energy, aware as we are of the hostility of the outside. We can think of ourselves as a people accepting and embracing our differences or identitarian nuances. Because what threatens all of us is too cruel.

Notes

1. *LGTTTBIQ*+ stands for Lesbiana, Gay, Travesti, Transexual, Transgénero, Bisexual, Intersex, Queer + (in English, Lesbian, Gay, Travesti, Transsexual, Transgender, Bisexual, Intersex, Queer, and others). The three *T*'s follow a historical order: first there was *travesti* activism, then a transexual subdivision, and eventually the term *transgender* came into the conversation.

2. Identidades cloacalizadas: This concept is very dear to me in the way that Latin American travesti theory has articulated it. It is a neologism that Lohana Berkins constructed, demonstrating travesti spoken word in action. It speaks of the complexity of a process by which the social body fabricates, molds, cooks, plots, and constructs the travesti identity in the gutter, not as an architectonic device so much as a signifier: the excrement. That detritus that circulates and is contained in the gutter. The travesti body is transformed into excrement and the collective identity, in turn, into the worst of society. Berkins enumerates: "sidosa, ladrona, escandalosa, infectada, marginal" ["AIDS-carrier, thief, scandalous, infected, marginal"]. See Lohana Berkins, "Travestis: Una identidad política," *emisférica* 4, no. 2 (2007): https://hemisphericinstitute.org/es/emisferica-42/4-2-review-essays/lohana-berkins.html. Thus, she amalgamates the most condemned and feared social positionalities of a moralist society that would project the worst of itself onto this collective, thereby constructing via this projection of a disposable totality with an ethical justification for disposing of it. There is the shadow of a recognition of being a part of humanity, but that part has to be expelled as its feces.

3. This is a reference to Marlene Wayar's book titled *Travesti: A Good Enough Theory* (Marlene Wayar, *Travesti: Una teoría lo suficientemente buena* [Buenos Aires: Muchas Nueces, 2018]), which in turn is a reference to Donald Winnicott's theory of a good enough mother, to reimagine politics from the premise that humans have a need for attachment and belonging at the emotional level and in material terms, an irreducible interdependence, both of which account for the unspeakable pain of feeling and being excluded, respectively. [This and all the following notes are by the translator.]

4. Some of these words are offensive slang for different types of queer people, although in these cases, the insult was reappropriated by the insulted community to create a positive identity affirmation, and so they are also terms of endearment in queer contexts.

5. The gerund in Spanish is often translated as the English suffix *-ing* following a verb root. Grammatically speaking, the English suffix *-ing* can create a noun, while in Spanish, the gerund is only used as an adverb or to compose verbal tenses often translated as "present continuous" and "past continuous," which means that the action is taking place or was already taking place at the moment referred to by the

storyteller (either in the past or present). This means that the action had started and would continue for a time completely undetermined or open-ended. In this regard, the gerund in travesti theory refers to the impermanence of identity inasmuch as it is only happening "for now" until something else happens, and who knows how that identity can eventually change.

6. It is impossible to translate *lo hombre* and *lo mujer* because Wayar is introducing a grammatical "error" (combining a neutral article with nouns that are respectively masculine and feminine) in order to call attention to the fact that men and women are not people so much as abstract cultural constructs that limit the freedom of persons to be who they are if left to their own devices and desires. It creates an uncanny grammatical experience not far from those horror movies in which an abstract monster occupies the bodies of men and women, moving them from within as puppets, to pass as real people. The neutral article has this alienating effect, in contrast with the common use of articles *el hombre* ("the man") or *la mujer* ("the woman") to indicate universal categories or a specific man or woman. In this regard, it is no different from Martin Heidegger's use of "das Man" to account for the alienation created by social norms. The novelty is to think of this construct as gendered (while Heidegger did not speak of "das Frau") and, moreover, to think of gender itself and patriarchy as the core matrix of this sort of alienation, in line with thinkers like María Lugones or bell hooks. Martin Heidegger, *Being and Time* (New York: Harper-Collins, 2008); María Lugones, "Heterosexualism and the Colonial/Modern Gender System," *Hypatia* 22, no. 1 (Winter 2007): 186–209; bell hooks, *Feminism Is for Everybody: Passionate Politics* (Boston: South End Press, 2000).

7. Overadaptation *(sobreadaptación)* is a concept taken from Argentinean social psychology, coined by Enrique Pichon-Rivière, to refer to the circumstance and means of assimilating oneself to a reality that is unhealthy or unjust, instead of actively fighting to change it (which would be a more sustainable and desirable form of adaptation). While overadaptation might allow a person to survive in a hostile environment, in the long run it is maladaptive since it enables the situation to perpetuate itself. See Enrique Pichon-Rivière and Ana P. de Quiroga, "Del psicoanálisis a la psicología social (Octubre, 1972)," *Área 3: Cuadernos de temas grupales e institucionales* 9 (Spring 2003). See also David Liberman, Elsa Grassano de Piccolo, Silvia Neborak de Dimant, Lía Pistiner de Cortiñas, and Pola Roitman de Woscoboinik, *Del cuerpo al símbolo: Sobreadaptación y enfermedad psicosomática* (Buenos Aires: Trotta, 1982).

8. Methodologically speaking, there is no way to measure the average death age of a population that is partially still alive. However, thirty-five is the number that is most often cited as an estimation based on

more nuanced data such as the following quoted in *La gesta del nombre propio*: "Respecto de la edad de las amigas o conocidas fallecidas, el 35% murió cuando tenía entre 22 y 31 años y el 34% entre los 32 y 41 años." ["Regarding the age of friends or acquaintances who had died, 35% of them had died between the ages of 22 and 31, and 34% were between 31 and 41 years old."] Lohana Berkins and Josefina Fernández, eds., *La gesta del nombre propio: Informe sobre la situación de la comunidad travesti en la Argentina* (Buenos Aires: Madres de Plaza de Mayo, 2005), 12.

9. Berkins and Fernández, *La gesta del nombre propio,* 111.
10. All this data was gathered by a trans-feminist team led by Lohana Berkins since the Argentine government did not collect data for trans women as they misclassified them as men who have sex with men. Lohana Berkins produced two books—the first one in collaboration with cis feminist sociologist Josefina Fernández, who trained her, and the second on her own—to fill this gap in the data and to begin to do the work of gathering concepts for a travesti theory. Berkins and Fernández, *La gesta del nombre propio*; Lohana Berkins, ed., *Cumbia, copeteo y lágrimas* (Buenos Aires: Madres de Plaza de Mayo, 2015).
11. Josefina Fernández and Mónica D'Uva, eds., *Cuerpos Ineludibles* (Ediciones Ají de Pollo, 2004).
12. Cornelius Castoriadis, *The Imaginary Institution of Society,* trans. Kathleen Blamey (Cambridge: Polity Press, 1987), 204.
13. "Man is a rope, tied between beast and overman—a rope over an abyss. A dangerous across, a dangerous on-the-way, a dangerous looking-back, a dangerous shuddering and stopping." Friedrich Wilhelm Nietzsche, *Thus Spoke Zarathustra: A Book for All and None* (Cambridge: Cambridge University Press, 2006), 15.
14. "The only activity that goes on directly between men without the intermediary of things or matter." Hannah Arendt, *The Human Condition* (Chicago: University of Chicago Press, 1985), 7.
15. Corte Suprema de Justicia de la Nacion [CSJN] [National Supreme Court of Justice], 21/11/2006, "Asociación Lucha por la Identidad Travesti – Transexual c. Inspección General de Justicia," Nro. Interno: A2036 XLRH, Fayt Id SAIJ: FA06000695 (Arg.), available at Sistema Argentino de Información Jurídica, http://www.saij.gob.ar/corte-suprema-justicia-nacion-federal-ciudad-autonoma-buenos-aires-asociacion-lucha-identidad-travesti-transexual-inspeccion-general-justicia-fa06000695-2006-11-21/123456789-596-0006-0ots-eupmocsollaf.
16. Fray Bartolomé de las Casas, cited in Guilhelm Olivier, "Conquistadores y misioneros frente al pecado nefando," *Historias* 28 (1992): 47–64, https://www.estudioshistoricos.inah.gob.mx/revistaHistorias/wp-content/uploads/historias_28_47-64.pdf.

17. "Historia general y natural de las Indias: Part 1 (1535) Gonzalo Fernández de Oviedo y Valdés," Research at King's College London: Early Modern Spain, chap. 3, accessed January 31, 2024, https://ems.kcl.ac.uk/content/etext/e026.html.

18. Francisco López de Gomara, *Historia General de las Indias,* chap. 33, available at Biblioteca Virtual Miguel de Cervantes, accessed January 31, 2024, https://www.cervantesvirtual.com/obra-visor/historia-general-de-las-indias--0/html/fef81d62-82b1-11df-acc7-002185ce6064_2.html#I_0_.

19. "Rome Statute of the International Criminal Court, 17 July 1998," International Humanitarian Law Databases, https://ihl-databases.icrc.org/en/ihl-treaties/icc-statute-1998/article-6#.

20. The author refers to the "edictos policiales." In the 1990s in Argentina, the travesti movement was organized around the urgency of a struggle to fight police brutality. During those years, the movement was a network of sex worker travesti political leaders in the red districts in the City of Buenos Aires and its periphery. The police had the legal authorization to detain and imprison trans women with the argument that they were dressed in violation of the public order. There was a piece of legislation called the "edictos policiales" authorizing police to exercise sovereign power to judge and punish anyone who might be found violating the so-called public order, even if their actions were not technically crimes as defined by the penal code. The travesti movement fought this legislation, which they rightly called unconstitutional, until the legislature of the City of Buenos Aires had to abolish its validity and write a new code for the city. During those years of struggle, travesti sex workers built strategic alliances with other marginal subjects who were also harassed by the police. The edictos policiales, far from being solely an instrument of transphobia, were a systematic way of criminalizing poverty in the city. This history of struggle is what prompted many travesti thinkers to frame certain forms of transphobic violence in a broader framework of the production of social space and the right to the city or, as Berkins eloquently puts it, the question of who has the right to inhabit public space. See Lohana Berkins, "Un itinerario político del travestismo," in *Sexualidades migrantes: Género y transgénero,* ed. Diana Maffia (Buenos Aires: Feminaria Editora, 2003), 127–37; Lohana Berkins, "Travestis: Una identidad política," in *Escrituras, polimorfías, e identidades,* ed. Paula Viturro (Buenos Aires: Libros del Rojas, 2008), 17–24. See also Rocío Pichon-Rivière, "Nudes and Naked Souls: Critical Phenomenology of Skin Disclosure and Hemispheric Trans Theory," *GLQ: A Journal of Lesbian and Gay Studies* 27, no. 3 (2021): 431–50.

21. See "Rome Statute of the International Criminal Court," art. 6 and 7.

22. Lohana Berkins and Josefina Fernández eds., *La gesta del nombre propio* (Buenos Aires: Ediciones Madres de Plaza de Mayo, 2005).

23. "Rome Statute of the International Criminal Court," art. 6 and 7.
24. The expression that Wayar uses is "campos de concentración a cielo abierto," which plays with the resonance of "minería a cielo abierto" (which refers to surface mining but literally means "mining in open sky," and it also echoes the idea of an occupied territory, such as Palestine, as operating as an open-air prison for its Indigenous people). The implicit parallel to mining compares traditional concentration camps to the closed space of mines while this form of concentration camp requires no enclosure or vigilance, as it is, too, a development of late-capitalist dispossession and desperation. In Argentina, the issue of surface mining is an urgent concern as it has taken the lives of many people, with its toxic fumes causing deadly illness in nearby populations. And yet, even progressive governments act as if the country were too poor to afford refusing this extraction.
25. "Crimes against Humanity," United Nations Office on Genocide Prevention and the Responsibility to Protect, https://www.un.org/en /genocideprevention/crimes-against-humanity.shtml. All the cited terms in the current paragraph are references to that definition.
26. Wayar is referring to the "Edictos Policiales," a piece of unconstitutional legislation that ruled in Buenos Aires until the travesti movement took to the streets and pressed the legislature of Buenos Aires until their abolition. For details on this history, see Berkins, "Travestis"; Paula Viturro, ed., *Escrituras, polimorfías e identidades* (Buenos Aires: Libros del Rojas, 2008).

Acknowledgments

A book like this—a book that aspires to mark the coalescing of a subfield—will necessarily have innumerable, and often unnameable, debts. It is with pleasure, then, that we turn gratefully to acknowledge some of the people without which this book would not be what it is or be happening at the time and in the way that it is.

Our thanks go to feminist and gender-variant literatures that were instrumental in our own journeys to find (and engage increasingly critically with) feminist, queer, and trans studies. Our thanks also to early trans philosophers (e.g., Talia Mae Bettcher, Loren Cannon, Miqqi Alicia Gilbert, and C. Jacob Hale) who worked in philosophy departments and as trans people at a time when this was largely unheard of. Scholarship like this has provided important groundwork for what is possible today. Thanks also to early nontrans feminist philosophers working on trans issues (e.g., Cressida J. Heyes, Gayle Salamon, and Naomi Scheman) who modeled a care and attentiveness to trans lives in their philosophical work that continues to be all too rare. We also acknowledge with passion the many visionaries whose antiracist, postcolonial, decolonial, crip, and mad work has paved, and continues to pave, the way for a kind of theorizing that transforms trans philosophy from within and without.

Our thanks to Megan Burke, Fulden İbrahimhakkıoğlu, and Amy Marvin for organizing that first fateful Trans* Experience in Philosophy Conference at the University of Oregon in 2016. And to organizers and attendees of trans philosophy conferences and workshops since. Thanks also to those organizing around the globe under the name of "trans" (or its variants, or incommensurable apposites) and "philosophy" (or its others) as a way to illuminate gender-variant life, both before and since.

To the many gender-variant communities that have lived and theorized their lives in contexts of devastation, survival, or flourishing, we recognize that you have both made us possible and possibilized our capacities to make each other today and for many tomorrows. There are ancestral lines we are eager to learn and some we will never know.

Thank you to our contributors for joining us not only in this small project but in the larger work of generating philosophy and theory accountable to trans and gender-disruptive lives and communities. It has been a delight to walk beside you.

Thanks, too, to Leah Pennywark and Anne Carter for welcoming this project at the University of Minnesota Press and for being committed to supporting work by trans and especially junior trans scholars at the Press. Thanks also to Ziggy Snow for so keenly copyediting the manuscript and to Doug Easton for indexing.

Perhaps our final thanks go to each other for navigating this project through what were tumultuous years for all of us, personally and professionally.

We would also like to note how important Perry Zurn has been in these final stages of this volume, ushering the project forward in ways that have improved the collection as a whole. We are sincerely grateful for his editorial labor, time, and expertise in bringing this collection into the world.

May there be more and more work like this coming out in future years, work that builds on and challenges what we have been able to see and do here.

Contributors

Talia Mae Bettcher is professor of philosophy at California State University, Los Angeles. She is the author of *Berkeley: A Guide for the Perplexed*; *Berkeley's Philosophy of Spirit: Consciousness, Ontology, and the Elusive Subject*; and *Beyond Personhood: An Essay in Trans Philosophy* (Minnesota, 2025).

Megan Burke is associate professor of philosophy at Sonoma State University. They are the author of *When Time Warps: The Lived Experience of Gender, Race, and Sexual Violence* (Minnesota, 2019).

Robin Dembroff is associate professor of philosophy and of women's, gender, and sexuality studies at Yale University. They are the author of *Real Men on Top: How Patriarchy Weaponizes Gender*.

PJ DiPietro is associate professor of women's and gender studies and the director of LGBTQ studies at Syracuse University. They are the author of *Sideways Selves: The Decolonizing Politics of Transing Matter across the Américas* and the coeditor of *Speaking Face to Face: The Visionary Philosophy of María Lugones*.

Marie Draz is associate professor of philosophy and women's studies and director of the LGBTQ+ Studies Program at San Diego State University.

Che Gossett is a Black nonbinary femme writer and the associate director of the Center for Research in Feminist, Queer, and Transgender Studies at the University of Pennsylvania.

Ryan Gustafsson is a writer and researcher based at the University of Melbourne.

Stephanie Kapusta is associate professor of philosophy, cross-appointed with gender and women's studies, at Dalhousie University.

Tamsin Kimoto is assistant professor of women, gender, and sexuality studies at Washington University in St. Louis.

Hil Malatino is associate professor of women's, gender, and sexuality studies and philosophy at Pennsylvania State University and a senior research associate at the Rock Ethics Institute. He is the author of *Queer Embodiment: Monstrosity, Medical Violence, and Intersex Experience*; *Trans Care* (Minnesota, 2020); and *Side Affects: On Being Trans and Feeling Bad* (Minnesota, 2022).

Amy Marvin is Louise M. Olmsted Fellow in Ethics at Lafayette University and the editor of *APA Studies on LGBTQ Philosophy*.

Andrea J. Pitts is associate professor of comparative literature at the University of Buffalo. They are the author of *Nos/Otras: Gloria E. Anzaldúa, Multiplicitous Agency, and Resistance* and the coeditor of *Beyond Bergson: Examining Race and Colonialism through the Writings of Henri Bergson* and *Theories of the Flesh: Latinx and Latin American Feminisms, Transformation, and Resistance*.

Marlene Wayar is an Argentinian social psychologist, activist, performer, journalist, and writer. She is the author of *Travesti: Una teoría lo suficientemente buena* (Travesti: A good enough theory) and *Furia travesti: Diccionario de la T a la T* (Travesti rage: A dictionary from T to T).

Perry Zurn is Provost Associate Professor of Philosophy at American University. He is the author of *Curiosity and Power: The Politics of Inquiry* (Minnesota, 2021) and *How We Make Each Other: Trans Life at the Edge of the University* (forthcoming) and the coauthor of *Curious Minds: The Power of Connection*. Zurn is the coeditor of *Active Intolerance: Michel Foucault, the Prisons Information Group, and the Future of Abolition*; *Curiosity Studies: A New Ecology of Knowledge* (Minnesota, 2020); and *Intolerable: Writings from Michel Foucault and the Prisons Information Group (1970–1980)* (Minnesota, 2021).

Index

faces: features of, 199; feminizing, 193, 194–98, 206; masculine, 195
facial feminization surgery (FFS), 193, 194–98, 206, 207n3; literature on, 196; overview of, 195
facial gender, 197, 206, 208n14
facial masculinization surgery (FMS), 207n3
familiarity, 83, 92; cultivated, 85; sense of, 88
Family Guy, 64
Fanon, Frantz, 130, 246
Fantasia Fair, xiv
Fausto-Sterling, Anne, 236
Feinberg, Leslie, xvi, 33
female, 106, 141; biological role of, 107; sex-only, 107
femininity, 50, 51, 60, 193, 203, 262, 263, 267; beauty and, 195; caricature of, 143–44; condition of, 155; Latina, 64; masculinity and, 196; patriarchal form of, 140
feminism, viii, 32, 99, 238, 244, 257, 261; Anglo-American, 248; antitrans, 234; Asian American, 202; Black, 102, 127, 244; cyborg, 60, 147–48; decolonial, 21, 234, 235, 241, 242, 243, 245, 246, 248; gender-critical, xii, xxvin8, 233; Latina, xv, xxviin16, 83; postcolonial, 251n29; transnational, 119n28; trans-neutral, 236; trans of color, 193; transphobic, 250n10; women of color, 102, 193, 251n29
feminist philosophy, x, xiii, 3, 11, 12, 20, 100, 237, 248; trans studies and, xiv
feminist theory, xx, 101, 142, 240–41; Black, 238; trans philosophy and, 11
feminization: facial, 195; hormones, 27; procedures for, xxiii, 195
femmes, 26, 28, 112, 156, 202, 213
Fernández, Josefina, 275n10

FFS. *See* facial feminization surgery
First Nations, 257
Flaming Faggots, 184
Fleetwood, Nicole R., 121
FMS. *See* facial masculinization surgery
Foucault, Michel, 173
freedom, 124, 129; aesthetic imaginings of, 121; Black, 121, 123; generative dream of, 131; slavery and, 122
Freeman, Elizabeth, 159
Frye, Phyllis Randolph, 65–66
FTMs, 66, 84, 148
fuckability, 193–94
fundamentalism, 258, 264
future-sex, 242
futurism, white trans, 136, 149, 150
Futuro Trans, 265, 266, 267

Galarte, Francisco J., xv
Garfinkel, Harold, 36, 235
Garland-Thomson, Rosemarie, 201
Garry, Ann, xiii–xiv
Gates, Henry Louis, Jr., 124
Gay Activist Alliance, 184
Gay Liberation Front (GLF), 179, 180, 181, 182, 184
gay men, 112, 263
Gell-Mann, Murray, 43
gender, 29, 48, 113, 141, 158, 201, 219, 226, 236, 244; beauty and, 204; binary view of, 42, 242; at birth, 159; coloniality of, 162, 238, 239, 240, 246, 247; concept of, 197, 200, 238, 240; criteria for, 144; dispossession by, 126; disrupting, x, 28, 103; distinctions/differences, 110; facial, 195; fantasy, 74; fundamental rules of, 27; gender-inclusive accounts of, 42; genre and, xxv, 146; history of, 38n13, 163; masquerading, 62–63; medicalized aesthetics of, 193; misrecognition and, 164–65;